D1448128

THE ECONOMICS OF KANSAS AGRICULTURE

Andrew Barkley

Ag Econ Books

Copyright © 2007 Ag Econ Books, All Rights Reserved.
International Standard Book Number: 978-1-60458-090-7
Library of Congress Catalog Card Number: 2007938749

All rights reserved. No part of this publication may be reproduced or transmitted in any form or by any means, electronic or mechanical, including photocopy, recording, or any information storage and retrieval system, without permission in writing from the author.

A Note on how to use this book.

Questions to test readers for comprehension are found throughout this book, and are labeled, "Quick Quiz" questions. These questions should be read, analyzed, and answered correctly before the reader continues. These questions should allow the reader to gain a better grasp of how well he or she is learning the material as it is read.

Special thanks to Professor David Smit, Department of English, Kansas State University, and Suzanne Goering, Teaching Assistant, Department of Agricultural Economics, for their useful comments. Also, thanks to the numerous students in AGEC 120 who provided input to previous editions of this book.

This book is dedicated to my parents:

Paul and Lela Barkley

who taught me to seek the truth and live well.

THE ECONOMICS OF KANSAS AGRICULTURE
TABLE OF CONTENTS

DETAILED TABLE OF CONTENTS

CHAPTER ONE
INTRODUCTION TO THE ECONOMICS OF KANSAS AGRICULTURE

1. Economics is Important and Interesting!

It is an exciting time to be alive and to study the *Economics* of *Agriculture*, or *Agricultural Economics*. Economics is a timely and relevant field because it allows us to gain a greater understanding of current events and issues. Changes in the global economy and in agriculture abound: agriculture is changing at a faster pace than any other time in history, with huge implications for the Kansas economy.

On 9-11, terrorist attacks changed our world. Economics provides a useful tool for understanding why the attacks took place, what the economic implications are, and how agricultural and food markets have been affected. The agricultural industry has increased security of the nation's food supply in response to the heightened threat of bioterrorism. Wheat produced in Kansas was air lifted to Afghanistan, and used as a tool to gain support of the citizens of that war-torn nation during the battle with the Taliban. Food is used to help the victims of hurricane Katrina in New Orleans. An increasing amount of food is imported from China, given their low labor costs.

Events that happen in the rest of the world often have a large impact on our lives in Kansas. In recent years, China has made a transition from a centrally-planned, Marxist economy to a free-market economy. This transformation has led to unprecedented economic growth and huge increases in the standard of living for Chinese workers and families. This growth has allowed many Chinese people to purchase automobiles, and oil consumption has increased tremendously. The increased oil demand has caused the price of oil to rise. Car owners in the United States are faced with higher fuel costs, and are looking for a substitute for oil-based fuels. Ethanol is an alternative fuel that has had a truly enormous influence on the agricultural economy of Kansas and the Great Plains. Ethanol is typically produced using corn, or maize. As our economy switches out of fossil fuels and into ethanol, the demand for corn has grown, and the price of corn has increased significantly, causing large increases in the profitability of grain producers in Kansas.

The rapid economic development of Japan since World War II is another example of how international events affect Kansas agriculture. For many centuries, rice was the staple food of the Japanese people. Rice even had religious implications due to its importance in the

1

Japanese diet. In the past few years, rice is no longer the number one food consumed in Japan: beef has taken over. Today, the per-capita consumption of beef in Japan is actually greater than the per-capita consumption of rice. As the Japanese economy prospered in the years following World War II, the income levels of Japanese households increased dramatically, resulting in a shift out of rice and into more expensive goods such as beef. This shift in Japanese eating habits has had a large impact on the Kansas beef industry. As income levels in low-income nations increase, individuals often shift out of less expensive foods such as grains and into more expensive goods such as beef. Understanding how and why consumers purchase goods provides information for better decision-making by persons employed in agriculture and agribusiness.

Not only can business decisions be enhanced with economics, but political decisions can provide for a stronger nation by considering economic principles in the democratic process. Interestingly, there are a number of individuals from Kansas who have a major impact on agricultural policy in Washington D.C. The Secretary of Agriculture during the Clinton administration, Dan Glickman, is from Wichita, and was a Kansas congressperson in the U.S. House of Representatives for many years. Senator Sam Brownback (a graduate of the KSU Department of Agricultural Economics) had a large impact on shaping the 1996 and 2002 Farm Bills. In September 2002, Brownback voted in favor of drought relief legislation that authorized $5.8 billion to farmers affected by the dry weather. Senator Pat Roberts from Dodge City, a member of the Senate Agricultural Committee, held a seat in the U.S. House of Representatives representing Western Kansas for many years.

The 1996 Farm Bill drastically changed agricultural policy, and the relationship between the federal government and Kansas. Since 1933, agricultural producers had received large subsidies (government payments) each year. The 1996 Farm Bill removed these subsidies in a movement toward free markets and free trade. The 2002 farm legislation reversed this course by increasing the role of the federal government in agricultural production decisions and payments. This policy shift has angered our trading partners, and members of the World Trade Organization (WTO). The economic principles that we will learn in this course will allow us to understand the reasons behind this drastic change in agricultural policy, and the impacts of the new policy on Kansas agricultural producers, consumers, and taxpayers. In the remainder of this section, we will examine current examples that reveal the importance of understanding agricultural economics.

Example One. The meat processing industry, which earns profits by purchasing cattle and selling meat, has undergone huge consolidation through mergers and acquisitions over many years. Due to several decades of merging small packing companies into larger ones, today there are only three remaining beef packers: IBP, Excell (owned by Cargill), and ConAgra. Many individuals and firms in the beef business would like to know if the "structure" of the beef industry (the number of firms) has an effect on the profits of the Kansas livestock industry. With only three packers, there is less competition in buying cattle from livestock producers, which could result in downward pressure on the price of cattle. However, there are potentially positive price effects from having big packers. Larger packing plants allow the meat production process to become more efficient, resulting in lower costs to meat consumers, who in turn purchase more meat. Enhanced meat sales place upward pressure on the price of beef. The study of economics allows for a deeper understanding of the causes and consequences of mergers and acquisitions in the agricultural and food industries.

   Example Two. Free trade agreements such as NAFTA (the North American Free Trade Agreement), the GATT (the General Agreement on Tariffs and Trade), and the WTO (the World Trade Organization) have had a major influence on agricultural producers and consumers in the United States and throughout the world by reducing and eliminating trade barriers between nations. Trade barriers are laws that restrict the movement of goods across national borders. These free trade agreements have increased exports of grain (wheat, corn, milo, and soybeans) through the elimination of trade barriers. The United States can now sell grain to Russia, Japan, Mexico, and many other buyers of Kansas grain products without legal restrictions or taxes. This course will demonstrate that this movement towards free trade has benefits for agricultural producers in the Great Plains. The 1999 rioting at the World Trade Organization (WTO) meetings in Seattle and Washington D.C. was primarily about the impact of world trade on agriculture and the environment! More recently, the breakdown of trade negotiations in the WTO Doha Round, held in Cancun, Mexico was due to low-income nations anger at agricultural subsidies to farmers in high-income nations.

   Example Three. Environmental issues have an increasingly important role to play in agriculture. Northeast Kansas is an area well suited to growing corn. Modern corn production uses an herbicide called Atrazine to eliminate weeds. Atrazine provides large agronomic and economic benefits to corn farmers in Kansas. Unfortunately, the chemical is also associated with health problems when it enters the water supply. The farmers of the Delaware River Valley in Northeastern Kansas have voluntarily reduced their use of Atrazine, to reduce the level of the chemical in the Delaware River, which flows into Lake Perry, Northeast of Topeka. The impacts of Atrazine are mixed. On the one

3

hand, the chemical provides efficient removal of weeds, resulting in higher levels of profits for corn farmers. On the other hand, Atrazine contaminates the ground water, possibly causing health problems for not only the corn farmers and their families, but also for all water drinkers downstream. This kind of "tradeoff" between economic benefits and environmental degradation is what economics is all about. Successful decision making for individuals, firms, and governments involves understanding how to choose the "correct" level of Atrazine to apply to cornfields in Kansas.

Example Four. Since World War II, the use of fertilizer and agricultural chemicals (such as herbicides, pesticides, and fungicides) has increased dramatically. In recent years, environmentalists and others who are concerned about chemical residuals in the food supply and in the water have criticized this practice. As a result, the large chemical companies that produce agrochemicals (Monsanto, Dow, Novartis, Union Carbide) are looking to the future where chemical use is likely to diminish drastically as environmental laws will likely be strengthened. An example of this is the business strategy of Monsanto, the company which sells the very profitable herbicide Round Up, which recently purchased a large agricultural seed business. This form of diversification is a prudent business strategy for a large chemical company, since environmental laws and regulations may impose huge costs on the producers of agricultural chemicals in the future. As the standard of living increases, consumers are likely to become more interested in organic food, causing a major chemical company to switch from chemical production to biotechnology development. Recent growth in the consumption of food produced without chemicals has led to large investments in organic food products by several large agribusiness corporations (for example, General Mills, Heinz, ConAgra, and Gerber).

Each of the examples described above is an issue that affects our lives in Kansas. Economics can help us understand the causes and consequences of each of these situations and events. All of these issues will be carefully studied in this course, and economics will be used to further our knowledge and understanding of our rapidly-changing world. Economics can be used to better understand our complex society, agriculture, and food consumption choices. *Economic principles and the economic framework help us make better business, career, and personal decisions.* Not only can we use economics to make better decisions, but we can also use economics to better understand other people's behavior and world events. Once an individual learns economics, she will look at the world in an entirely new, interesting, and useful way. Economics is also fun: some individuals have found economics so interesting that they devote their entire career to it!

4

The goal of this course is to learn to "think like an economist." Throughout this course, we will apply simple economic principles to current events and issues that we hear of in newspapers, television, and online. Since the economy is changing rapidly, to be a successful player in the global agricultural economy of the future, we need to be well informed, and understand how world events shape our lives. Thinking like an economist provides a framework for understanding economic events, career decisions, and personal situations in a clear and precise manner.

2. What is Economics, and What Is It About?

Economics is a **Social Science**, the study of human behavior. We will be studying how humans act and interact with one another. This is what makes economics interesting: we are studying people and what they do. In this section, we will define and explain several economic concepts, and then use these ideas to provide a formal definition of economics.

1.2.1 Producers and Consumers.

Economists are particularly interested in how people produce items such as food, clothing, and housing, and how people consume these items. Economists divide all people into two broad groups, Producers and Consumers.

Producer = An individual or firm that produces (makes; manufactures) a product.
Consumer = An individual or household that purchases a product.

These two groups of people are so important in economics that we have several names for them:

Producers = Firms = Business Firms = Sellers

Consumers = Households = Buyers = Customers

We can think of agricultural producers as individuals, families, or firms that grow and sell agricultural products. In Kansas, these include both field crops and animal products. Grains produced in Kansas include wheat (Kansas is often called the "Wheat state"), corn (used for both human consumption and animal feed), sorghum (also called milo, a feed grain), soybeans, sunflowers (another name for Kansas is the Sunflower State), and canola (a grain used to make cooking oil, also called rapeseed). Cotton has been planted on an increasing number of acres in Southwest Kansas in the past year. Kansas is the number one state in the number of cattle slaughtered. Increasingly, large hog production plants locate in the Great Plains.

A consumer is any person who buys something. Consumers buy food items, such as pepperoni pizza and milk. They also buy houses, cars, cell phones, computers, and real estate. Consumers drive the economy, since their purchases allow producers to earn revenues.

One important point to be made at this point in our study of economics is that most individuals are simultaneously producers and consumers. For example, a wheat producer from Sumner County, Kansas produces wheat and sells it to make a living. This same person buys food at the grocery store (whole wheat bread), clothing (Wranglers), and perhaps a pick-up truck (Ford). Since most individuals are both producers and consumers, we will need to look at individuals in one of the two roles at a time.

1.2.2 Macroeconomics and Microeconomics.

Economics is divided into two major categories: *Macroeconomics* and *Microeconomics*.

Macroeconomics = The study of economy-wide activities such as economic growth, business cycles, inflation, unemployment, recession, depression, boom, etc.

Microeconomics = The study of individual decision-making units such as individuals, households, and firms.

This course will mainly cover microeconomic behavior, or the actions and choices of individuals. For example, we will take a look at the behavior of feedlot owners, and how they might react to a change in the price of cattle. Here, we are studying Microeconomics, since the feedlot is an individual decision-making unit (in this case, a business firm).

1.2.3 Positive and Normative Economics.

As a social science, economics deals with topics of major consequence to public policy. There are many divergent opinions about issues such as the minimum wage, affirmative action, NAFTA, welfare, animal rights, environmentalism, the War on Terrorism, etc. Since economics deals with all of these issues, it is important to distinguish between value judgments, which are opinion statements, and neutral statements, which are factual and descriptive, rather than opinions. Two categories of economics are *Positive Economics* and *Normative Economics*.

Positive economics = Statements that are factual; these statements contain no value judgments. Positive economic statements describe, "what is."

Normative economics = Statements that contain opinions and/or value judgments. This type of statement contains a judgment about "what ought to be" or "what should be."

(Quick Quiz 1.1: Check out the following statements, and determine if each statement represents a positive or normative statement. See if you can get them all correct, to start the course off with a bang!)

1. The market price of wheat is $3.82 per bushel.
2. The market price of wheat should be higher.
3. The market price of corn should be higher.
4. Abortion is legal in the United States.
5. Environmentalists have an increasing voice in   agricultural policy.
6. Abortion should be outlawed in the USA.
7. Unemployment is a major economic issue.

Answers:
1. Positive 2. Normative 3. Normative 4. Positive 5. Positive 6. Normative 7. Normative.

Notice in the first three examples that price changes can be both good and bad, at the same time. If the price of a good increases, the producer of that good is made better off, while the consumer of that good is made worse off. For example, when the price of oil increases, oil companies earn higher levels of profits.

Meanwhile, agricultural producers who must purchase oil and petroleum-based products (gasoline, diesel, fertilizer, chemicals, etc.) are made worse off by oil price increases, since petroleum products are a major input into the production of food. Thus, economists seek to be very careful when making normative statements and normative judgments because "facts" have different implications for different persons. Economists, as social scientists, attempt to eliminate normative statements from their economic discussions, because what is good for one individual can often be bad for another. Economists try to retain objectivity in their work as social scientists by purging normative statements from their discussions.

3. Scarcity.

Economics is about *Scarcity*. Scarcity simply means that there is less of something than we desire of it. Scarcity reflects the idea that we have fixed resources and unlimited wants and desires. As humans, we typically want more than what we have: more money, more material goods such as cars, trucks, football championships, higher grades, more time, etc. The notion of scarcity applies to both material goods (computers and palm pilots) as well as intangible goods (fame, respect). The bottom line is that humans want more than they have.

An interesting issue related to scarcity is that the major religions of the world (Judaism, Christianity, Islam, Buddhism) suggest that it is better to give than to receive. This important ethical principle seems to be in direct contradiction with the economic principle that "people always desire more." Mother Teresa was a Catholic nun who devoted her life to helping the poorest of the poor in Calcutta, India. Did Mother Teresa fall victim to the idea that "more is better than less?" Yes, even philanthropists would like to have more resources to feed the hungry and help poor people. These activities require large amounts of resources and money. So, the desire to have more than we currently have is shared by both capitalists who use money to acquire fame and fortune, as well as deeply religious persons who desire to improve the lot of humanity.

Consumers are insatiable: we always want more! Many of us can't afford to eat out every night. We often would like to have more than 24 hours in a day, since we need time for studying, partying, sleeping, etc.

We will devote much time to talking about "goods" in economics. A "good" that is scarce is called an *Economic Good*. Any good that we would have more of, if it were free, is scarce. Examples include steaks, clothes, houses, time, and vacations. Any good that you would consume more of if it were free is scarce.

Noneconomic Goods are not scarce: they are free goods. This means that you can have as much as you want at no cost. Watching a beautiful Kansas sunset is a noneconomic good, because it is free. Air is free. We can consume as much as we want. However, air is not a free good in every circumstance. Mountain climbers, scuba divers, submariners, and test pilots would consume more air if it were free. Is

8

the air in a lecture room totally free? Indirectly, we are paying for it with tuition and fees, since the air is heated and/or cooled and forced into the room through the ventilation system. Clean air is not always free: people who live in urban areas would like more clean air, if it were available. Anything that people desire more of is scarce.

Since we can't have everything that we want, we must choose. For example, a certain middle-aged college professor could go on a nice exotic vacation if he were willing to sell the family Subaru, or give up his children's education, so he must choose between a vacation and a car.

The fundamental problem of economics is: "*scarcity forces us to choose*." Economics is defined as "the allocation of scarce resources among competing ends." How does the economic system allocate resources, goods, and services to different people? We will study how our economic system solves the economic problems of production, consumption, and the distribution of resources. Scarcity constantly forces us to make decisions, or choose, between what goods to buy, how to spend our time, and which career activities to pursue. *Economics is all about making informed decisions.* The study of economics allows individuals to make more informed personal, career, and business decisions.

4. Economic Organization.

There are many different forms of economic organization, or different ways that a society can choose to organize an economy. Nations can choose what type of economic system will be used to allocate resources. Three fundamental ways of organizing an economy include: (1) a *Market Economy* (capitalism; free markets); (2) a *Command Economy* (dictatorship, communism); and (3) a *Mixed Economy* (a combination of a market economy and a command economy). These three forms of economic organization will be described in this section. Before we discuss economic organization, we must take a diversion to define and explain what *Resources* are.

1.4.1 Resources.

Above, we noted that an economy must "allocate resources." But, what are these *resources* that are allocated? *Resources* are productive items used to produce goods and services to satisfy human wants and desires. Resources, together with the letter abbreviation used in economics, are listed in table 1.1.

Table 1.1 Resources.

1. Land (A)	Natural and biological resources, climate.
2. Labor (L)	Human resources.
3. Capital (K)	Manufactured resources, which include buildings, machines, tools, and equipment.
4. Management (M)	The entrepreneur, or individual, who combines the other resources into outputs.

A *Market Economy* is an economic organization where prices determine how resources and goods are allocated. Consumers in a market economy base decisions on how much to buy on the price of goods. For example, if the price of chicken increases, many consumers will eat fewer chicken products and eat more pork and beef. Similarly, in a market economy producers use prices to determine what to produce. If the price of wheat increases relative to soybeans and corn, many farmers will plant more acres to wheat than they did previously, to earn higher levels of profits. Prices drive the entire economy in a market system by conveying value, or how much things are worth to producers and consumers. In a free market economy (capitalism), *Resources* are allocated to the use characterized by the highest returns. For example, crops are generally grown in Kansas, but the Flint Hills are too rocky and too steep to grow crops on, so the land is devoted entirely to grazing, which provide the highest return for land located in the rocky hills. Prices allocate resources; prices affect the incentives and behavior of both producers and consumers.

In a *Command Economy*, resources don't automatically flow to the highest return. Resources are allocated by whoever is in charge. Examples of command economies include Cuba, where resources are allocated by a dictator (Fidel Castro), and the former USSR, where high-ranking members of the Communist Party allocated resources. Note that in a command economy, the individual or group with authority to allocate resources is not necessarily a dictator. In many socialist countries such as Sweden, resources are allocated by an elected group of decision makers. However, a dictator who has complete control of the economic system could allocate resources. In either case, resources are allocated according to the discretion of the decision-maker(s).

In a command economy, decisions are made by considerations other than price. Resources don't always flow to the highest return. For example, suppose that the people who live in a command economy desire more cars and airplanes. If the government's goals are different from the citizen's goals, then these cars and airplanes will not be built. The steel, glass, rubber, and other resources may be used in the production of missiles or public transportation, rather than private automobiles. The economic returns to building cars may be higher, but it is up to the decision-maker as to whether or not to build automobiles.

Most economic systems have elements of both market economies and command economies. These are called *Mixed Economies*. The United States has many markets that are free from government interaction. However, industries such as agriculture, transportation, and banking are regulated and subsidized. Therefore, the economy of the USA is a Mixed Economy, although the nation prides itself on being a capitalist democracy. The former Soviet Union and China were both considered to be command economies, where elected officials planned what goods were to be produced. However, recent changes in both countries have moved their economic systems towards free markets, particularly in agriculture. Therefore, the economies of these two nations are mixed economies, with elements of both market economies and command economies. Even in nations considered to be command economies, market forces are at work.

So, all real-world economies are a mixture of free market and command economies. We will spend most of our time in this class studying markets since they organize and allocate resources in the United States. In a free market economy, goods are produced and consumed according to price. Prices are all-important to producers and consumers.

5. A Model of an Economy.

The model developed in this section could be any economy: market, command, or mixed. The individuals in the economy are divided into two categories: Firms (producers) and Households (consumers). In a subsistence economy, like Robinson Crusoe, stranded on an island, producers and consumers are the same people: they must consume only what they produce. If there were no trade of economic goods, then individuals would have to produce all of their own food, clothing, and housing. These individuals would be able to consume only what they produced, since trade with others would not be possible.

11

The major feature of the flow of goods and services in a market economy is voluntary exchange. Producers and consumers do not have to buy or sell if they don't want to. No one is forced to do anything that they do not want to do.

Goods and services that consumers wish to purchase and consume must be produced. Resources are used to produce output. *Resources* are also called *Inputs*, *Factors of Production*, or *Factors*. All of these terms are used interchangeably in economics. Table 1.2 lists the major types of resources employed in agriculture.

The resources shown in table 1.2 are used to produce agricultural outputs: food and fiber. The model of an economy presented in figure 1.1 is a simplified version of the real world. The real world is extraordinarily complicated. It needs to be simplified in order to understand it. One of the key elements of the scientific method is simplification. The scientific method makes the complicated real world easier to understand.

Table 1.2 Agricultural Resources.

Inputs = Resources = Factors of Production	Payments
L = Labor = Operators, Family, Hired	Wages, Salaries
K = Physical Capital = Machines, Buildings, Tools, Equipment	Interest
M = Management	Profit
A = Land	Rent

The arrows in figure 1.1 show the flow of goods and services between households and firms. The two arrows across the top of the diagram show the movement of goods and services from producers (firms) to consumers (households). Households must make payments to the firms to take possession of the goods and services. The term, "*Goods*" refers to physical goods, whereas "*Services*" are not physical, but nonphysical items like haircuts and phone calls. In order to produce goods, firms must use *Inputs* (also called resources, factors, and factors of production). These resources are supplied by households, and include: *Capital* (K), *Labor* (L), *Land* (A), and *Management* (M). In economics, the term *Capital* refers to physical capital, which includes machines,

12

tools, buildings, and equipment. Contrast this with the typical use of the term "capital" for financial capital, which simply refers to money.

The payments that the firms make to the households for the use of the inputs are: interest (payment to capital), wages and salaries (payment to labor), rent (payment to land), and profits (payment to management).

If the lower box labeled "government" were omitted from the diagram, the model would be one of a market economy. All real-world economies have government intervention into the economy. By adding the government sector to the diagram, we convert a market economy to a mixed economy, in order to reflect the large role of government in real-world economies. Both business firms and households must pay taxes to fund the government sector, as shown in the diagram. However, legislation allows for subsidies (government payments) to be paid to selected firms. These subsidies might include payments to family farms, or welfare checks to low-income households.

Figure 1.1

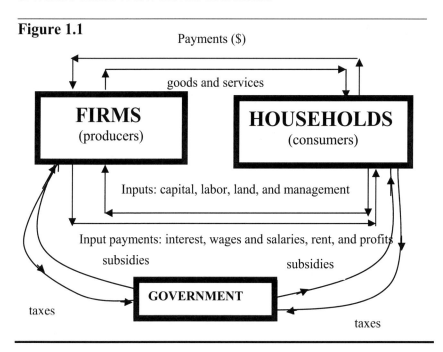

6. Trends in the Agricultural Economy.

In this course, we will apply our economic knowledge to agriculture. This will allow us to learn both economic principles and information about the agricultural sector at the same time. In this section, some background information is provided about the characteristics of modern agriculture in the United States. There are five major trends in the agricultural economy of the United States. In this remainder of this course, we will learn the causes and consequences of these five important trends.

1. **Fewer and larger farms.** The continuing consolidation of small farms into larger units is primarily due to technological change, including mechanization, agricultural chemicals and fertilizers, and improved seeds. These changes allow for larger farms to have lower costs than small farms. Since the production costs of large-scale operations are lower than small farms, there has been a huge change in the structure of agriculture since World War II. Currently, approximately two percent of all farms in the United States produce over fifty percent of all of the agricultural output.

2. **Agriculture is not just farming.** Production agriculture is approximately 1% of the US workforce, but the food and fiber industry represents approximately 16%. Although it is true that "everyone eats food," the number of persons involved in production agriculture has decreased steadily since the turn of the century, so that roughly one percent of the people in the United States and other high-income nations in North America and Western Europe are farmers. However, the food and fiber sector of the economy comprises approximately 16 percent of the workforce, demonstrating that there continue to be many employment opportunities in food processing, handling, and distribution.

3. **Substitution of capital for labor.** Over the past several decades, there has been an enormous movement toward replacing workers with machines through a process known as mechanization. This movement has been based on relative prices: if it is cheaper to use machines than labor, we will use machines. For example, combines are used to harvest wheat. These large machines are expensive, but cheaper than hand-shocking (harvesting) wheat on a per-bushel basis, due to the huge number of acres that a modern combine can harvest in a single day. A second example is the fast food giant, McDonalds. If there is an increase in the minimum wage, McDonalds will use more machinery, and hire fewer workers (think of the automatic French fry machines and drink dispensers).

4. **Off-farm income has increased enormously.** Farming used to be the sole source of income for most farm families. In today's agricultural economy, most farm families rely not only on income from agricultural

sources, but also on income from nonfarm jobs. Typically, one individual in the family will do farm work, and another will work in a nonfarm position. With this arrangement, a family's total income will not be dependent on farm income alone, which can fluctuate based on weather, production conditions, and price movements. It is interesting to note that farm families in the United States have, on average, higher levels of income and wealth than nonfarm families.

5. **Exports are increasingly important to the agricultural sector.** As our agricultural productivity continues to increase through biological breakthroughs, mechanization, and management improvements, our ability to produce ever-larger amounts of food has increased. In fact, our ability to produce food has grown more rapidly than our consumption of food. As a result, we need to export, or sell food to consumers in other nations, to sell all of the food that is produced in Kansas and the USA.

  The agricultural economy is changing rapidly. The material in this class will help you make good decisions in a rapidly-changing economy. By learning economic principles, we will learn how to approach management decisions in our careers and personal lives.

7. Graph Review.

  Economists often use graphs to summarize and interpret information. Graphs can communicate a lot of information in a small space, which makes them a useful tool to quickly see the most important aspects of a situation or decision. One characteristic of graphs is that they simplify data. Remember that social scientists must simplify the real world in order to understand it. The real world is extremely complicated, and as a result, we must look at the major driving forces behind any situation to begin to understand it. Most graphs allow the viewer to look at the relationship between two variables, holding everything else constant. In economics, we have a special name for this: *Ceteris Paribus*, which is Latin for "holding all else constant."

  Much of economics, a study of human behavior, has to do with looking at the relationship between two variables. For example, prices determine both producer and consumer behavior in a market economy. There is a relationship between price (P) and quantity (Q). A graph isolates the relationship between price and quantity, holding all else constant (*Ceteris Paribus*). On a two-dimensional surface such as the blackboard or a page in your notebook, we can only look at two things at once. Thus, in a two-dimensional graph, we hold all of the variables that impact a relationship constant, and focus our attention on the two most

15

important variables.

In a graph, the numerical value of one variable is measured along the horizontal axis (x-axis), at the bottom of graph, starting from the origin (the point labeled 0). In figure 1.2, the quantity (Q) is the variable on the x-axis. The numerical value of a second variable is measured along the vertical axis (y-axis), on the left-hand side of the graph, also starting at the origin. In the graph below, price (P) is measured on the vertical axis.

All graphs must show the labels and units of both variables. The reader could not understand what is going on in a graph unless each axis has two items: *LABELS* and *UNITS*. In the graph below, the label for quantity is Q (pizza), and the units are slices. The label for price is P and the units are ($/slice). Units are typically placed in parentheses.

Figure 1.2

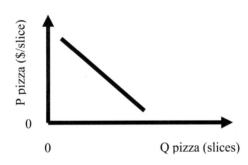

---

8. Absolute Prices and Relative Prices.

We have learned that in a market economy, prices determine the decisions of both producers and consumers. It is important to point out that it is not a single price that is used to make decisions, but rather the price of a good relative to other goods that both producers and consumers use to make choices.

1.8.1 The Difference Between Absolute and Relative Prices.

Absolute Prices = These refer to a single price level. Example: The price of wheat is $3/bushel.

Relative Prices = The prices of goods relative to each other. Example: the price of wheat increased relative to the price of corn.

16

When making a production decision about which crop to plant, the fact that the market price of wheat is equal to $3/bushel doesn't mean much. Producers need to know the price of wheat relative to the price of alternative goods such as corn, milo, and hay. This is because the land used to produce wheat could also be used to produce these alternative crops. The farmer desires to earn the highest possible level of profits on this land. A good economic decision is one that takes into account the relative prices of all of the crops that can be grown on the land. In general, producers will react to a relative price increase by producing more of a good, since they will earn higher levels of profits by doing so. Consumers, on the other hand, will react to a price increase by buying less of a good.

If you can remember these two facts about how producers and consumers react to price changes, you know a lot of economics already! The remainder of the course will pursue how producers and consumers react to price changes in detail. Try to remember the following intuition, as it will serve you well in the study of economics, as well as in business and career decisions.

Producers prefer higher prices of the goods that they produce.

Consumers prefer lower prices for the goods that they purchase.

Suppose that all crop prices went up by the same percentage due to an increase in oil prices. In this case, the relative prices for all crops remained the same, even though the absolute prices increased. The reason: all of the prices moved up together, so the relative prices all remained constant.

Consider the following statement: if all prices in an economy doubled, nothing would happen. At first glance, this does not seem to make sense. However, if we consider that all of the prices in the entire economy increased by the same amount, then relative prices remained constant, so producers and consumers would not change their decisions. Everything would cost the same relative to everything else. This is because the "price" of labor went up: wages and salaries are prices, they are the price that the firm must pay for labor services.

Likewise, if inflation were 10% for all goods in the economy, then the prices of everything would increase by 10%. This would be true for all goods, including labor services, so wages and salaries would increase by the same amount as goods. Nothing would happen, because all items in the economy would have the same value. However, if oil prices were to increase due to a war in Iraq, then consumers would use less oil and more energy from other sources. To summarize, absolute

17

prices are accounting devices, whereas relative prices are actually used to make actual decisions.

1.8.2 Price Units.

The units that prices are expressed are crucial to understanding how producers and consumers behave. The price of a good is not just a number of dollars, it is dollars per unit ($/unit). Although this seems simple, it is very important. The price of bread at Dillons is not just $1, but rather it is $1/loaf. Other examples can be seen in the table:

Bread	$1/loaf
Wheat	$4/bushel
Pizza	$10/large pizza
Blue jeans	$30/pair
Car	$19,000/car

Prices are not expressed in dollars alone! Prices are expressed in **DOLLARS PER UNIT**.

1.8.3 Constant-Quality Prices.

When we mention the price of a good in economics, we are talking about constant-quality units. We can't just say, "a pair of jeans," or "a large pizza." We must be more specific. We often discuss specific qualities in everyday life. For example, "I sold two pens of cattle," or "10,000 cars were sold today;" or "Five billion bushels of wheat were exported to Russia in February." With constant-quality units, we must be more specific. We must specify the type of good we are speaking of, for example:
"I sold 2 pens of heifers of average quality."
"10,000 Jaguars were sold last month."
"5 billion bushels of US #2 Hard Red Winter Wheat were exported in February."
Notice again: we are simplifying the real world in order to understand it.

9. Graph Examples.

1.9.1 A Graph of the Demand for Hamburger in Dodge City, Kansas.

Let's take a look at the demand (consumption) for hamburger from a mathematical perspective: We are considering consumer behavior. How do consumers respond to a change in the price of hamburger in Dodge City, Kansas? The numbers in the Demand Schedule in table1.3 show the relationship between the price of hamburger and the quantity of hamburger purchased in grocery stores in Dodge City.

Units are very important: we are assuming constant-quality units, which means that the entire quantity of hamburger sold is of the same quality. The units used for the hamburger price are dollars per pound (not just dollars!) P = $/lb, and the units used for the quantity of hamburger purchased are thousand pounds of hamburger, Q = 1000 lbs. Notice that figure 1.3 has both labels and units.

(Quick Quiz 1.2: what are the labels and units in figure 1.2?).

As fewer pounds of hamburger meat are placed on the market in Dodge City, consumers are willing to pay a higher price for it. This is due to scarcity: the less of something that there is, the more valuable that it is, *ceteris paribus*. Figure 1.2 demonstrates the relationship between the price and quantity of hamburger, and nothing else. It tells us the price of hamburger and the quantity demanded of hamburger, no more and no less. We are holding everything else constant.

___

Table 1.3 Hamburger Demand Schedule in Dodge City, Kansas.

Price($/lb)	Quantity Purchased (1000 lbs)
2.30	0
2.10	20
1.90	40
1.70	60
1.50	80
1.30	100
1.10	120
0.90	140
0.70	160
0.50	180
0.30	200
0.10	220
0 (free!)	230

The graph simplifies the real world: many details are left out. For example, if wages in Dodge City increased, is more hamburger sold? To answer this question, we would need to know income levels, and how they are associated with changes in the consumption of hamburger. Also, the demand for hamburger is seasonal: people buy more hamburger during the summer months for outdoor cooking. We have totally ignored this in the graph above. We must simplify the real world in order to understand it.

Figure 1.3

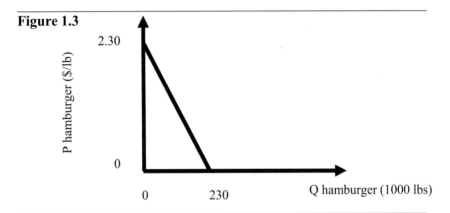

1.9.2 The Slope of a Line.

We can look at this same situation in a slightly different way using algebra. Let's review some simple algebra dealing with the slope of a line. Remember that a function relates two variables, say x and y:

$y = f(x)$.

We can read this, "y is a function of x." The variable x is called the independent variable, since the value of x does not depend on any other variable. The y variable is called the dependent variable, since the value of y depends on the value that x takes. In other words, x causes y.

x = independent variable

y = dependent variable

The expression $y = f(x)$ is a general function, which could take any form, linear or nonlinear. A more specific functional form is the linear form, which just means that the relationship between the two variables is a straight line. The linear functional form is:

20

$$y = b + mx$$

We now read, "y is a function of x, where b is the y-intercept, and m is the slope." Armed with this simple algebra, we can characterize the demand for hamburger in Dodge City using an equation, where P is the price of hamburger in dollars per pound, and Q is 1000 lbs of hamburger purchased in Dodge City:

$$P = 2.30 - 0.01Q.$$

We can now graph the demand for hamburger in Dodge City using a different method. First, we will calculate the slope of hamburger demand in Dodge City. The slope is the rate at which a relationship increases or decreases. The slope is sometimes called the "rise over the run," or the "change in y divided by the change in x." In the graph above, we would like to calculate the slope of the demand line, or how much hamburger price changes when the quantity of hamburger purchased changes. The symbol for change is a delta: Δ. The slope is equal to:

$$\Delta y / \Delta x = \Delta P / \Delta Q.$$

In the case of hamburger in Dodge City in figure 1.3, the slope equals: $-2.30/230 = -0.01$. Therefore, the slope of the demand line (m) equals -0.01, and the y-intercept (b) equals 2.30. This can be clearly seen in the equation of the line, $P = 2.30 - 0.01Q$. The graph of this economic relationship can be derived from either the demand schedule or the equation of the line.

1.9.3 Example: Veterinary Clinic in Hutchinson, Kansas.

Suppose that a veterinarian charges $50 for an appointment in her clinic in Hutchinson, located close to the Cosmosphere. The vet's total revenues (TR) are equal to the number of hourly appointments (Q) multiplied by the price of an appointment (P = $50/hour):

$$TR = P*Q = 50*Q.$$

This economic relationship is quite simple to graph, since it is a linear relationship. The slope of the line (m) equals 50, and the y-intercept equals zero.

Figure 1.4

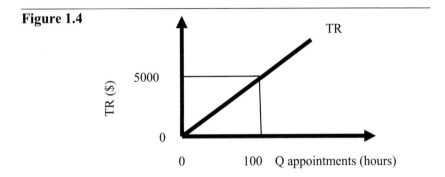

Graphs can be used to study relationships between variables other than price and quantity, as we will see in the next example. Notice that the units for total revenue (TR) are in dollars. This is because we have multiplied the price P, in dollars per hour ($/hr), times the quantity, in hours (hrs). The dollars represented by TR are the bills found in the clinic's cash register at the end of the working day.

1.9.4 Example: The Impact of Nitrogen Fertilizer on Wheat Yields.

A good example of a **nonlinear** relationship is the impact that nitrogen (N) fertilizer has on wheat yields. Nitrogen increases plant growth, allowing for higher yields in wheat and other crops. However, this increase occurs at a decreasing rate: the impact is largest for the first application of fertilizer, and decreases after that. After a certain point, additional application of fertilizer actually decreases crop yield, since the fertilizer actually "burns" the wheat plant. Too much of a good thing is a bad thing! We will come back to this theme often in our study of production processes. This relationship can be seen in figure 1.5.

Figure 1.5

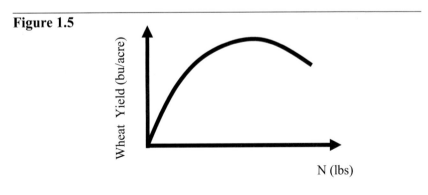

In figure 1.5, the slope is positive at small levels of N, zero at maximum point, and then becomes negative as N is increased beyond the maximum point. What is the best point on the graph for the wheat farmer to locate? Many students who have not studied economics might find that the optimal (best) point to locate would be the top of the hill, or the point of maximum wheat yield. However, this is not necessarily the profit-maximizing point for the wheat producer. In many situations, it costs too much to maximize yields: the nitrogen costs farmers money, and the profit-maximizing point may be to the left of the top of the yield hill. To maximize profits, we must compare both the benefits of using fertilizer, which are the higher crop yields, with the costs of using fertilizer, which are the payments that must be made to purchase the fertilizer. To make good economic decisions, we must compare the benefits of any activity with the costs of that activity.

The slope of this relationship is equal to the slope of a line that is just tangent to the curve. So, the slope of the relationship is positive but decreasing as the curve becomes less steep with more nitrogen use. At the top of the yield hill, the slope is exactly equal to zero. To the right of the maximum yield point, the slope of the curve is negative. This simply means that an increase in nitrogen fertilizer results in a decrease in wheat yield.

Graphs are useful tools to help organize our thoughts about economic relationships.

We must be careful when we use graphical analysis: every axis must include *labels* and *units*. Also, remember that prices are always in $/unit, not just in dollars, and they units are constant-quality units. We will be emphasizing several of the concepts that we have discussed in this introductory chapter throughout the remainder of the course. Since the course is cumulative (all of the new concepts build on the old concepts), students who learn each concept thoroughly in the beginning of the course will have a huge advantage as the course progresses. Chapter Two will introduce the concept of production, or how we turn inputs into economically useful outputs.

Chapter One Summary

1. Economics is important and interesting.
2. Economics helps us make better business, career, and personal decisions.
3. Goal of course: to learn to "think like an economist." Thinking like an economist provides a framework for understanding economic events, career decisions, and personal situations in a clear and precise manner.
4. Economics is a social science, which is the study of human behavior.
5. A producer is an individual or firm that produces (makes; manufactures) a product.
6. A consumer is an individual or household that purchases a product.
7. Individuals are both producers and consumers.
8. Macroeconomics is the study of economy-wide activities.
9. Microeconomics is the study of individual decision-making units.
10. Positive economics are statements that are factual and contain no value judgments ("what is").
11. Normative economics are statements that contain opinions and/or value judgments ("what should be").
12. Price increases help producers and hurt consumers, whereas price decreases help consumers and hurt producers.
13. Economics is about scarcity. Scarcity means that there is less of something than we desire of it: we have fixed resources and unlimited wants and desires.
14. An economic good is any good that we would desire more of if it were free.
15. A noneconomic good is a good that is not scarce (a free good).
16. Scarcity forces us to choose: we can't have everything that we want.
17. Economics is the allocation of scarce resources among competing ends.
18. A market economy is an economic organization where prices determine how resources and goods are allocated (capitalism; free markets).
19. A command economy is an economic organization where resources are allocated by whoever is in charge (dictatorship; communism; socialism).
20. A mixed economy has elements of both a market economy and a command economy.
21. Resources are productive items used to produce goods and services to satisfy human wants and desires. Resources include: land (A), labor (L), capital (K), and management (M).

22. Firms combine resources (K, L, A, and M) to produce goods and resources. Consumers make payments to firms to obtain these goods and services.
23. The agricultural economy is changing rapidly. Important trends include: (1) fewer and larger farms, (2) agriculture is not just farming, (3) substitution of capital for labor, (4) off-farm income has increased enormously, and (5) exports are increasingly important to the agricultural sector.
24. Graphs are useful tools to summarize and interpret information.
25. Absolute prices refer to a single price level, whereas relative prices refer to the prices of goods relative to each other. The economic decisions of producers and consumers depend on relative prices.
26. Prices of goods are expressed in constant-quality prices.
27. Every graph must have units and labels on each axis.

Chapter One Glossary

Absolute Price. An absolute price refers to a price in isolation, without reference to other prices. (Also see Relative Price).

Agricultural Economics. Economics applied to agriculture and rural areas.

Agriculture. The science, art, and business of cultivating the soil, producing crops, and raising livestock useful to humans; farming.

Capital. Physical capital; machinery, buildings, tools, and equipment.

Ceteris Paribus. Latin for "holding all else constant." We use this assumption to simplify the real world in order to understand it.

Command Economy. A form of economic organization where resources are allocated by whoever is in charge, such as a dictator or an elected group of officials. (Also see Market Economy and Mixed Economy).

Consumer. An individual or household that purchases a product.

Economic Good. A good that is Scarce. (Also see Noneconomic Good).

Economics. The study of the allocation of scarce resources between competing ends.

Good. An economic good.

Macroeconomics. The study of economy-wide activities such as economic growth, business cycles, inflation, unemployment, recession, depression, boom, etc. (Also see Microeconomics).

Market Economy. A form of economic organization where resources are allocated by prices. Resources flow to the highest returns in a free market system. (Also see Command Economy and Mixed Economy).

Microeconomics. The study of the behavior of individual decision-making units such as individuals, households, and firms. (Also see Macroeconomics).

Mixed Economy. A form or economic organization that has elements of both a Market Economy and a Command Economy.

Noneconomic Good. A good that is not scarce; there is as much of this good to meet any demand for it; a free good. (Also see Economic Good).

Normative Economics. Statements that contain opinions and/or value judgments. This type of statement contains a judgment about "what ought to be" or "what should be." (Also see Positive economics).

Positive Economics. Statements that are factual; these statements contain no value judgements. Positive economic statements describe "what is." (Also see Normative Economics).

Producer. An individual or firm that produces (makes; manufactures) a product.

Relative Price. The price of a good relative to prices of other goods. (Also see Absolute Price).

Resources. Inputs provided by nature and modified by humans using technology to produce goods and services that satisfy human wants and desires. Also called Inputs, Factors of Production, or Factors. Resources include Capital (K), Labor (L), Land (A), and Management (M).

Scarcity. Because resources are limited, the goods and services produced from those resources are also limited, which means consumers must make choices, or trade-offs between different goods.

Service. A type of economic good that is not physical. For example, a haircut or a phone call is a service, whereas a car or a shirt is a good.

Social Science.   The study of society and of individual relationships in and to society, generally regarded as including sociology, psychology, anthropology, economics, political science, and history.

Chapter One Review Questions

1. Economics is:
   a. an agricultural science
   b. a social science
   c. a physical science
   d. not a science, but a field of study
2. A producer is:
   a.   a person who purchases a product
   b.   the seller of a product
   c.   the buyer of a product
   d.   a good sow
3. A consumer is all of the following except:
   a.   a buyer   b. a household   c. a customer   d. a firm
4. A Kansas wheat farmer is an example of a:
   a.   producer   b. consumer   c. both a and b   d. neither a nor b
5. The study of growth in Mexico's standard of living is an example of:
   a.   Macroeconomics
   b.   microeconomics
   c.   political science
   d.   consumer behavior
6. The study of how a single beef producer uses growth hormones is an example of: a.   macroeconomics
   b.   microeconomics
   c.   biological science
   d.   consumer behavior
7. The statement, "the market price of soybeans is $2.50 per bushel" is an example of:
   a. positive economics
   b. normative economics
   c. a value judgment
   d. consumer behavior
8. The statement, "the price of wheat should be higher" is an example of:
   a.   positive economics
   b.   normative economics
   c.   a factual statement
   d.   consumer behavior
9. If the price of wheat rises, who is made better off:
   a.   producers   b. consumers   c. both a and b   d. neither a nor b
10. An increase in the price of wheat is good for:
    a.   wheat producers
    b.   milling and baking firms

    c.   bread consumers

    d.   cattle producers

11. Scarcity affects:

    a.   Industrial firms

    b.   agricultural producers

    c.   internet users

    d.   everyone

12. Scarcity:

    a. reflects limited resources and unlimited desires

    b. affects religious persons

    c. forces us to choose

    d. all of the other three answers

13. An example of an economic good is:

    a.   a cookie b. pollution c. garbage d. disease

14. The following is a noneconomic good:

    a.   a cookie

    b.   a sunset

    c.   a football

    d.   a Lexus automobile

15. In a market economy, resources are allocated by:

    a.   prices

    b.   whoever is in charge

    c.   an elected group of officials

    d.   a disaster

16. The United States is an example of:

    a.   a command economy

    b.   a market economy

    c.   a mixed economy

    d.   none of the other three answers

17. Production agriculture in the USA has what percent of employment?

    a.   16 b. 3   c. 1   d. 25

18. If the price of corn increases relative to the price of other crops:

    a.   farmers will plant more corn

    b.   farmers will plant less corn

    c.   farmers will plant the same amount of corn

    d.   a corn consumer will purchase more corn

19. If the price of all crops increases, then:

    a.   farmers will plant more corn

    b.   farmers will plant less corn

    c.   farmers will plant the same amount of corn

    d.   a corn consumer will purchase more corn

20. The price of corn is given by:

    a. $2 b. $/bushel c. 2 bushels d. 2 bushels/$

CHAPTER TWO
THE ECONOMICS OF PRODUCTION

1. The Production Function.

We will begin our study of the agricultural economy with a look at how goods and services are produced. Firms, or producers, combine inputs into outputs, which are then sold to consumers. We will devote the next several chapters of this book to production by firms. We will then shift our focus to the behavior of consumers, or households. Then, we will study the interaction of consumers and producers: markets, or supply and demand.

Production is the process of producing goods and services, or the relationship between inputs and outputs. The production process requires scarce resources, which cost the firm money to purchase and use. We have seen that these resources have several different names:

Inputs = factors = factors of production = resources = A, L, K, M

(Quick Quiz 2.1: what do the letters A, L, K, M refer to?)

2.1.1 Wheat Production in Sumner County, Kansas.

We will begin our study of production by studying how inputs are combined into outputs, or the production process. First, let's take a look at a wheat producer in Sumner County, Kansas. We choose this county just south of Wichita because it produces more wheat than any other county in Kansas or the USA (in most years).

Let Y = output = wheat (bu)

Notice that when we speak of an economic variable such as output, we need units. In the case of wheat, the units of output are measured in bushels (bu) of wheat.

Output = f(inputs)

where f = the mathematical relationship between inputs and output

Y = f(inputs)

$$Y = f(K, L, A, M)$$

Our wheat producer uses the inputs of K, L, A, and M to produce wheat (Y). As discussed in Chapter One, we need to simplify this complex relationship in order to understand production. To allow us to graph and understand this production function, we reduce the number of inputs that are allowed to vary to just one. We will look at the relationship between outputs and inputs by concentrating on just one input: capital.

(Quick Quiz 2.2: how is capital defined in economics? What four types of capital are included in this definition?)

We will use the assumption of *ceteris paribus* to isolate the relationship between output and a single input, capital.

(Quick Quiz 2.3: what does *ceteris paribus* mean?)

To show that we are holding all inputs constant other than capital, we use a vertical bar in the mathematical equation. The variable to the left of the vertical bar (in this case, K) is allowed to vary (or change). All of the variables to the right of the vertical bar (L, A, and M) are held fixed, or constant. This allows us to graph the multidimensional relationship on a two-dimensional surface, such as the chalkboard or a page in your notebook. The real physical production process is complicated; we must *isolate* one input and one output at a time to further understand the production process.

$$Y = f(K \mid L, A, M)$$

Now we are in a good position to define a **Production Function**.

Production Function = The physical relationship between inputs and outputs.

There are no prices in the production function. The production function is a purely physical relationship between inputs and outputs. The production function tells us exactly what quantity of inputs are required to produce a given quantity of output. Therefore, the production function is a ***physical*** relationship only: it refers to what we study in Agronomy or Animal Sciences. There are no economics in production functions, since they refer to physical processes only.

Since real-world production processes are very complicated, it would be difficult to understand if we allowed all variables to change at once. We need to isolate one variable, *ceteris paribus*. An example of this is the way that scientific experiments are conducted for wheat crops. To determine the optimal use of the fertilizer Nitrogen on wheat fields, the Agronomy Department runs a controlled experiment to determine what happens to wheat yields as the amount of Nitrogen is altered. They do this type of controlled experiment on test plots, or small wheat fields that are typically adjacent to each other to keep the weather, growing conditions, and soil constant across all of the plots. The idea behind the controlled experiment is to hold all inputs constant except for Nitrogen, and measure how the different levels of N affect the wheat yields.

The wheat production function would look like this:

$$Y = f(x_1, x_2, \ldots, x_n)$$

Where Y is wheat output, measured in bushels (bu), f is the production function, or the physical relationship between inputs and output, and the x_i are inputs, which include land, labor, machinery, seed, and Nitrogen. If we specify each of the inputs, we can write the following production function:

$$Y = f(N, L, K, M, A)$$

(Quick Quiz 2.4: what do each of the letters in this production function stand for?)

To isolate the relationship between Nitrogen and wheat yields, the agronomists will hold all inputs constant other than the one that they are isolating to study: Nitrogen.

(Quick Quiz 2.5: what is the term that economists use for "holding all else constant?")

The controlled experiment will provide the agronomists information on the following physical relationship:

$$Y = f(N \mid L, K, M, A)$$

Knowledge of this relationship will allow agronomists to find the optimal level of Nitrogen for wheat producers in Kansas to apply to their wheat fields. Too little Nitrogen, and the yields will be lower than the potential, and too much Nitrogen will burn the crop, causing smaller yields.

Figure 2.1

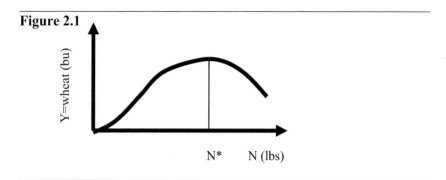

Here is one of the main points of this course: the point of maximum *physical* wheat yield (N*) is not always the optimal *economic* wheat yield. This is because nitrogen is a scarce resource, and costs money to purchase. In fact, fertilizer is one of the largest costs of production for farmers in the Great Plains. If nitrogen were free, then the optimal number of pounds of nitrogen to apply to a wheat field would be N*, since this is the level of nitrogen that maximizes production. However, since it costs money to purchase and use fertilizer, the farmer will stop applying N at a point to the left of N*. We will find the exact point in this course: where the benefits of using N are greater than the costs. For now, we can note that producers will never maximize production, because it costs too much!

A second example of a production function is a controlled experiment in the Department of Animal Sciences and Industry to find the impact of growth hormones (H) on beef production. Growth hormones are controversial, since some consumers believe that the hormones are unhealthy for human consumption. Europeans do not import American beef for this reason. Cattle producers continue to use the hormones because they increase output significantly. A production function for beef can be written: Y = f(H, K, L, A, M).

(Quick Quiz 2.6: what do these letters stand for? How do we isolate the growth hormones' influence on beef output?)

The controlled experiment would use several pens of cattle with identical inputs, with the exception of the level of growth hormone. The scientists would carefully measure and record the weight of each animal, and find the physical relationship between the growth hormone and the amount of muscle on the animal.

Figure 2.2

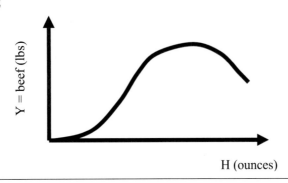

Note that the shape of this graph is similar to the Agronomy experiment: there is an "optimal" level of growth hormone for cattle production. This is because larger amounts of input will increase output only up to a certain point. After that, the input causes production to fall.

(Quick Quiz 2.7: will the cattle producer use the level of growth hormones that maximizes production? Why or why not?)

The study of production functions can be applied to many situations, events, and circumstances. For example, think of a college student studying for an exam. We can think of this situation as a production process, where output (=Y) is the test performance, or grade, and the input (=X) is the number of hours that the student studies. The output of this production process will depend on how many hours the student studies. However, if the student drinks a bunch of coffee (or Mountain Dew) and stays up all night, the test performance may actually fall. Too much studying can result in a loss of sleep, which in turn results in poor test performance. Thus, the relationship between the number of hours studied and the grade on a test will have the same shape as the graphs for wheat production and beef production.

Figure 2.3

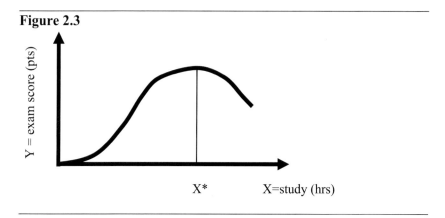

We are now equipped to make a prediction about human behavior. Will students always study the number of hours that will result in the highest test score possible (X*)? Unfortunately not. Why? Because studying is not free! It requires a great deal of time and effort, and there are many other activities that college students can spend their time on (sleep, television, beer, etc.). Economics has been used to make a prediction: students are able to study enough hours to get perfect test scores, but choose to get a less than perfect test score in order to spend their time in other activities. Is economics correct? We will continue to apply economic principles to real-life situations for the remainder of this course.

2.1.2 Profit Maximization.

In economics, we assume that the goal of all producers is to maximize profits. This is a simplification of the real world, since there may be producers who have other goals, such as a nice lifestyle, a clean environment, or to pay employees more than the market wage rate. Although there are many producers who may not do everything in their power to maximize profits, it is a very good assumption to make. Why? Because any business owner who does not pay attention to the bottom line (profits) is unlikely to be able to remain in business for long.

Profits have special meaning in economics: total revenues minus total costs:

$$\pi = TR - TC$$

where the symbol π (the Greek letter pi) stands for Profits, TR are total revenues and TC are total costs.

***Profits* [π]** = Total revenues minus total costs: π = TR − TC. The value of production sold less the cost of producing that output.

Total revenues are simply the dollars earned by a producer from the sale of a good. Let the quantity of a good sold be given by Q units, and the price of the good is P dollars per unit. Then, the total revenues earned by the producing firm are equal to TR = P*Q. The units for total revenue are in dollars, since P is in (dollars/unit) and Q is in (units), when we multiply P by Q, the units cancel and TR are in (dollars). Total costs represent the total costs of production of the good, and are also in dollar units.

2. Short Run and Long Run.

We often hear people speak of the "long run." In economics, this term has a very specific meaning. The most important thing to remember about the long run is that it does not refer to a length of time. The length of the long run depends on the specific situation, as will be explained further below.

2.2.1 Immediate, Short, and Long Runs.

In the **Immediate Run**, all of the inputs (also called factors or resources) are fixed. This simply means that the producer cannot change the quantity of any input. We say that all resources are fixed in this case. Think of a wheat producer who purchases land, labor, seed, machinery, fertilizer, and chemicals. In a one-month period, this producer is unlikely to be able to alter the quantity of these inputs, so this is defined as the immediate run.

Immediate Run = IR = A period of time in which all inputs are fixed.

As time passes, the farmer will have more flexibility to change the quantities of inputs. Suppose that in a three-month period, this producer is able to alter the number of hours of work hired, but cannot change the number of acres of land that are in production. This situation is called the **Short Run**, defined as a period when some inputs are fixed (the quantities of inputs used can not be altered) and some inputs are variable (the quantities of inputs can be changed).

Short Run = SR = A period of time in which at least one input is fixed.

Some inputs cannot be changed in the short run. A common example is land in agricultural production. Most producers can not quickly acquire more land in a short length of time, as it typically takes a long time to purchase or sell agricultural land that is adjacent or nearby. Therefore, we can think of the quantity of acres of land as fixed in the short run (SR). Similarly, machinery and equipment (combines, tractors, plows) are very expensive, and many producers are unable to rapidly increase or decrease the number of these inputs. When a farmer is unable to alter the quantity of these inputs, they are called fixed inputs, and the farmer is in the **Short Run** (SR). However, in the short run, some inputs are variable. For example, the producer could alter the level of chemicals, fertilizer, labor, or management.

In the **Long Run** (LR), all inputs are variable.

Long Run = LR = A period of time in which all inputs are variable.

Over a longer period of time, a producer could buy or sell machinery and land. Producers can adjust the size of their farm. An agribusiness example is the agricultural implement manufacturer, John Deere, of Moline, Illinois. In the short run, Deere could not build a plant to produce more combines since this would require purchasing land and building a factory. However, in the long run (several years), Deere could build a new factory. The crucial aspect to remember about the short run and long run definitions is that there is not a set length of time of the long run: the long run is defined as however long it takes to adjust the levels of inputs. This is different in each situation.

The John Deere Implement Division may require three years to finance and build a new plant. In the long run, everything is variable, including plant size. So in this case, the long run is defined as three years, and the short run is any length of time less than three years.

Now suppose that a farmer in Northeast Kansas is able to increase his land holding in only two weeks (he is also a real estate broker). If all of the inputs on this farm are variable in a two-week time period, then the length of the long run is only two weeks for this producer. The length of time that defines the long run depends on the situation, and the willingness of the neighbors to sell land. Most farmers face a much different situation, as it can take many years to acquire new land. So, there is no set number of years for long run: it just depends on the situation.

A last example is a lemonade stand set up by my children on our street. For this business firm, the long run is very short. This is because the children can alter the quantities of all inputs (water, glasses, lemonade mix, stirring spoon) very quickly by coming into the house. For this business, the long run may only be five minutes long.

(Quick Quiz 2.8: how long is the short run and the immediate run for the lemonade stand?)

2.2.2 Fixed and Variable Inputs.

Given our discussion above, we can now define fixed and variable inputs.

Fixed Input = An input whose quantity does not vary with the level of output.

A fixed input is one that does not change with the level of output. This is a short run concept, because in the long run, all inputs are variable (by definition).

Variable Input = An input whose quantity does vary with the level of output.

A variable input is one that when changed, affects the level of output.

(Quick Quiz 2.9: in our examples above, were nitrogen and growth hormones fixed or variable inputs?)

3. Physical Production Relationships.

We will now study the production function in more detail, to achieve a greater understanding of how inputs are converted into outputs. We will look closely at the production function facing a corn farmer in Iola, a small city in southeastern Kansas. Suppose that this corn farmer uses the inputs capital, labor, land, and management to produce corn:

$$Y = f(L, K, A, M).$$

To study the impact of labor on corn output, we can isolate labor by holding all of the other inputs constant:

$$Y = f(L \mid K, A, M).$$

This allows us to specifically define the production concepts needed to understand production efficiency.

2.3.1 Constant, Increasing, Decreasing, and Negative Returns.

The level of inputs and the production function determine the level of output. Recall that the production function is the physical relationship between inputs and output. The physical production process can take on several different forms: **Constant Returns**, **Increasing Returns**, **Decreasing Returns**, and **Negative Returns**. The word "returns" refers to how much additional output is produced as inputs are increased incrementally. Think of increasing the level of inputs by one unit at a time, and measuring what the change in output is due to the change in input.

In a production process characterized by **Constant Returns**, each additional unit of input is equally productive as all other units of input.

Constant Returns = For each additional unit of input used, output increases at a constant rate (the rate of change in output remains constant).

An example could be the number of cattle it takes to produce cattle hides: one animal produces one hide, no more, no less (figure 2.4).

Each additional unit of input (in this case steers) produces exactly one additional leather hide. The slope of the production function for leather hides (=)Y/)X) remains constant as more inputs are used, graphically demonstrating the concept of **Constant Returns**.

Increasing Returns occur when an additional unit of input yields more additional output than the previous unit of input.

Figure 2.4. Leather Production: Constant Returns.

Y = Leather (hides)	X = Cattle (steers)	Added Output = $(\Delta Y/\Delta X)$
0	0	--
1	1	1
2	2	1
3	3	1
4	4	1
5	5	1

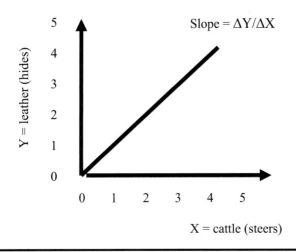

Figure 2.5. Wheat Production: Increasing Returns.

Y = Wheat (bu)	X = Workers (persons)	Added Output = $(\Delta Y/\Delta X)$
0	0	--
10	1	10
30	2	20
60	3	30
100	4	40
150	5	50

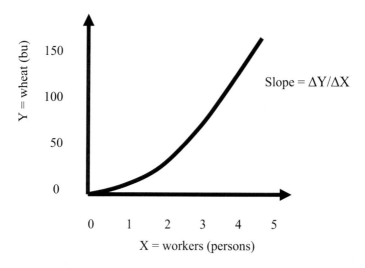

Increasing Returns = When each additional unit of input added to the production process yields more additional product than the previous unit of input.

The managers of business firms look favorably upon this type of production process, since each additional unit of input is more productive than the last, meaning that the firm is becoming more efficient with each unit of input. An example is harvesting a crop (figure 2.5). If only a single person tries to run the combine and the truck to haul the crop to the grain elevator, the production process is inefficient. When a second worker is hired to drive the truck, then the first person can spend all of her time operating the combine.

As more workers are added to the harvest crew, the output increases at an increasing rate, as depicted in figure 2.5. In a situation of increasing returns, each additional unit of input causes the level of output to increase more than the last unit of input.

(Quick Quiz 2.10: Figures 2.4 and 2.5 show an upward slope. Do both graphs demonstrate increasing returns?)

Decreasing Returns occur when the addition of one more unit of input results in a smaller increase in output than the previous unit.

Decreasing Returns = When each additional unit increases the production level, but with a smaller increase than the previous unit.

A production function that exhibits decreasing returns is shown in figure 2.6: the case of a kitchen. As more chefs are added, the productivity of the cooks increases, but at a decreasing rate. The first cook is the most productive, and as more cooks are added, the additional productivity declines.

Negative Returns occur when an additional unit of input actually decreases total output. This is a situation where the input is actually causing harm to the production process. Using our cooks in a kitchen example, if the kitchen were very small, then the addition of the second cook would lower cook number one's ability to prepare meals. In many situations, adding inputs results in a loss in output. Although this may sound strange at first, we have already encountered situations where negative returns have been at play. Do you remember the wheat farmer who applied Nitrogen fertilizer to her field? If too much fertilizer was applied, then the Nitrogen actually burned the wheat plants, and lowered yield. Also, we saw that cattle ranchers who use too large of doses of growth hormones can actually lower the weight gain by steers, as they can become sick if too many hormones enter the bloodstream. Negative returns are illustrated in figure 2.7.

Negative Returns = When each additional unit of input added to the production process results in lower total output than the previous unit of input.

Figure 2.6. Food Production: Decreasing Returns.

Prepared Food (meals)	Cooks (persons)	Added Output = $(\Delta Y/\Delta X)$
0	0	--
10	1	10
18	2	8
24	3	6
28	4	4
30	5	2

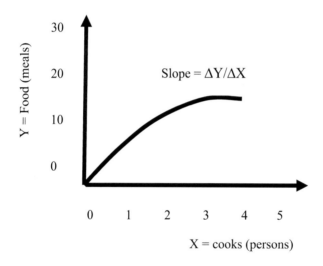

Figure 2.7. Small Kitchen Example: Negative Returns.

Prepared Food (meals)	Cooks (persons)	Added Output = ($\Delta Y / \Delta X$)
0	0	--
10	1	10
9	2	-1
7	3	-2
4	4	-3
1	5	-3

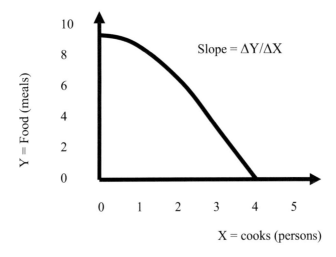

The negative slope in figure 2.7 corresponds to a production function characterized by negative returns. Any time there is "too much of something," then it is a condition of negative returns.

2.3.2 A "Typical" Production Function.

Most production processes can be characterized by increasing returns, decreasing returns, and then negative returns. Why do economists believe that this production pattern is so prevalent? Remember the production function that we are describing: we are looking at the relationship between output (Y) and a single input (X), *ceteris paribus* (holding all else constant).

Think of our wheat farmer, who used land, labor, capital, and management to produce wheat. Suppose that this farmer has several hundred acres of wheat, and holds all of the inputs constant except one: the number of combines. During harvest time, the first combine will allow this farmer to produce a large amount of grain. In fact, the mechanized combine was given its name because it combined the reaping function (cutting grain) with the threshing function (separating the wheat from the chaff). Compared to harvesting wheat by hand, combines can boost production enormously.

(Quick Quiz 2.11: what is the Wichita State University mascot? How does it relate to our example?)

Getting back to our story, the first combine will provide a very large amount of output. A second combine will be really helpful, and will allow the farmer to take advantage of having two combines going at once. This can actually increase production by even more than the first combine. This remains true for the first several combines. After several combines are used on the same field, however, the efficiency begins to fall: decreasing returns set in, as combines begin to get in each other's way. When many combines are used, production can actually decrease, since the farm operator must manage too many machines. This process can be seen in figure 2.8.

Figure 2.8

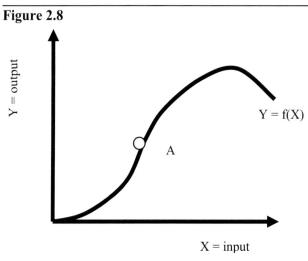

In real-world production processes, the "typical" production function almost always holds. As a single input is increased, holding all other inputs constant, the productivity will typically increase as more units of the input are used in the production process. At a certain point, adding more of the input will cause the increase in productivity to increase at a decreasing rate. This is the point in the graph where the slope of the production function turns from increasing to decreasing (point A).

2.3.3 Total Physical Product.

The **Total Physical Product** (TPP) is the relationship between output (in this case corn) and one variable input (labor), holding all other inputs constant (figure 2.9). It is measured in physical terms and represents the maximum amount of output brought about by each level of input use. Below is a table and graph of the TPP relationship for the corn farmer in Iola.

Total Physical Product [TPP] = The relationship between output and one variable input, holding all other inputs constant. It is measured in physical terms and represents the maximum amount of output brought about by each level of input use.

2.3.4 Average Physical Product.

The **Average Physical Product** (APP) refers to the average productivity of each unit of variable input used (see figure 2.10). The APP is calculated by dividing the quantity of output by the quantity of input (Y/X). Average Physical Product tells how much output is produced by the entire quantity of input.

Average Physical Product [APP] = The average productivity of each unit of variable input used [=Y/X].

The concepts of TPP and APP must be graphed on two separate graphs. The reason is that TPP is expressed in different units than APP. Specifically, TPP is expressed in units of output, whereas APP is expressed in units of output per unit of input.

Figure 2.9. Corn Production: Total Physical Product.

Labor (workers)	TPP = corn (bu)
0	0
1	100
2	210
3	330
4	405
5	475
6	500
7	490

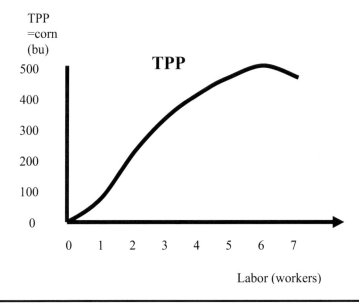

2.3.5 Marginal Physical Product.

The **Marginal Physical Product** is the amount of additional, or marginal, total physical product obtained from using an additional, or marginal, unit of variable input (see figure 2.10). This concept tells us how much more output we get from the last, or marginal, unit of input. We will use the word, "marginal," throughout the rest of the course. The word marginal refers to a small incremental change. Using mathematical notation, marginal is a "small change," which we symbolize with the Greek letter Delta (Δ). The MPP is the change in output (ΔY) brought about by a change in input (ΔX), or:

$$MPP = \Delta Y / \Delta X.$$

Marginal Physical Product [MPP] = The amount of additional, or marginal, total physical product obtained from using an additional, or marginal, unit of variable input [$=\Delta Y/\Delta X$].

Figure 2.10. Physical Product of Corn: Average and Marginal Product.

Labor (wkrs)	TPP (bu)	APP (bu/wkr)	MPP (bu/wkr)
0	0	-	-
1	100	100	100
2	210	105	110
3	330	110	120
4	405	101.25	75
5	475	95	70
6	500	83.33	25
7	490	70	-10

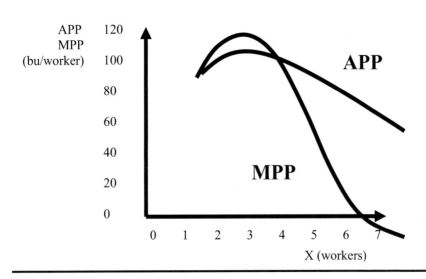

48

In figure 2.10, we can see that **Average Physical Product** (APP) and **Marginal Physical Product** (MPP) are derived from the information on inputs (X) and outputs (Y). Notice that output is identical to TPP, and in this case is corn in bushels. To derive APP, we divide TPP in the second column by the number of workers found in the first column for each input level. In the first row, note that if there are zero workers, no corn is produced, which makes good sense. If there are no workers, the corn cannot be planted or harvested. To calculate APP for the first row, we divide TPP (=0) by the number of workers (=0), which is not easy. Any number divided by zero is undefined, so we place a dash in the first row for APP. In the second row, we divide TPP=100 by X=1 to get APP=100. Similarly for the remaining rows, we can calculate average productivity by dividing Y by X [APP=Y/X]. The graph shows that APP increases up to a given level, then decreases. Remember that the APP refers to the average productivity of all inputs used.

Marginal Physical Product (MPP) can be calculated in a similar fashion. The MPP is the change in output given a small change in input ($\Delta Y/\Delta X$). To calculate MPP, we must look at a change in the input level, and find out how much the output level changed as a result of the input change. In figure 2.10, we note that when we increase the number of workers from zero to one [$\Delta X=1-0=1$], output increases from zero bushels to 100 bushels of corn [$\Delta Y=100-0=100$]. By definition, MPP=$\Delta Y/\Delta X$=100/1=100, as can be seen as the first entry in the MPP column in the table above. The MPP refers to the productivity of the last unit of input, or the additional unit of input. By calculating MPP, we are asking ourselves the question, "how much more output will be produced by adding one more input?"

Let's take a look at the MPP of using a second worker: the change in input is one [$\Delta X=2-1=1$], and the change in output is 110 [$\Delta Y=210-100=110$]. The marginal productivity of labor increased when a second worker was added.

(Quick Quiz 2.12: be sure that you can calculate the APP and MPP columns in the table above. To test your ability, complete the following table for a beef producer. In this example, the input is bushels of corn (which is fed to cattle) and the output is meat in pounds. Graph TPP, APP, and MPP.)

Table 2.1 Data for Quick Quiz 2.12.

Corn (bu)	TPP (lbs)	APP (units=?)	MPP (units=?)
0	0		
10	10		
20	40		
30	65		
40	80		
50	90		
60	80		

2.3.6 Relationship between Average and Marginal Physical Product.

The APP and MPP are both directly derived from the TPP. Therefore, APP and MPP are intimately related to each other. Their close relationship is worth noting, and can be described as follows:

If MPP > APP then APP is increasing.
If MPP < APP then APP is decreasing.

An easy way to remember this is: "*AVERAGE CHASES THE MARGINAL*." This can be seen in the graph of APP and MPP.

Figure 2.11

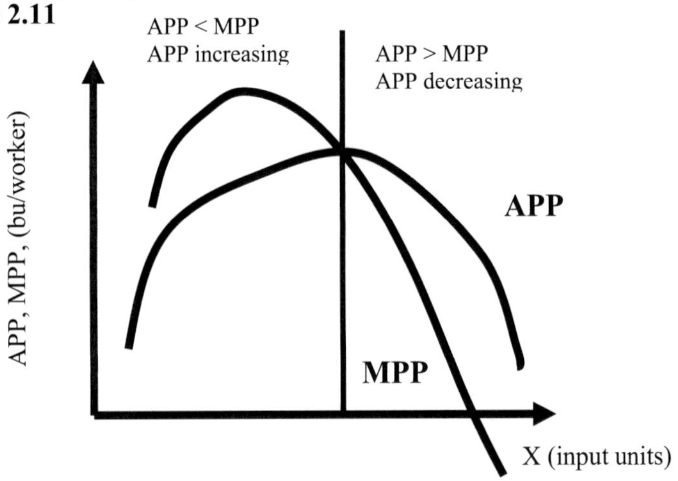

APP < MPP
APP increasing

APP > MPP
APP decreasing

APP, MPP, (bu/worker)

APP

MPP

X (input units)

An example of this is L.A. basketball player Kobe Bryant's average productivity and marginal productivity. We can think of Kobe's productivity as the number of points that he scores in a season. Think of Kobe's APP as the average number of points that Bryant scored in a game, and his MPP as the number of points that he scored in his last (marginal, or additional) game.

TPP = total season points scored
APP = Average Points per game
    = season points/games = TPP/X
MPP = Marginal Points per game
    = change in season points/change in games = $\Delta TPP/\Delta X$
    = points scored in the last game.

Suppose that Kobe's average points per game = 40 points/game. If Kobe scores 80 points in last game, then his Average increases.

MPP > APP (80 > 40), so APP increases
If Kobe scores 20 points in last game, then his Average decreases.

MPP < APP (20 < 40), APP decreases.

This simply states that the incremental, or marginal, change pulls the average up or down. "The average chases the marginal."

Another example is the wheat farmer adding Nitrogen to the wheat field. In this case, Y is output of wheat in bushels.

TPP = Total Physical Product
    = Y = wheat (bu)
APP = Average Physical Product
    = Y/N = wheat/nitrogen (bu/lb)
MPP = Marginal Physical Product
    = $\Delta Y/\Delta N$ = Δwheat/Δnitrogen (bu/lbs)

The Average Physical Product refers to the productivity for all pounds of nitrogen applied. The Marginal Physical Product refers to the additional number of bushels of wheat that are produced from one additional pound of nitrogen. Do you understand the difference?

When the marginal physical product is greater than the average physical product, the APP will increase. The relationship between the average and marginal physical product curves will look like those in the graph above.

51

In the case of a cattle feedlot, the production process is to add pounds of muscle to a steer by feeding it feed corn.

TPP = Total Physical Product
    = Y = beef (lbs)
APP = Average Physical Product
    = Y/X = beef/corn (lbs/bu)
MPP = Marginal Physical Product
    = $\Delta Y/\Delta X = \Delta beef/\Delta corn$ (lbs/bu)

In this example, the units are different, but the relationship between average and marginal physical products is the same.

(Quick Quiz 2.13: draw the TPP, APP, and MPP graphs for the feedlot example in table 2.1).

A last example is the productivity of Homework Assignments: we can all relate to this example, since the output is the scores on assignments. Here, TPP refers to all of the points scored on all of the assignments. Let's take a look at scores on the first three assignments. In this case, TPP is the total points scored on the three assignments, APP is the average points scored, and MPP is the number of points scored on the last (marginal) assignment. Suppose that you score 8, 8, and 10 on the first three assignments. Your average score is 8 for the first two assignments, then the marginal score rises above the average, which causes the APP to increase, as can be seen in figure 2.12.

Table 2.2. Assignment Scores Example One.

Assignment	Score	TPP	APP	MPP
1	8	8	8	8
2	8	16	8	8
3	10	26	8.67	10

Figure 2.12

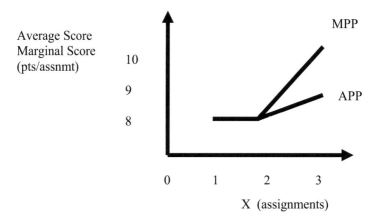

The marginal score is the incremental, or additional score on last assignment. The average score is the average for all assignments. Now suppose that after scoring two 8's, you receive a score of 6 on assignment number three (table 2.3, figure 2.13). In this situation, the marginal score is below the average, and as a result, the APP must decrease (the average chases the marginal).

Table 2.3. Assignment Scores Example Two.

Assignment	Score	TPP	APP	MPP
1	8	8	8	8
2	8	16	8	8
3	6	22	7.33	6

Figure 2.13

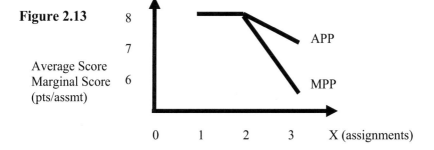

2.3.7 Technological Change.

Our newly gained knowledge of productivity and the production function can now be put to use to understand an important issue: technological change. Think of all of the wonderful and amazing technologies that have been developed in our lifetimes! The Internet and the information age have all occurred in the past few years, and have changed the world forever. **Technological Change** allows production processes to become more efficient.

Technological Change = allows the same level of inputs to produce a greater level of output. Restated, technological change allows the same level of output to be produced with a smaller number of inputs.

Graphically, technological change is an upward shift in the production function, as in figure 2.14. Technological change shifts the wheat production function from Y_0 to Y_1.

Figure 2.14

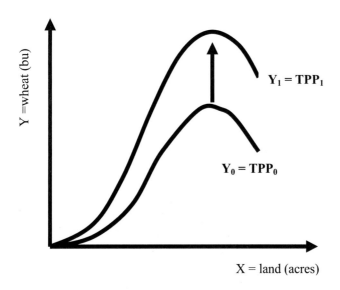

A good example of technological change in wheat production is the wheat breeding program in the Agronomy Department of Kansas State University. Through genetic selection and biotechnology, the wheat breeders have been able to develop new varieties of wheat seeds

54

that result in higher wheat yields (more bushels per acre) in the Great Plains region. All of the other inputs used in the production of wheat (land, chemicals, fertilizer, labor, etc.) can be held constant (ceteris paribus), yet the new seed varieties result in higher yields. Technological change is pervasive in agriculture: output continues to increase as new methods of farming and raising animals for food are developed and adopted.

4. The Law of Diminishing Marginal Returns.

We have now learned enough economics to propose a "law," which just means that the production relationship is universal. The name of this law is the **Law of Diminishing Marginal Returns**, which simply states that as we use more of a single input, holding all other inputs constant, the increase in productivity will eventually decline.

Law of Diminishing Marginal Returns = As additional units of one input are combined with a fixed amount of other inputs, a point is always reached at which the additional output produced from the last unit of added input will decline.

Why is this true? The answer comes from the foundation of economics: scarcity. As we add more of a single input, we are holding all other inputs fixed. This means that there are not enough other resources to accommodate the input that we are increasing. If scarcity did not exist, we could increase the use of ALL inputs, and we could continue producing more and more goods and services. There would be no need for economics in this case: we could produce more than enough of every good! In that case, choices would not need to be made, because we would have everything that our heart desired.

Think of some examples: the first hour of studying is the most productive. After studying for several hours, our energy runs low and our productivity declines. This holds true for all productive activities. We can think of crop production in the United States as another example. As the USA was settled by Europeans, the most productive lands were cleared and planted to crops first, because they produced the largest output. As more acres of land came into production, productivity fell, since the best lands were settled first. This is in accordance with the Law of Diminishing Marginal Returns. Note that productivity need not be negative for the Law to hold, as we can see in figure 2.15.

Figure 2.15

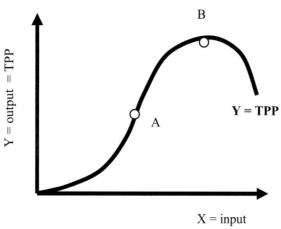

X = input

Diminishing Returns begin when the rate of productivity begins to fall (point A), or when we move from a situation of increasing returns to decreasing returns. A common mistake is to think that the Law of Diminishing Marginal Returns means that the returns to adding one additional unit of input are negative, which occurs to the right of point B. The Law says that additional productivity must decline, or the *slope* of the TPP curve must decline, which occurs at point A.

5. Geometry of Physical Product Curves.

So far, we have only spoken of the physical relationships between inputs and outputs. We have not spoken of economic relationships yet.

In this chapter, we have been describing the production activities that take place in Departments such as the Agronomy Department and the Department of Animal Sciences and Industry, but we have not yet included the *dollar value* of these productive activities. Therefore, we are looking at what is physically possible given the current state of technology. Our next task is to use geometry to graph the physical product curves, to gain a better understanding of the relationships between total, average, and marginal products.

Figure 2.16

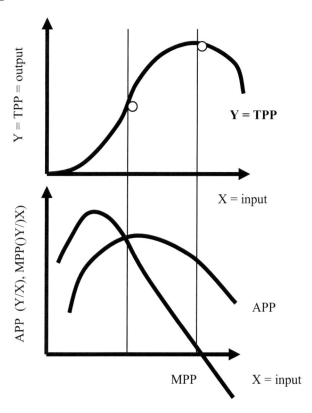

In figure 2.16, the Total Physical Product (TPP) has the "typical" construction of increasing, decreasing, and then negative returns. Two points have been identified in the TPP graph to make it easier to draw the APP and MPP graphs below it. Remember that the TPP curve must be drawn separately from the APP and MPP curves, since the units are different: TPP is in units of output, and APP and MPP are in units of output per unit of input.

Average Physical Product (APP) is defined as output divided by input, or Y/X. To graph the APP curve, select a point on TPP curve (X_o, Y_o) in the graph below. By definition, APP is equal to Y_o/X_o. The slope of any line is equal to the "rise over the run," or the change in Y divided by the change in X ($\Delta Y/\Delta X$). Therefore, the slope of a ray through origin is equal to the APP at the point where the ray through the origin meets the TPP curve. As the slope of the ray through origin increases, it will eventually reach a maximum, and then decrease.

Figure 2.17

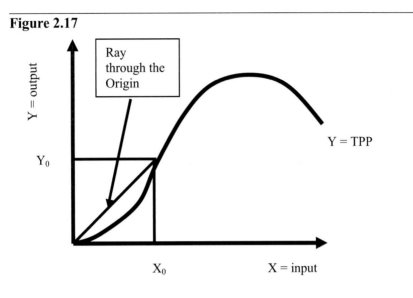

Ray through the Origin

Y = output

Y_0

Y = TPP

X_0

X = input

Starting at X=0 and moving from left to right, we can see that the slope of the ray through the origin increases as we move from rays A to B to C in figure 2.18.

Since the slope of the ray through the origin is increasing from A to B to C, the APP function drawn immediately below the TPP function is increasing. The APP function continues to increase until the vertical line is reached. At that point, the slope of ray through the origin reaches its highest point. This occurs at ray D, where the slope of the ray through the origin is at its highest point. To the right of the vertical line, as we move from rays D to E, the slope of the ray through the origin decreases, thus the APP decreases also. The APP curve is tightly linked to the TPP curve: the same information is plotted in both curves; they are drawn using different units. The TPP curve is drawn in units of output (Y), and the APP curve is drawn in output per unit of input (Y/X).

Now we turn to the Marginal Physical Product curve. Marginal Physical Product (MPP) is defined as the change in output brought about by a small change in input ($\Delta Y/\Delta X$). Notice that this definition is identical to the definition of the slope of a line. Therefore, the MPP is equal to the slope of the TPP function. Note that this differs from the slope of the ray though the origin, which is the definition of the APP curve. We can use the graphs below to derive the MPP curve. Since MPP is the slope of the TPP curve, we can use the top diagram to derive the MPP curve in the bottom diagram.

Figure 2.18

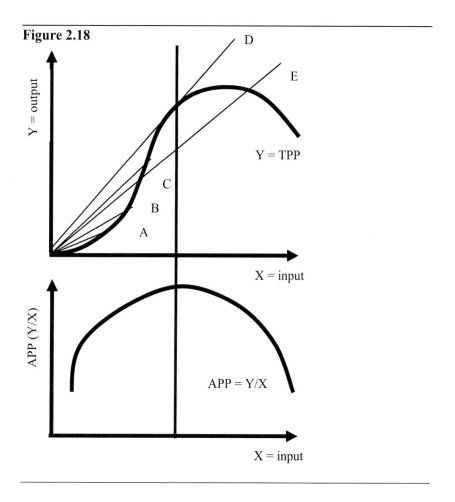

(Quick Quiz 2.14: why are the two functions not drawn on the same graph?)

In the top diagram, notice that the TPP function is increasing at an increasing rate until point C is reached. At that point, diminishing returns set in, and the TPP function continues to increase, but at a decreasing rate. The Total Physical Product continues to increase at a decreasing rate until the maximum TPP is reached at point D, then the TPP declines as more input is added to the production process.

(Quick Quiz 2.15: State the Law of Diminishing Returns, and explain why it must hold for the TPP function figure 2.19)

The slope of the TPP curve can be found at any point along the curve by looking at a line that is tangent (tangent means, "touching at only one point") to the curve. By taking a close look at the TPP curve, we can see that the slope of the TPP curve increases from the origin to point C, where the slope of the TPP function reaches its highest point. To the right of C, the slope is decreasing, but positive until point D is reached. At D, the slope is equal to zero. To the right of D, the slope of TPP is downward-sloping, or negative. This pattern is reflected in the MPP curve drawn below the TPP panel.

Figure 2.19

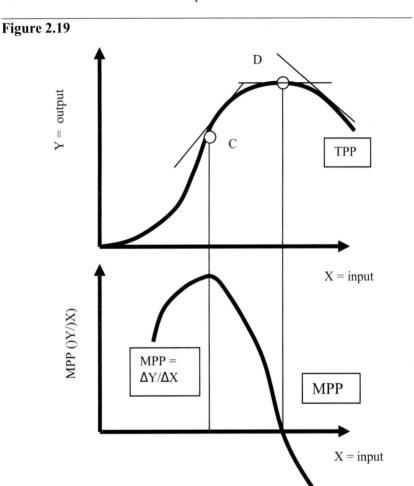

By combining both APP and MPP curves onto one graph, we can see the relationship between the average and marginal curves. Specifically, the APP and MPP curves intersect at the point when the slope of TPP (MPP = $\Delta Y/\Delta X$) is equal to the slope of the ray through origin (APP = Y/X). At this single point, the slope of TPP and the slope of the ray through the origin are equal, so $\Delta Y/\Delta X = Y/X$.

Figure 2.20

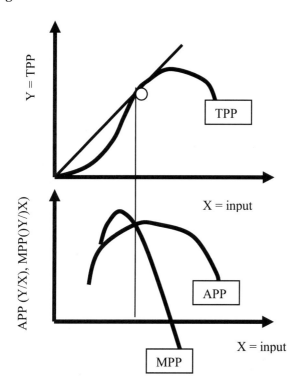

---

6. The Three Stages of Production.

Assume that producers are "rational," which simply means that they desire to maximize profits. If a producer's objective is to maximize profits, we can use production economics to show that she will always operate within a certain range of input use, as shown in the diagram below.

Stage I of production is defined by a level of input use that is to the left of point A, where APP = MPP (identified in the preceding section). Stage I is considered to be an "irrational" stage of production, because the producer can become more efficient if she increases the quantity of input used. This can be seen by the APP curve in Stage I. The APP curve is the average productivity of the production process. Since the average productivity is increasing, the producer can get more productive outcomes by increasing the level of input use. Therefore, the rational producer will never locate in Stage I, because productivity could increase by using more inputs.

Figure 2.21

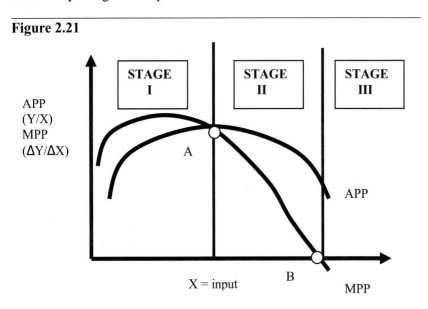

Stage III is also an "irrational" stage of production. The third stage of production is defined by input levels greater than point B, where MPP becomes negative. In this stage, the producer is using "too much" input, since total productivity is decreased due to the input use. Total output would increase if the quantity of inputs were decreased! In other words, higher levels of productivity would be achieved at lower levels of input use (think of too many cooks in the kitchen actually lowering the number of meals cooked). Stage III is considered to be irrational, since the producer could produce greater levels of output in by using fewer inputs.

Stage II is found between Stage I and Stage III. Stage II is considered to be the "rational" stage of production, since the producer is operating in the region of input use that is most productive. The exact point of input use that is "optimal," or profit-maximizing depends on the price of the input, or the cost of acquiring the productive resource. We will find this profit-maximizing point in Chapter 4.

Chapter Two Summary

1. Production is the process of combining scarce resources into outputs.
2. A production function is the physical relationship between inputs and outputs.
3. The point of maximum physical output is not always the optimal economic level of output.
4. To graph a production function in a two-dimensional graph, we look at the relationship between one output and one input, *ceteris paribus* (holding all else constant).
5. In economics, we assume that the goal of all producers is to maximize profits. Profits are equal to total revenues (the value of production sold) minus total costs of production.
6. The immediate run is a period of time in which all inputs are fixed. In the short run, at least one input is fixed. The long run is a period of time in which all inputs are variable.
7. The length of time that defines the long run depends on the specific situation: it is the length of time that it takes for all inputs to become variable.
8. A fixed input does not vary with the level of output. A variable input does vary with the level of output.
9. A constant returns production function is characterized by output increasing at a constant rate for each additional unit of input used. Increasing returns occur when an additional unit of input results in more additional output then the previous unit of input. A production function characterized by decreasing returns is one where each additional unit of input increases output, but at a smaller rate than the previous unit. Negative returns occur when output decreases as additional units of input are added.
10. A typical production process is characterized by increasing returns,
decreasing returns, and then negative returns.
11. Total Physical Product (TPP) is the relationship between output and one variable input, holding all other inputs constant. Average Physical Product (APP) is the average productivity of each unit of variable input (Y/X). Marginal Physical Product (MPP) is the amount of additional, or marginal, total physical product obtained from using an additional, or marginal, unit of variable input.

12. If MPP is greater than APP, then APP is increasing; if MPP is less than APP, then APP is decreasing. The average chases the marginal.

13. Technological change is an upward shift in the production function. Technological change allows more output to be produced with the same level of inputs.

14. Stage I occurs when APP<MPP, or when APP is increasing. It is an irrational stage of production, since productivity could be enhanced by increasing the level of input use. Stage II occurs when MPP<APP, and MPP>0. This is the rational stage of production. Stage III occurs when MPP<0. Stage III is an irrational stage, since increased input use results in lower levels of output. The rational producer will locate input use in Stage II.

Chapter Two Glossary

Average Physical Product [APP]. The average productivity of each unit of variable input used [=Y/X].

Constant Returns. For each additional unit of input used, output increases at a constant rate (the rate of change in output remains constant).

Decreasing Returns. Each additional unit increases the production level, but with a smaller change than the previous unit.

Fixed Input. An input whose quantity does not vary with the level of output.

Immediate Run (IR) = A period of time in which all inputs are fixed.

Increasing Returns. Each additional unit of input added to the production process yields more additional product than the previous unit of input.

Law of Diminishing Marginal Returns. As additional units of one input are combined with a fixed amount of other inputs, a point is always reached at which the additional output produced from the last unit of added input will decline.

Long Run [LR]. A time span such that no inputs are fixed; all inputs are variable.

Marginal Physical Product [MPP]. The amount of additional, or marginal, total physical product obtained from using an additional, or marginal, unit of variable input [=$\Delta Y/\Delta X$].

Negative Returns. When each additional unit of input added to the production process results in lower total output than the previous unit of input.

Production Function. The physical relationship between inputs and outputs.

Profits [π]. Total revenues minus total costs; the value of production sold less the cost of producing that output.

Short Run [SR]. A time span such that some factors are variable and some factors are fixed.

Technological Change. Allows a greater level of output to be produced with fewer inputs, or the same level of output to be produced with fewer inputs. An upward shift in the production function.

Total Physical Product [TPP]. The relationship between output and one variable input, holding all other inputs constant. It is measured in physical terms and represents the maximum amount of output brought about by each level of input use.

Variable Input. An input whose quantity does vary with the level of output.

Chapter Two Review Questions

1. The production function is a(n):
    a.   economic relationship
    b.   physical relationship
    c.   mathematical property
    d.   party for producers
2.   In the following production function:
    $Y = f(L| K, A, M)$:
    a.   ceteris paribus does not hold
    b.   labor is held constant
    c.   land is allowed to vary
    d.   labor is allowed to vary
3.   In economics, we assume that producers attempt to:
    a.   do the best that they can to get by
    b.   maximize profits
    c.   feed the world
    d.   produce enough food to feed their family
4.   Profits are equal to:
    a.   costs of production minus revenues
    b.   total revenues minus total costs
    c.   average revenues minus average costs
    d.   marginal revenues minus marginal costs
5.   The long run is defined as:
    a.   ten years
    b.   one year
    c.   depends on the situation
    d.   when at least one input is fixed
6.   If all inputs are variable except land for a wheat producer, then:
    a.   the firm is in the short run
    b.   the firm is in the long run
    c.   the firm is in the immediate run
    d.   the firm is not in production
7.   A variable input is one that:
    a.   changes with the weather
    b.   moves up and down
    c.   varies with the level of output
    d.   varies with the level of other inputs

8. In decreasing returns, as an additional unit of input is added to a production process:
   a. output increases at an increasing rate
   b. output decreases
   c. output increases, but at a decreasing rate
   d. output remains constant

9. When too much of an input is used, and output decreases, the production process is:
   a. constant returns
   b. increasing returns
   c. decreasing returns
   d. negative returns

10. If average productivity is 20 bu/acre, and marginal productivity is 30 bu/acre then:
   a. average productivity is increasing
   b. average productivity is decreasing
   c. average productivity is constant
   d. average productivity is negative

11. The relationship between average and marginal is:
   a. average causes marginal
   b. marginal causes average
   c. average chases marginal
   d. marginal chases average

CHAPTER THREE
THE COSTS OF PRODUCTION

1. Profits.

In our study of production, we assumed that the goal of a business firm is to maximize **Profits**. We make this assumption about all firms, whether they are a large multinational corporation such as Microsoft or Cargill, or a small family-owned business such as a family farm in Western Kansas or a family restaurant in Topeka. We begin our study of the costs of production in this chapter by reviewing what profits are, and how the level of profits is affected by the costs of production. Profits (π) are defined as total revenues (TR) minus total costs (TC).

$$\pi = TR - TC$$

Total revenues simply refer to how much money a firm earns from the sale of its output (Y). Total Revenues are found by multiplying the number of units of output (Y) by the per-unit price of the output (P).

$$TR = P*Y$$

The units for TR are in dollars, since output (Y) times price ($/Y) is in terms of dollars, as the units of output cancel each other.

The level of Total Costs (TC) is determined by the payments that a firm must make to purchase the factors of production. The previous chapter emphasized that the production of a good or service requires inputs to be transformed into output by a business firm. These inputs are not free, but require payments because they are scarce. The sum of all of the payments for inputs are the Total Costs that a firm must pay to produce a good.

(Quick Quiz 3.1: define scarcity. What implications does scarcity have on the production process?)

In many counties in Kansas, an award is presented to the corn or wheat producer who attains the highest yield in the county. The award winner typically wins a cash prize and publicity in the local newspaper. What does an economist think about these awards? Not much, as we shall see. One of the main concepts that economists and agricultural economists can offer to family farmers and agribusinesses is the idea that the maximum level of *profits* differs from the highest level of *production*.

A county yield contest encourages farmers to grow the maximum level of output. This requires large amounts of scarce inputs, and is a costly activity. To grow the highest-yielding crop in the county, a farmer will apply a huge amount of inputs, and devote a large amount of time to picking every single weed out of the field, and nurturing every single plant to its highest level of production. The contest winner will have total costs (the costs of those scarce inputs) that are much higher than the value of the crop on the marketplace (TR). Let's use a simple graph of Total Revenues and Total Costs to see why.

Figure 3.1

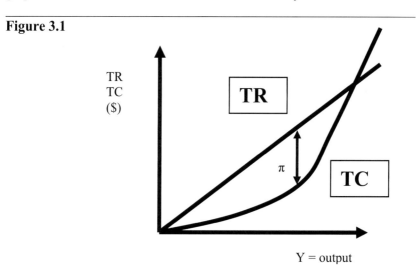

In Figure 3.1, we can see that profits (π) are the vertical difference between the TR curve and the TC curve, because by definition, profits equal TR minus TC. Total Revenues are defined as price times output, so TR are an increasing function of output, which is located on the horizontal axis of figure 3.1. Note that this is the same output level that was found on the vertical axis of the production function in Chapter Two. Total Revenues are a linear function of output, since the price of output is constant ($/Y). The more output that the firm produces and sells, the higher the level of TR.

Total Costs also rise with increasing levels of output, but at an increasing rate. This is due to the Law of Diminishing Marginal Returns: the production process will at some point become less productive, which means that it will become more costly. What does this say about county

69

yield contests? This analysis indicates that a farmer could very well be spending way too much money on the inputs necessary to win the award.

From an economist's point of view, the emphasis would be better placed on *profits* rather than *yields*. An economist would advise the producer to weigh the benefits and the costs of producing a higher yield: the maximum yield is often not the highest level of profits. It costs too much to get there. To win the award, the farmer is spending too much on inputs, especially labor. The producer may be better off backing off of production and looking at both benefits and costs of each activity.

This is how economists think: to determine the level of input use, an economist will compare the benefits of the input to the costs. If the benefits of using one more unit of input are greater than the cost of the input, then the unit of input should be purchased and used. If the costs of the input are higher than the benefits, then the input should not be purchased.

The comparison of benefits and costs is the most important "take home lesson" from this course in the economics of agriculture! In every activity that we undertake, an economist will ask himself or herself the question, "do the benefits of this activity outweigh the costs?" If the rewards of the activity are bigger than the costs, then the activity should be undertaken! This is true for producers deciding how much fertilizer to apply to their fields, or how much corn to produce, or for consumers trying to decide how many slices of pizza to eat, or for students trying to decide how many hours to study for an upcoming test.

This economic approach to decision making is enormously useful, and the ability to think like an economist is scarce. Therefore, this ability is very valuable! The salaries of Agricultural Economics and Agribusiness majors provide evidence that this is true: learning to think like an economist can provide you with many rewards in life, including greater financial rewards, better personal decision making, and more career choices. Our study of the costs of production will allow us to gain a better understanding of how to make solid economic decisions.

2. Opportunity Costs.

When we speak of costs in economics, we need to specify exactly what we are talking about. In economics, total costs include two types of costs: **Accounting Costs** and **Opportunity Costs**. Accounting costs are explicit costs, or payments that a business firm must actually make in order to obtain factors of production.

Accounting Costs = Explicit costs of production; costs for which payments are required.

Bookkeepers, or accountants consider only **accounting costs**. Economists include **opportunity costs**, which are the value of a resource in its next-best alternative use.

Opportunity Costs = The value of a resource in its next-best alternative use. What an individual or firm must give up to do something.

Opportunity costs exist for every activity that we undertake. By studying economics, you are giving up your "next-best alternative," which might be studying biology, listening to music, partying, or seeing a movie. Farm operators are giving up the opportunity to be a Professor, or a mechanic, or whatever their next-best occupation might be.

My son Charlie wants to be both a soil scientist and an Architect. The trouble is, he can't be both. If he becomes a soil scientist, his opportunity cost would be how much he was giving up by not being an Architect. My daughter Katie takes dance lessons, but would also like to take Tae Kwon Do (karate) lessons with Charlie and I. Since we are a busy family, she must give up martial arts in order to take dance lessons. Therefore, the opportunity cost associated with taking dance lessons is the cost of not taking Tae Kwon Do. The concept of opportunity cost is quite powerful, and can be used to explain all kinds of economic (and noneconomic) behavior.

All resources have opportunity costs associated with them, not only labor. For example, the opportunity cost of planting one acre of land into wheat would be the value of planting the next-best alternative crop on that acre of land. Every resource has a "next-best use," which is its opportunity cost. The key idea to remember is that in economics, total costs (TC) always include both the accounting (or explicit) costs, and the opportunity costs, or what must be given up to use the resource. We will use examples below to gain more confidence with this concept.

3.2.1 Profits (Again!).

Returning to our definition of **profits** $[\pi = TR - TC]$, we can now see that we must be careful about the definition: what types of costs are included in the term, "TC?" Which costs are included in the definition of profits? We can answer these questions with some simple definitions and then an example.

3.2.2 Accounting Profits.

Accounting Profits are profits that subtract only explicit costs from total revenues. This type of profits are what accountants calculate, and reflect only the explicit monetary costs of producing and selling a good.

Accounting Profits (π_A) = Total revenues of a firm minus explicit costs. $\pi_A = TR - TC_A$.

Notice that accounting profits do not take opportunity costs into account. When we include opportunity costs in our calculations of profit, we are speaking of economic profits.

3.2.3 Economic Profits.

Economic Profits are the pure profit left over after all costs, including the full opportunity costs of all inputs, are deducted from total revenues.

Economic Profits (π_E) = Total revenues of a firm minus both explicit and implicit costs. $\pi_E = TR - TC_A$ - opportunity costs.

Remember that the opportunity cost refers to the value of a resource in its next best alternative use.

3.2.4 Opportunity Cost Example: Wheat Grower in Atwood, Kansas.

Our example will illustrate the difference between accounting profits and economic profits. Consider a wheat farmer in Atwood, Kansas, in the Northwest corner of the Sunflower State.

CASE ONE.

Suppose that this producer grows and sells 25,000 bushels of wheat at a price of $4/bu. Also assume that the wheat production function requires 10 months of managerial labor to produce.

(Quick Quiz 3.2: define a production function.)

An easy calculation can be made to find that TR=$100,000.

(Quick Quiz 3.3: show how this calculation was made.)

72

Let's turn to the costs of production. [Note: we will use simplified cost numbers here to make our example simple. Actual cost data could be easily used for any farm or agribusiness operation]. First, the explicit, or accounting costs only:

Costs:
1. Chemicals	$20,000
2. Machinery	$20,000
3. Seed, fertilizer	$20,000
4. Land (rent)	$20,000
5. Hired Labor	$10,000
TC=	$90,000

Continuing with our story, suppose that an accountant adds up all of the accounting costs (explicit costs, which are the costs on the books) for this wheat producer. The accounting costs are explicit costs: things that you write a check for. The total accounting costs (TC_A) are equal to $90,000, the sum of all of the payments made for the inputs to produce wheat.

Accounting profits can now be easily calculated:

$\pi_A = TR - TC_A = \$100,000 - \$90,000$
$\pi_A = \$10,000.$

Next, we can calculate the level of economic profits, and compare the results to accounting profits. Remember that economic profit is what is left over after all costs including opportunity costs are deducted ($\pi_E = TR - TC_A$ - opportunity costs). Restated, economic costs include both accounting costs and opportunity costs.

To calculate economic costs, we use the following formula:

$TC_E = TC_A +$ opportunity costs
$TC_E = \$90,000 +$ opportunity costs

Opportunity costs are simply the value of a resource in its next best alternative use. Suppose that this owner-operator could earn $1,000/month in town as a salesperson with a farm implement dealer. In this case, we can calculate the opportunity cost of being a wheat farmer for this individual, remembering that the wheat production process required ten months of managerial labor:

73

Opportunity cost = 10 months*$1,000/month = $10,000
Opportunity cost = $10,000.

The levels of economic costs and economic profits can now be found:

TC_E = $90,000 + $10,000 = $100,000

π_E = TR - TC_E
π_E = $100,000 - $100,000 = 0.

At first glance, it appears that this wheat producer is not doing very well, since his economic profits are equal to zero. In reality, this is not a bad thing. The farmer is earning exactly what he is worth, or exactly his opportunity cost. The farmer's accounting profits are positive (=$10,000), which is exactly what he could be making in his next-best alternative job. So, oddly enough, when economic profits equal zero, all resources are paid exactly what they are worth! To confirm this idea, let's continue with our example.

CASE TWO.

For the second case, assume that the farmer continues to grow and sell 25,000 bushels of wheat at the prevailing market price of $4/bu. Therefore, total revenues (TR) remain equal to $100,000. Suppose that the federal government increases the minimum wage, so that the wages paid to the hired help increase. Now, the cost of hired workers to help out with wheat harvest increases to $15,000. To keep our example simple, assume that the minimum wage increase is the only change in the costs of production facing this firm.

TR = $100,000

Costs:
1. Chemicals	$20,000
2. Seed, fertilizer	$20,000
3. Hired Labor	$15,000
4. Land (rent)	$20,000
5. Machinery	$20,000
TC=	$95,000

π_A = $100,000 - $95,000 = $5,000
π_E = $100,000 - $95,000 - $10,000 = -$5,000

In this second case, the increase in the minimum wage has resulted in negative economic profit for this producer. Interestingly, the farmer might stay in business anyway. Why? Many farmers have strong ties to the occupation of agriculture, and will try to stay in farming even if they are subject to negative economic profits. This is possible because the accounting profits are positive, so the bills are being paid. In this case, the farmer is giving up the possibility of earning more money in his next best alternative job: he gives up $5,000 to remain in agriculture. This is a very realistic scenario for many persons employed in jobs such as agricultural production or teaching, where income levels are often lower than in other areas.

If the farmer remains in agriculture with negative economic profits, however, he is violating the assumption that the objective of all producers is to maximize profits. Many individuals are content to work in a job that has rewards other than money. In our study of economics, we will continue to assume profit maximization, as it simplifies our analysis greatly, and the major conclusions of economics remain the same with or without the assumption.

REMEMBER THAT ALL COSTS IN ECONOMICS INCLUDE OPPORTUNITY COSTS!!!

Another example of economic costs that is close to home is the full costs of attending Kansas State University. The explicit, or accounting costs of attending college include tuition, fees, together with room and board, textbooks, football tickets, etc. The opportunity cost is the value of a resource in its next-best alternative use. In this case, the resource is you, and the opportunity cost is how much you could earn in another field with a high school diploma. So the full, or economic, cost of attending college is not only the high costs of paying for your undergraduate education, but also what you must give up to be here: your annual salary in the job that you gave up to come here.

3. Costs and Output.

In this section, we will explore the relationship between the level of output produced by a firm and the costs of producing that output. Total costs will increase as more of a good is produced, since resources are scarce and must be paid for.

(Quick Quiz 3.4: should a firm always strive to produce the highest level of output?)

Recall the definition of the short run: a period of time when at least one input is fixed. A fixed input is one that the quantity of input cannot be changed. An example is the number of acres of land in an agricultural business. In the short run, it is often impossible to change the size of a farm, as agricultural real estate may not be up for sale. Another example is the plant size of a business firm in Aggieville. If one of the many pizza restaurants in the 'Ville desired to increase its size, it may be difficult to accomplish in the short run due to a lack of building space available. These examples demonstrate that some inputs are fixed in the short run.

Also in the short run, other inputs are variable, which means that their quantity can be changed. For a wheat farm, variable inputs might include: chemicals, labor, fertilizer, etc., since the items in this list are easy to change, even in a short amount of time. Using the knowledge that some inputs are fixed and some are variable, we can break total costs down into two categories: fixed costs and variable costs.

Total Fixed Costs (TFC) = The total costs of inputs that are fixed (inputs that do not vary with the level of output).

Total Variable Costs (TVC) = The total costs of inputs that are variable (inputs that vary with the level of output).

Total Costs (TC). The sum of Fixed Costs and Variable Costs. TC = TFC + TVC.

Fixed Costs are payments to fixed factors such as land or machines that can not be altered in the short run. Variable Costs are payments to variable factors, such as chemicals, labor, or management, that can be changed in the short run.

(Quick Quiz 3.5: how long of a time period is the long run?)

In the Long Run, all factors are variable. This is because over a longer period of time, a producer can buy more machines and more land. Producers can adjust the size of their farm. There is no set number of years for the long run, it just depends on the situation (which is the answer to Quick Quiz 3.5!).

Since fixed factors do not vary with output, fixed costs must be paid regardless of output. Examples include (1) rent to landlord that must be paid no matter what, and (2) a payment to the bank for a loan taken out to purchase machines. These **Fixed Costs** must be paid, no matter how much you produce. Therefore, the key item to remember about fixed costs is that they do not vary with output. Restating for emphasis: ***FIXED COSTS DO NOT VARY WITH THE LEVEL OF OUTPUT.***

As can be seen in figure 3.2, fixed costs do not vary with output: these costs must be paid whether the firm produces zero units of output or a huge amount of output or any level of output in between.

Figure 3.2

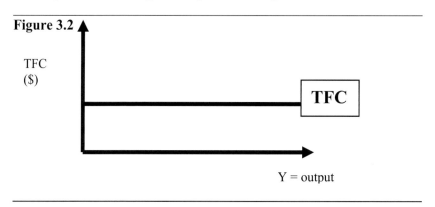

Variable Costs, on the other hand, increase with the level of outputs, due to the fact that producing firms must purchase more of these resources to increase the quantity of output produced. This can be seen in figure 3.3 below.

Figure 3.3

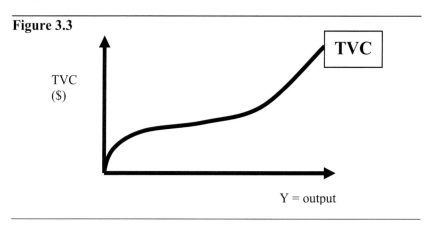

These costs increase for a wheat farmer, for example, because more labor and more chemicals are required to produce more wheat output. The interesting shape of the TVC curve is due to the "typical" shape of the production function that we studied in the previous chapter. Notice that the slope of the TVC curve is positive, but decreasing in the range of output near the origin. This reflects the increasing productivity of a production process as more inputs are added. Further to the right, the total variable cost curve begins to increase at an increasing rate, reflecting the Law of Diminishing Marginal Returns.

(Quick Quiz 3.6: state the Law of Diminishing Marginal Returns, and explain the shape of the TVC curve.)

3.3.1 Standard Cost Curves.

Total Costs (TC) are the sum of Total Fixed Costs (TFC) and Total Variable Costs (TVC). Graphically, we can add TFC and TVC together to get TC, as in figure 3.4.

Figure 3.4

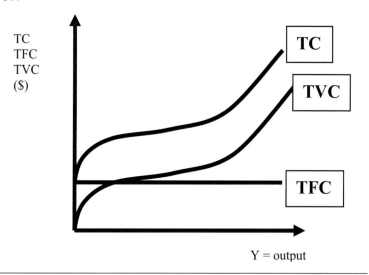

In addition to total costs, the average, or per-unit, costs of producing goods are of interest. Average Costs (AC) can be calculated by dividing the Total Costs (TC) by the level of output (Y): AC = TC/Y. **Average Total Costs (ATC)** allow us to calculate how much it costs to produce a single unit of output. We are also interested in **Average Fixed Costs (AFC)** and **Average Variable Costs (AVC)**. The formal definitions of these concepts are:

Average Fixed Costs (AFC) = The average cost of the fixed costs per unit of output. AFC = TFC/Y.

Average Variable Costs (AVC) = The average cost of the variable costs per unit of output. AVC = TVC/Y.

Average Total Costs (ATC) = The average total cost per unit of output. ATC = TC/Y.

The concept of **Marginal Cost** is the additional cost of producing one more unit of output. The marginal, or incremental, cost helps us to think like economists, since we can ask ourselves the question: do the benefits of producing one more unit of output outweigh the costs? We will emphasize this "marginal way of thinking" in the next chapter on profit maximization.

Marginal Costs (MC) = The increase in total cost due to the production of one more unit of output. MC = ΔTC/ΔY.

The average, or per-unit, costs and marginal costs can all be graphed all on the same graph, because they all share the same units: dollar per unit of output. Note that the total cost curves (TC, TFC, and TVC) can be graphed on the same graph (figure 3.4) because all of the total costs are in dollars.

Figure 3.5

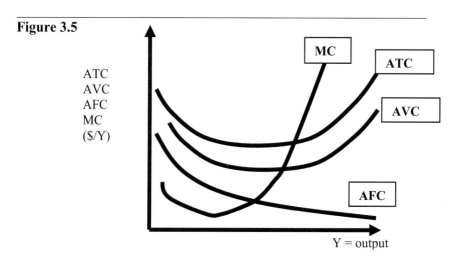

The per-unit cost curves shown in figure 3.5 are intimately related to the total cost curves in figure 3.4. These curves are the "typical" cost curves for a business firm that has the "typical" production function of increasing returns followed by decreasing returns. Notice in figure 3.5 that the average total costs decrease, reflecting an increase in

79

productivity, and then increase, due to decreasing returns. The marginal cost curve cuts through the AVC and ATC curves at the minimum point on each curve. To get some practice at deriving these curves, we will use an agricultural example in the next section.

4. Cost Curve Example: A Dairy Farmer in Ottawa, Kansas.

In this section, we will use an example of a dairy farm to derive the cost curves introduced above numerically and graphically. To begin this example, think about what the fixed costs and variable costs would be for a milk producer. Fixed costs might include a rental payment to the landlord, or a payment to the bank for a loan on milking machines.

(Quick Quiz 3.7: what are fixed costs? Why would a loan payment be a fixed cost? List one more input for this dairy that could be a fixed cost.)

Variable costs might include payments for cows, feed, the veterinary services bill, medicine, electricity, etc.

(Quick Quiz 3.8: what are variable costs?
Why is electricity a variable cost? In the long run, what will the variable costs be?)

Now, let's use the definitions of costs given above to calculate the total, average, and marginal costs for the dairy farmer. We will use small numbers to illustrate the cost curves for a dairy farm, to make our math simpler. Real-world dairy farms could use their cost data to calculate the same cost curves. The total fixed costs for this firm are the payments that must be made to (1) the landlord for pasture rent, and (2) the payment that must be made to the bank for the loan on the milking machines. Suppose that each of these payments is equal to $5, so TFC = $10.

(Quick Quiz 3.9: if the dairy were to shut down in the short run, what would the fixed costs be equal to? If the dairy were to double the number of cows milked in the short run, what would the fixed costs be?)

Here are the cost curve definitions, and a table of costs. If you know the first three columns on the left side of the table (Y, TFC, and TVC), the rest of the table can be easily derived with the formulas below.

$$TC = TFC + TVC$$
$$ATC = TC/Y$$
$$AVC = TVC/Y$$
$$MC = \Delta TC/\Delta Y$$

Note that the units of output for the Ottawa Dairy Farm are 1000 pounds of milk. Each unit of Y is equal to one thousand pounds of milk produced on the farm.

Table 3.1 Dairy Farm Production Costs.

Y = milk (1000 lbs)	TFC($)	TVC($)	TC($)	ATC($/Y)	AVC($/Y)	MC($/Y)
0	10	0	10	--	--	--
1	10	10	20	20	10	10
2	10	18	28	14	9	8
3	10	23	33	11	7.67	5
4	10	30	40	10	7.5	7
5	10	40	50	10	8	10
6	10	56	66	11	9.33	16
7	10	74	84	12	10.6	18

We will begin our description of table 3.1 with the left column, and move toward the right across the table. The first column is output (Y), in units of 1000 pounds. The second column is Total Fixed Costs (TFC), which by definition, do not vary with output. The TFC are constant at $10 for all units of milk produced.

(Quick Quiz 3.10: why do fixed costs not vary with the level of output? What do the fixed costs for this dairy farmer in Ottawa represent?)

Total Variable Costs (TVC) appear in the third column. Variable costs do change with the level of output, and increase as more output is produced. To follow the "standard" production process for a firm, the Total Variable Costs increase at a decreasing rate, then at an increasing rate, as will be seen momentarily when we graph these costs. Total Costs (TC) are simply the sum of the Total Fixed Costs and Total Variable Costs (TC = TFC + TVC). Notice that all of the total costs (TC, TFC, and TVC) are in units of dollars.

Average Total Costs (ATC) are simply per-unit total costs, or TC/Y. These per-unit costs decrease, then increase. Average Variable Costs are the Total Variable Costs (TVC) divided by output (TVC/Y). The AVC follow the same pattern as the ATC. The next column is AFC, or Average Fixed Costs. This represents the payments to fixed factors per unit of output, found by dividing Total Fixed Costs by the amount of milk produced (AFC = TFC/Y). The average fixed costs decline as more output is produced: the dairy farmer is spreading these fixed payments over more output, so average fixed costs decline with larger quantities of milk produced. This is a major explanation as to why agribusiness firms continue to increase in size: bigger output means lower per-unit costs. Expansion of output can lower per-unit costs in many circumstances. We will return to this theme throughout the semester. Graphing these costs will provide us with a better understanding of their shapes and meaning.

Figure 3.6

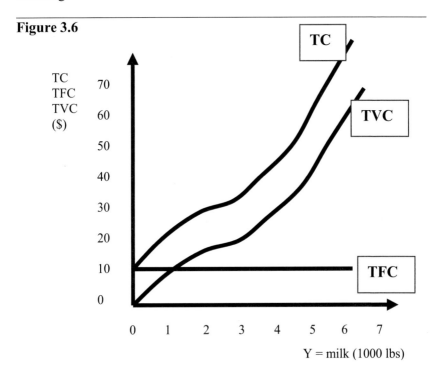

Total Cost curves for the Ottawa Dairy Farmer can be seen in Figure 3.6. The TFC curve is perfectly horizontal, demonstrating that fixed costs are constant at all levels of output. Notice that even in the extreme case of the dairy shutting down and producing no milk at all, the fixed costs must be paid. The Total Variable Cost (TVC) curve shows the pattern of costs increasing at a decreasing rate over the first units of output, then costs increasing at an increasing rate at output levels increase. Total Costs (TC) are the sum of fixed and variable costs, which is why the TC curve lies directly above the TVC curve. The vertical distance between the TC and TVC curves is exactly the level of fixed costs. Next, we turn to a graph of the per-unit costs.

(Quick Quiz 3.11: why are total, average, and marginal costs all shown in the table 3.1, but we use a separate graph for (1) total and (2) average and marginal costs?)

Figure 3.7

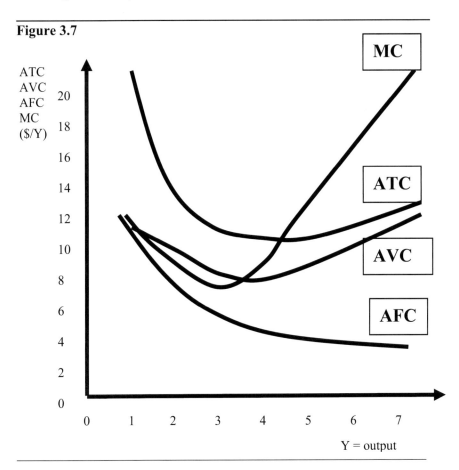

The cost curves for the dairy farmer have the same shape as the cost curves derived above in figures 3.4 and 3.5, due to the typical production function relationship of productivity increasing at an increasing rate, then at a decreasing rate due to the Law of Diminishing Marginal Returns. This relationship between the costs of production and the production curves will be explored in the next section.

5. Where Do Cost Curves Come From?

The costs of production are intimately related to the productivity of a firm. A firm that is more efficient will have lower costs of production. In this section, we will make the connection between the physical product curves from Chapter Two with the cost curves introduced in this chapter. Recall that the production function is the physical relationship between inputs (X) and output (Y).

$$Y = f(X_1, X_2, ... X_n)$$

Since graphs and paper only have two dimensions to work with, we isolate the relationship between one input and output by holding all of the other inputs constant.

$$Y = f(X_1 | X_2, ... X_n)$$

We can see in figure 3.8 the typical production relationship of increasing then decreasing returns in production, together with cost curves that are increasing at a decreasing rate, then increasing at an increasing rate.

Figure 3.8

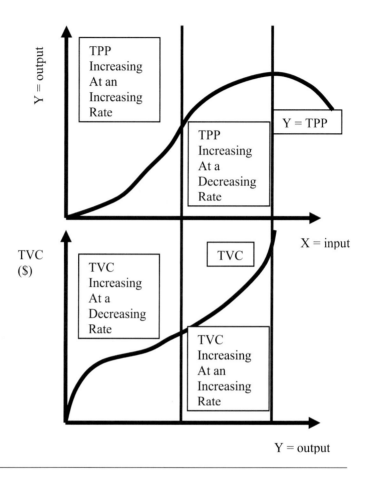

The relationship between physical product curves and cost curves can also be seen in the per-unit graph, shown in figure 3.9. The average and marginal product curves in the top half of the diagram are the exact mirror image of the average and marginal cost curves in the bottom half of the diagram. Mathematically, we can derive this inverse relationship by noting that the total variable costs of a firm are the payments made to the variable inputs. In this case, we have isolated a single input (X_1) as variable, and held all other inputs constant. Let P_1 be the price of input X_1.

Figure 3.9

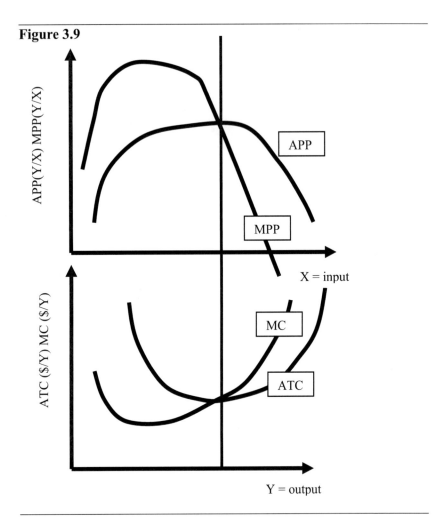

$$TVC = P_1 * X_1$$
$$AVC = TVC/Y$$
$$APP = Y/X_1$$

$$AVC = TVC/Y = P_1*X_1/Y = P_1*(X_1/Y) = P_1/(Y/X_1) = P_1/APP$$

This result shows that the AVC curve is inversely (oppositely) related to the APP curve, just as in the diagram. We can also show that the marginal cost curve is inversely related to the MPP curve:

$$MC = \Delta TC/\Delta Y = \Delta(P_1*X_1)/\Delta Y = P_1*(\Delta X_1/\Delta Y) = P_1/(\Delta Y/\Delta X_1) = P_1/MPP$$

Now that is a cool result! It shows that marginal costs and marginal physical products are inversely related, as in the graph. Figure 3.9 summarizes the close connection between physical product curves and cost curves: an increase in productivity (increase in APP) is identical to a decrease in costs (decrease in ATC). The relationship between average and marginal costs is the same as the relationship between average and marginal physical products, as explained in the next section.

3.5.1 The Relationship Between Average and Marginal Costs.

As we noted in Chapter Two, *"The average chases the marginal."* This simply means that:

(1)   If MC > AC, then AC is increasing
(2)   If MC < AC, then AC is decreasing

Here, average costs (AC) can refer to either Average Total Costs (ATC) or Average Variable Costs (AVC). The result above occurs because the marginal cost reflects the additional cost of producing one additional unit of output, so if it is larger than the average, it "pulls" the average up. If MC, the additional costs of producing the last unit, are smaller than the average, it "pulls" the average down.

Figure 3.10

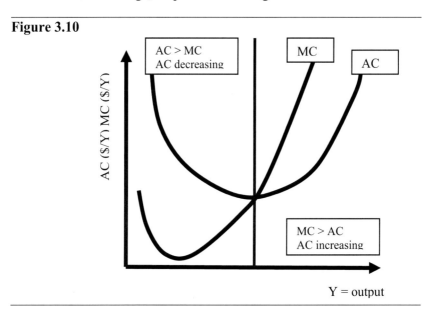

This relationship between average and marginal is true for anything: grades, costs, revenues.

(Quick Quiz 3.12: graph the relationship between average and marginal grades).

6. The Geometry of Cost Curves.

In this section, we will explore the relationship between TC, AC, and MC curves.

Figure 3.11

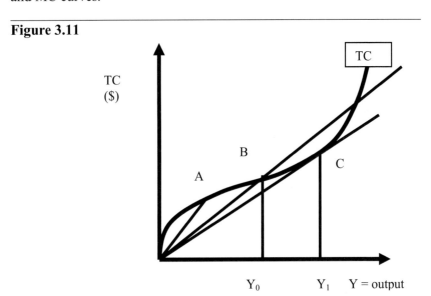

Average Total Costs are defined as: $ATC = TC/Y$. This simply states that we divide TC by Y_0 to find the average cost of producing Y_0 units of a good. Geometrically, this is found by a ray through the origin. Why? Because the slope of a ray through the origin is equal to the "rise" over the "run," which in this case is equal to $\Delta y/\Delta x = TC/Y$. For every quantity of output produced, the AC curve can be found by the slope of the ray through the origin to the point of the TC curve. In figure 3.11, from a quantity of 0 to Y_1, the AC curve is decreasing, since the slope of the ray through the origin decreases from O to A to B. Geometrically, the slope of the ray through the origin declines until it hits Y_1. At quantities larger than Y_1, the ray through the origin becomes steeper again. This results in the shape of the average cost curve being "U-shaped," with a declining portion and an increasing portion.

Marginal costs are: $MC = \Delta TC/\Delta Y$, which are the marginal, or additional, or incremental addition to costs, since the ")" refers to a "small change" in the total. Since the slope of any function is defined as the "rise" over the "run," the slope of the TC curve is equal to $\Delta y/\Delta x = \Delta TC/\Delta Y$ in figure 3.11. There, the slope of TC is positive but decreasing until point Y_0, then it increases again.

Figure 3.12

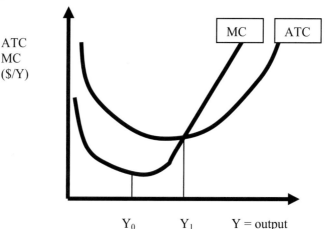

7. Constant, Decreasing, and Increasing Cost Curves.

Section Seven discusses four possible types of cost curves of a business firm: constant, decreasing, and increasing cost structures, as well as the "standard" cost curves that were explained above.

3.7.1 Constant Cost Firm.

A constant cost firm is one that faces constant production costs for all units of output produced. This means that the first unit of output produced has the identical costs of production as the last unit of output produced. An example is a feedlot in Western Kansas. A feedlot purchases cattle and fattens them until they are ready for slaughter. The fattening process is one of feeding the cattle large quantities of feed (corn, sorghum, soybean meal) together with some vitamins and nutritional supplements. A typical feedlot pays the same amount for each bushel of feed, no matter how many steers are being fed. The idea that the firm pays the same amount for inputs can be shown in figure 3.13.

Figure 3.13

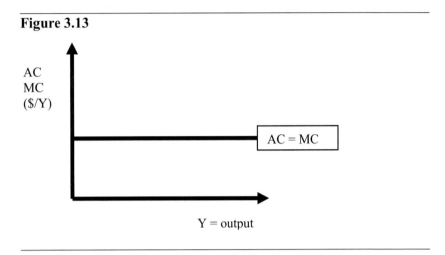

No matter how many units of output are produced, the per-unit cost is the same at a given point in time. Since the marginal cost of producing a unit of output is fixed (constant), then MC is horizontal and AC = MC. The average chases the marginal, but in this specific case, it has caught it! For a constant cost firm, the average costs (AC) equal the marginal costs (MC), as shown above.

3.7.2 Decreasing Cost Firm.

Decreasing costs occur when the per-unit costs of a firm decline as more output is produced. An example of a decreasing cost firm is the IBP packing plant in Emporia, Kansas. Packing plants, also called slaughterhouses, convert the fattened cattle from feedlots in Western Kansas into steaks, hamburger, and leather. These are very large facilities, with enormous electricity, water, and labor requirements. Due to this huge scale, the average costs of a meat packing firm decline as greater quantities of meat are produced. Each additional pound of meat can be produced at a lower per-unit cost, since the large fixed costs (the electricity, water, and labor) are spread over more units of output.

Since MC < AC, AC is decreasing. The huge fixed costs result in the outcome that more output means greater productivity and lower costs, as shown in figure 3.14.

Figure 3.14

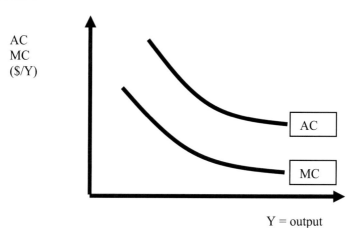

In the case of a decreasing cost firm, the MC always lie below the AC, and the AC are declining. Other examples of declining cost firms are: electric plants and cable television companies. These examples are of firms that have a huge network, or distribution system. The high costs of installing power generators and power lines to every house in the network region result in a decreasing cost structure for an electricity plant. This also holds true for cable television companies, who must invest a large amount of money in developing the cable network throughout town. The more customers who purchase electricity and cable television, the lower the per-unit costs of production will be.

3.7.3 Increasing Cost Firm.

An increasing cost firm is one whose per-unit cost of production increases as more output is produced. Firms that produce fixed natural resources, such as oil, lumber, or coal typically have cost structures that are increasing. This is because a fixed resource becomes more scarce as more is extracted from the earth, making the cost of production of the resource increase as more of the good is produced and used up. An increasing cost structure (figure 3.15).

For an increasing cost industry, the cost of obtaining the resource becomes greater as more of the resource is produced. This is because the lowest-cost resources are used first; with costs increasing as more resource is produced. For example, the costs of digging a mine deeper, or hauling lumber further increase as more resource is extracted.

Figure 3.15

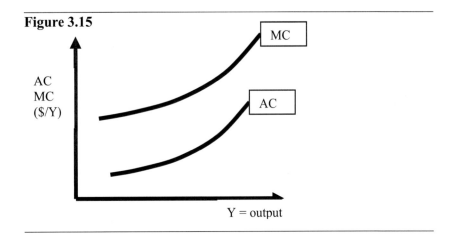

Note that the MC is everywhere above the AC curve, and that AC is increasing (average chases the marginal).

3.7.4 Standard Cost Curves Revisited.

The standard cost curves involve all three types of costs: decreasing AC, constant AC, and increasing AC.

Figure 3.16

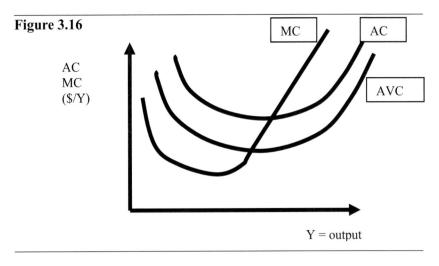

These cost curves are now familiar to us; we have used them throughout Chapter Three. In the next Chapter, we will find the profit-maximizing point.

Chapter Three Summary

1. Profits equal total revenues minus total costs. Total Revenues equal the product price times the level of output. Total costs are the payments paid to acquire factors of production.
2. Accounting costs are the explicit costs of production. Opportunity costs are the value of a resource in its next-best alternative use.
3. Accounting profits are total revenues minus explicit costs. Economic profits are total revenues minus explicit and opportunity costs.
4. When all resources are earning their opportunity costs, economic profits are equal to zero, and the resources are earning as much as they are worth.
5. Some farmers and ranchers remain in agriculture, even if they are earning negative economic profits, since they prefer a career in farming or ranching even if it pays less than what they could earn in a different occupation.
6. Total fixed costs do not vary with the level of output.
7. Average fixed costs are fixed costs per unit of output. Average variable costs are variable costs divided by the level of output. Average total costs are total costs divided by the level of output.
8. Marginal cost is the additional cost of producing one more unit of output.
9. A typical total cost curve increases at a decreasing rate, and then increases at an increasing rate, as diminishing marginal returns set in.
10. If MC>AC, the average costs are increasing; if MC<AC, then average costs are decreasing.
11. A firm's cost curves reflect the firm's productivity: an increase in productivity is identical to a decrease in costs.
12. A constant-cost firm faces constant production costs for all units of output produced.
13. A decreasing cost firm has per-unit costs that decrease as more output is produced.
14. An increasing cost firm has increasing per-unit costs as more output is produced.
15. A firm with "standard" cost curves is one whose average costs decrease, then increase.

Chapter Three Glossary

Accounting Costs. Explicit costs of production; costs for which payments are required.

Accounting Profits (π_A). Total revenues of a firm minus explicit costs. $\pi_A = TR - TC_A$. (Also see **Economics Profits**).

Average Costs (AC). Total costs per unit of output. $AC = TC/Y$. Note that **Average Costs** (AC) are identical to **Average Total Costs** (ATC).

Average Fixed Costs (AFC). The average cost of the fixed costs per unit of output. $AFC = TFC/Y$.

Average Total Costs (ATC). The average total cost per unit of output. $ATC = TC/Y$. Note that **Average Costs** (AC) are identical to **Average Total Costs** (ATC).

Average Variable Costs (AVC). The average cost of the variable costs per unit of output. $AVC = TVC/Y$.

Costs of Production. The payments that a firm must make to purchase inputs (resources, factors).

Economic Profits (π_E). Total revenues of a firm minus both explicit and implicit costs. $\pi_E = TR - TC_A -$ implicit costs. (Also see **Accounting Profits**).

Fixed Costs. Those costs that do not vary with the level of output; the costs associated with the fixed factors of production.

Marginal Costs (MC). The increase in total cost due to the production of one more unit of output. $MC = \Delta TC/\Delta Y$.

Opportunity Costs. The value of a resource in its next-best alternative use. What an individual or firm must give up to do something (the value of the next best alternative).

Profits (π). Total Revenues minus total costs. $\pi = TR - TC$. (Also see **Accounting Profits** and **Economic Profits**).

Total Costs (TC). The sum of Fixed Costs and Variable Costs. TC = TFC + TVC.

Total Fixed Costs (TFC). The total costs of inputs that are fixed (inputs that do not vary with the level of output).

Total Variable Costs (TVC). The total costs of inputs that are variable (inputs that vary with the level of output).

Variable Costs. Those costs that vary with the level of output; the costs associated with the variable factors of production.

Chapter Three Review Questions

1. Corn producers interested in maximizing profits should:
   a. maximize yield
   b. maximize revenues
   c. consider both costs and revenues
   d. minimize costs
2. Accounting costs include all of the following except:
   a. electricity payment
   b. payment to hired workers
   c. how much money the operator could earn as a plumber
   d. fertilizer costs
3. Opportunity costs are:
   a. explicit costs
   b. the value of a resource in its current use
   c. implicit costs
   d. the value of a resource in its previous use
4. Economic profits are:
   a. accounting profits
   b. total revenues minus accounting costs
   c. total revenues minus accounting costs and opportunity costs
   d. total revenues minus marginal costs
5. When economic profits equal zero:
   a. the firm should shut down
   b. the firm must increase profits
   c. the resources employed by the firm are underpaid
   d. resources are earning exactly what they are worth
6. In a situation of negative economic profits:
   a. the costs of production can not be paid
   b. accounting profits are negative
   c. accounting profits could be positive or negative
   d. the firm will shut down
7. In the short run:
   a. only fixed costs exist
   b. only variable costs exist
   c. both fixed and variable costs are present
   d. neither fixed nor variable costs are present
8. Variable costs:
   a. do not change with the level of output
   b. increase with the level of output
   c. decrease with the level of output
   d. fluctuate in a manner unrelated to the level of output

9. Total variable costs divided by output equal:
   a.   average variable costs
   b.   marginal costs
   c.   average fixed costs
   d.   total fixed costs
10. If MC > ATC, then:
   a. ATC are increasing
   b.   ATC are decreasing
   c.   ATC are constant
   d.   Can not be determined from the information given
11. All of the following are typical variable costs for a small business except:
   a.   Electricity
   b.   Hired labor
   c.   Paper
   d.   Rental payment
12. For a firm with typical cost curves:
   a.   The ATC increase then decrease
   b.   The ATC decrease then increase
   c.   MC is greater than ATC
   d.   ATC is greater than MC
13. A public utility such as Kansas Power and Light (KPL) is a:
   a.   Increasing cost firm
   b.   Decreasing cost firm
   c.   Constant cost firm
   d.   Can not be determined from the information given
14. A coal mining company is a:
   a.   Increasing cost firm
   b.   Decreasing cost firm
   c.   Constant cost firm
   d.   Can not be determined from the information given

CHAPTER FOUR
PROFIT MAXIMIZATION

In this chapter, we will learn how to make good economic decisions. The material in this chapter represents the "heart" of all economic decision making, and will provide a way of looking at the world that will be useful to you for the rest of your life... honest! This "economic way of thinking" is simply comparing the benefits and costs of every activity that we undertake, whether it is purchasing a new pickup truck, attending college, or studying late. Marginal analysis allows us to focus our attention on the advantages and disadvantages of each decision, resulting in better decision making and greater success.

We will learn how to select the profit-maximizing level of inputs to use in a production process, and the optimal level of output to produce. With a little imagination, we can see that marginal analysis, or the economic approach to decision making, can be usefully applied to a great number of decisions, choices, and issues.

1. Perfect Competition.

To determine the profit-maximizing levels of inputs and outputs, we will use the concepts of physical product curves and cost curves introduced in the two preceding chapters. An additional piece of information that must be known prior to learning to maximize profits is that of output price (P_Y). This price is the market price received by producers when they sell their output (Y) to consumers. The units of the output price are in dollars per unit of output ($/Y). The output price provides us with the value that consumers place on the firm's product.

When we introduce output price, we must also make some assumptions (simplifications) about the structure of the market in which the firm operates. This is done to simplify the analysis to something that we can easily learn and use, and later expand to fit the real world for specific situations. The major simplification that we will make is that the firm that we are studying is in an industry characterized by **Perfect Competition**. An "**Industry**" is a group of firms that all produce and sell the same product.

Industry = A group of firms that all produce and sell the same product.

Perfect Competition means something very specific in economics: it means that the industry has four characteristics:

1.   Large number of buyers and sellers,
2.   Homogenous product,
3.   Freedom of entry and exit, and
4.   Perfect information.

Let's take a close look at each of these characteristics.

1. Large number of buyers and sellers.

This condition states that there are numerous firms which sell a product, and many consumers who purchase it. This means that competition exists, so prices are assumed to be constant: each individual firm is so small relative to the market that it can not affect the price. This is due to competition: if one firm were to raise the price of a good above the competitive level, no buyers would pay the higher price, they would make their purchases from a different firm.

This is a key concept that we will make use of extensively:

UNDER PERFECT COMPETITION, OUTPUT PRICE IS FIXED.

In a perfectly competitive market, no individual firm can influence the output price. This means that we can assume that P_Y, the output price, is a constant in our study of profit maximization. No single seller or buyer has an influence on price.

(Quick Quiz 4.1: does agriculture have a "large number of buyers and sellers?")

2. Homogeneous product.

This concept refers to the idea that one firm's product is identical to the product sold by all other firms in the industry. The key idea is that a consumer can not tell which firm produced the good. Many agricultural products have this characteristic. Consider a truckload of wheat: a buyer could not distinguish who produced the crop.

(Quick Quiz 4.2: are cattle an example of a homogeneous good? Meat?)

3. Freedom of entry and exit.

Freedom to enter an exit an industry means that there are no "barriers to entry." Each firm can enter and leave the industry without encountering any government obstacles, or financial limitations to starting a business. Most small businesses, including farming, have freedom of entry and exit. A counterexample is a public utility, such as electricity production and distribution: this industry requires a government permit to enter. Medical doctors, dentists, professors, accountants, and many other professionals are required to obtain a license to practice their craft. In a competitive industry, a firm can enter and exit with ease.

(Quick Quiz 4.3: do farmers in Kansas have freedom of entry and exit?)

4. Perfect information.

Information is required in any business firm: a successful firm must know the prices of output and all inputs, and the quantities available of all inputs, in order to make good decisions. If a single firm had "inside information" about movements in future prices, that firm would have a distinct advantage over other firms, and would be able to earn higher profit levels. This form of cheating is what Enron, WorldCom, and Martha Stewart have recently been charged with. In a perfectly competitive industry, all buyers and sellers know all prices, quantities, qualities, etc. There are no informational advantages in an industry characterized by perfect competition.

(Quick Quiz 4.4: how realistic is the assumption of perfect information?)

Recall why scientists must make assumptions: the real world is extraordinarily complicated, and we must simplify the real world in order to understand it. All scientists use this type of simplification to acquire a better understanding of the world in which we live. The four characteristics of a perfectly competitive industry are unlikely to hold completely in the real world. However, the assumptions guide us toward solid knowledge by first using the assumptions, then later relaxing the assumptions and adding complexity to our simple analysis.

The major point to remember about perfect competition is that the prices are constant in a competitive industry.

PERFECT COMPETITION = FIXED, CONSTANT PRICES

A competitive firm is called a "price taker," since it must take price as fixed and given, and can not change the price. Firms in market structures other than competition may be able to influence the market price of a good, and these firms can be considered to be, "price makers." Competitive firms that meet the four criteria listed above, however, will always be price takers, having no influence on prices.

Price taker. A competitive firm that can not influence the price of a good.

Price maker. A non-competitive firm that can influence the price of a good.

We will draw upon the assumptions of perfect competition throughout the remainder of the course, and particularly in this chapter on profit-maximization.

2. The Profit-Maximizing Level of Input.

We will now turn to one of the fundamental exercises in all economics courses: maximizing profits! Sounds good, doesn't it? First, let's examine the economic approach to decision making.

4.2.1 Economics: How To Make Better Decisions.

What we are really doing in economics is learning how to look at business and/or personal decisions in a new way. The economic way of thinking is the idea that in everything that we do, every decision that we make, we should compare benefits and costs. If the benefits are greater than the costs of any activity, do it! For example, if your satisfaction of eating a slice of pizza is greater than the cost of the pizza, you should eat the slice! Pretty simple, huh? Seems logical, so why is it so useful? The usefulness comes from looking at decisions "on the margin," or incrementally.

Marginal decision making is looking at the benefits and costs of each additional unit. The economic way of thinking, or marginal decision making, will allow us to determine the profit-maximizing levels of inputs and outputs, one unit at a time. Let's make some of these ideas explicit by reviewing marginal decision making with an example from the livestock industry.

4.2.2 Feedlot in Jetmore, Kansas: Physical Production.

As we have seen, a feedlot is a business firm that purchases steers and feeds them until they are ready for slaughter. So, the output

(Y) of a feedlot is beef in pounds, and the output price (P_Y) is the price of beef in dollars per pound:

Y = beef (lbs)
P_Y = price of beef = $1/lb

The price of beef in this example is $1/lb. We are already using the assumption of perfect competition! We are assuming that no matter how much beef that the feedlot sells, it will always receive one dollar per pound, or whatever the market price of beef is at the time.

The inputs in the feedlot's production process include steers, feed, water, medicine, hormones, etc. We can write out the production function for beef:

Y = f(feed, steers, water, medicine, hormones, …)

To focus on the profit-maximizing level of feed, we isolate the relationship between beef and feed, while holding everything else constant.

(Quick Quiz 4.5: what is the economic term for "holding all else constant?" Why do we do this?)

Y = f(feed | steers, water, medicine, hormones, …)

Remember that everything to the left of the vertical bar is a variable input, and everything to the right of the bar is held fixed. Let X refer to the feed input, in bushels of feed. The feed price is given by P_X, in dollars per bushel of feed.

(Quick Quiz 4.6: what is used for cattle feed in a feedlot?)

X = feed (bu)
P_X = price of feed = $5/bu
P_Y = price of beef = $1/lb

When we study the profit-maximizing level of inputs, it can become tricky to keep straight what the inputs and outputs are, as well as their prices. If you become lost, try to remember the actual physical production process to remind you of what the feedlot is all about: feeding steers. Recall that Y = f(X), where Y is fattened beef ready for slaughter, and X is the feed input. Next, let's take a look at a table of the physical product relationships from Chapter Two.

Table 4.1 Feedlot Production Process.

X= Feed (bu)	Y= beef (lbs)	APP= Y/X (lbs/bu)	MPP= ΔY/ΔX (lbs/bu)
0	0	-	-
1	10	10	10
2	30	15	20
3	60	20	30
4	80	20	20
5	90	18	10
6	96	16	6
7	98	14	2
8	96	12	-2

(Quick Quiz 4.7: do you remember what APP and MPP are? Can you define the terms?)

The term APP refers to Average Physical Product, or the per-unit productivity of all units of feed that have been used. It is the average productivity of all of the inputs. The MPP, or Marginal Physical Product, is the productivity of the last unit of feed used. The "marginal" input is the "additional" unit of input, which is used in economic decision making: we will compare the benefits and costs of an activity such as feeding steers *one unit at a time*.

We can graph the physical product curves to get a feel for the feedlot's production process.

(Quick Quiz 4.8: could we graph the TPP, APP, and MPP on the same graph? Why or why not?)

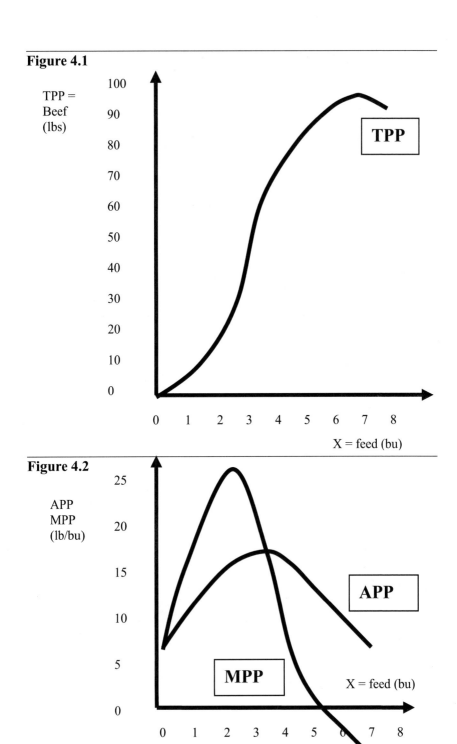

Figure 4.1

TPP =
Beef
(lbs)

100
90
80
70
60
50
40
30
20
10
0

TPP

0   1   2   3   4   5   6   7   8

X = feed (bu)

Figure 4.2

APP
MPP
(lb/bu)

25

20

15

10

5

0

APP

MPP

X = feed (bu)

0   1   2   3   4   5   6   7   8

4.2.3 Feedlot in Jetmore, Kansas: Value of Production.

The graphs in figures 4.1 and 4.2 show the physical relationships between inputs and outputs, or the production side of the firm, for the feedlot in Jetmore. The major activities of business firms can be broken down into two categories, (1) production, and (2) marketing. The marketing activity of the feedlot is what we will describe next. Once the beef has been produced, the feedlot converts physical units (pounds of beef) into values ($) by selling its product (fattened cattle) to the packing plant, or slaughterhouse.

To turn our discussion from production of physical units to the economic analysis of values, we must know how valuable the inputs and outputs are in dollar terms. To do this, we use the prices of the input (the price of feed, P_X), and the price of output (the price of beef, P_Y).

$P_Y = \$1/\text{lb}$ $\qquad\qquad$ $P_X = \$5/\text{bu}$

We also introduce a new term: the **Total Revenue Product (TRP)**, which is the total value of production. TRP converts our output from physical units (pounds of beef) to dollar values.

Total Revenue Product (TRP) = The dollar value of the output produced from alternative levels of variable input. TRP = TPP* P_Y.

The TRP is in dollars, since it is derived by multiplying the Total Physical Product (pounds of beef) by the price of output ($/pound of beef):

TRP = TPP(lbs)*P_Y($/lb) = ($).

We are now in a good position to study economic decision making because we know the value of the firm's output. Economic decision making is all about comparing the benefits with the costs of any activity. The benefits of feeding cattle in the feedlot are the revenues received from selling beef after production has occurred, or the TRP. The costs of feeding cattle are the **Total Factor Costs (TFC)** of feeding cattle. Remember that we have assumed that all inputs other than feed are fixed, or held constant.

Total Factor Cost (TFC) = The total cost of a factor, or input. TFC = P_X*X.

Using this definition, the costs are the total variable costs that must be paid for the feed:

$$TFC = P_X * X$$

The TFC are also in dollar units since we are multiplying the input (bushels of feed) by the price of the input (the price of feed, in dollars per bushel):

$$TFC = P_X(\$/bu) * X(bu) = (\$).$$

The benefits and costs for the Jetmore feedlot are shown in table 4.2.

Table 4.2. Feedlot Profit Maximization.

X	Y(=TPP)	TRP	TFC	Profits(=π)
(bu)	(lb)	($)	($)	($)
0	0	0	0	0
1	10	10	5	5
2	30	30	10	20
3	60	60	15	45
4	80	80	20	60
5	90	90	25	65
6	96	96	30	66
7	98	98	35	63
8	96	96	40	56

Starting with the left column, the number of units of input (X) is shown. The next column, TPP, is the number of units of output that can be produced with the corresponding level of inputs shown in the first column. The first two columns represent the production function shown in table 4.1 and figures 4.1 and 4.2: this is the *physical* relationship between inputs and outputs. To convert this technical, physical relationship into an economic relationship, we simply convert the physical units of output (pounds of Y, or TPP) into dollars by multiplying output by the price of output to get TRP in the next column. In this particular example, TRP has the same numerical values as TPP because the price of output is $P_Y = \$1/lb$.

(Quick Quiz 4.9: calculate TRP if the price of beef were equal to $2/lb.)

The next column shows TFC, or the feedlot's cost of production.

All costs are fixed, with the exception of the feed, which appears in the left column. Multiplying the left column by the input price gives us the total amount that the feedlot pays for feed.

Our goal as economists is to help the feedlot find the profit-maximizing, or optimal, level of input to purchase. To do this, we calculate the profits in the right column by simply subtracting the total factor costs (TFC) from the total revenue product (TRP) for each level of input (X). The profits are the amount of money left over after the inputs are paid for (π = TR – TC). To maximize profits, we just scan the profit column to find the highest value, which is equal to $66, when the feedlot uses 6 bushels of feed. Wow! We have just performed a major feat by calculating the profit-maximizing level of input for a business firm! This is exactly what economists do for real-world business firms. We have used simplified numbers, whereas economists in the real world would use the real cost and revenue data supplied by the firm, but the idea is much the same.

4.2.4 Feedlot in Jetmore, Kansas: Marginal Analysis.

The "trick" to economic analysis is to realize that we are finding the optimal (profit-maximizing) point by looking at input use ***ONE INPUT AT A TIME***, to find if the benefits of one more additional unit of input are greater than the costs. We do this with the help of the concepts of **Marginal Revenue Product (MRP)** and **Marginal Factor Cost (MFC)**.

Marginal Revenue Product (MRP) = The additional (marginal) value of output obtained from each additional unit of the variable input. MRP = MPP* P_Y.

The units for MRP are in units of dollars per unit of input: MPP is the per-unit quantity of output (lbs of beef per bu of feed), and the price of output is dollars per pound of beef.

MRP = MPP(lbs/bu)*P_Y($/lb) = ($/bu)

Marginal Factor Cost (MFC) is the additional cost of one more unit of input.

Marginal Factor Cost (MFC) = The cost of an additional (marginal) unit of input; the amount added to total cost of using one more unit of input. MFC = $\Delta TC/\Delta X$.

Notice that the same information is contained in the marginal revenue and cost concepts as in the total revenue and total cost concepts. This is true since the marginal concepts are derived from the total concepts. Therefore, the marginal analysis presented here will yield the identical profit-maximizing solution that was found in the previous section using total concepts. Let's find out if this claim is true by looking at the marginal analysis for the feedlot in table 4.3.

Table 4.3. Jetmore Feedlot Profit Maximization: Marginal Analysis.

X (bu)	TRP ($)	MRP ($/bu)	MFC ($/bu)
0	0	-	-
1	10	10	5
2	30	20	5
3	60	30	5
4	80	20	5
5	90	10	5
6	96	6	5
7	98	2	5
8	96	-2	5

The first two columns of table 4.3 replicate the input and TRP data from table 4.2. To calculate the MRP, we look at the changes in TRP according to each change in input use (MRP = ΔTRP/ΔX). We do this by taking a look at how the TRP column changes when we increase the feed input by one unit: when we increase feed from zero to one bushels ($\Delta X = 1 - 0 = 1$), TRP increases from zero to ten dollars ($\Delta TRP = 10 - 0 = 10$). Therefore, MRP = ΔTRP/ΔX = 10/1 = 10, our first entry in the MRP column. We can continue to calculate the change in TRP for each additional unit of feed used by the feedlot to generate the data in the MRP column.

A second method of calculating MRP is to calculate MPP, as we did in table 4.1, and simply multiplying by the output price. This follows from the definitions of MRP and TRP:

$$MRP = \Delta TRP/\Delta X = \Delta(TPP*P_Y)/\Delta X = (\Delta TPP/\Delta X)*P_Y = MPP*P_Y$$

(Quick Quiz 4.10: as a check, calculate the MRP using the definition: $MRP = MPP*P_Y$).

In the case shown here, the numerical values of MRP are equal to MPP, since the output price is equal to $1/lb. To find the profit-maximizing level of input use, the feedlot will continue to purchase feed as long as the benefits outweigh the costs. The marginal costs of purchasing a unit of feed are equal to the price of feed, five dollars per bushel ($P_X = \$5/bu$). Since we have assumed a perfectly competitive industry, the price of feed is fixed and constant at five dollars per bushel, for every bushel purchased by the feedlot.

(Quick Quiz 4.11: why does competition result in constant prices?)

The economist's advice is to continue with any activity as long as the marginal benefits are greater than the marginal costs. By comparing the MRP and MFC columns in table 4.3, we can determine the optimal number of bushels to feed by continuing to buy feed as long as MRP > MFC. The MRP is larger than the MFC for the first six bushels of feed. This shows that it is a good economic decision to continue feeding additional feed until the following condition is met:

Input Profit-Maximization Rule: MRP = MFC.

Once the marginal benefits (MRP) fall below the marginal costs (MFC), the feed input costs more than it is worth! Productivity eventually declines as more and more feed is bought and used, and at this point it is not a good decision to continue feeding cattle.

4.2.5 Feedlot in Jetmore, Kansas: Change in Input Price.

We have seen how a feedlot manager could use simple economic principles to find the profit-maximizing level of inputs to use in her operation in Jetmore. Real world feedlots do this same type of calculation every day. In the real world, the market prices of inputs and outputs change continuously, so the manager stays busy recalculating the optimal level of feed inputs. We can illustrate this by showing how the optimal feed decision changes when the price of the feed input changes. Suppose that there is an early frost that damages the corn and milo crops, resulting in a short supply of feed, and an increase in the feed cost from $5/bu to $10/bu. The feedlot manager must now recalculate the profit-maximizing level of feed to purchase.

Table 4.4. Feedlot Profit Maximization: Using Marginal Analysis.

$(P_X = \$10/bu)$

X (bu)	TRP ($)	MRP ($/bu)	MFC ($/bu)
0	0	-	-
1	10	10	10
2	30	20	10
3	60	30	10
4	80	20	10
5	90	10	10
6	96	6	10
7	98	2	10
8	96	-2	10

Table 4.4 shows that the feedlot will reduce the level of feed to 5 bushels: the sixth bushel would cost ten dollars, but would only increase the value of output by six dollars. The firm would continue to feed more input until the profit-maximizing condition (MRP = MFC) was reached at 5 bushels of feed.

Not only is this a nifty result for the feedlot manager, who is increasing her bottom line, but it is also important from the economist's perspective. We can now make a prediction about the agricultural economy: when the price of an input (P_X) increases, the quantity demanded of that input will decrease. Why? Because profit-maximizing managers will reduce the level of input, since it is more expensive! This is due to the "Law of Demand," which we will study in full in Chapter 8.

Another important and interesting outcome of this model is that the number of pounds of beef that will go to the packing plant will be reduced from 96 pounds to 90 pounds. Beef consumers will have less meat available to them in the grocery meat case, which will result in an increase in the price of meat. When the costs of production of a good increase, it results in an increase in the price of the good.

This explains why oil is such an important feature of our economy. Petroleum products are inputs to almost every good and service produced, so if there is an increase in the price of oil, the price of all goods that are produced with oil inputs will increase. Agricultural production is particularly sensitive to the price of oil, since farming requires a large amount of gasoline, diesel, and oil. Not only do tractors need fuel, but also fertilizer and agrochemicals are both petroleum-based products. Farmers are strongly affected by oil price changes.

4.2.6 Feedlot in Jetmore, Kansas: Change in Output Price.

Our analysis of input use can also be used to understand how producers will react to changes in output prices. Suppose that the National Cattleman's Beef Association (NCBA) is able to forge a deal with Russia to increase beef exports to the former Soviet Union. This would increase the price of beef in the USA, say, from one dollar per pound to three dollars per pound. Table 4.5 shows the results facing the feedlot when the output price increases to $P_Y = \$3/lb$.

Table 4.5. Feedlot Profit Maximization Using Marginal Analysis.

$$(P_Y = \$3/lb)$$

X (bu)	Y(TPP) (lb)	TRP ($)	TFC ($)	Profits(π) ($)
0	0	0	0	0
1	10	30	5	25
2	30	90	10	80
3	60	180	15	165
4	80	240	20	220
5	90	270	25	245
6	96	288	30	258
7	98	294	35	259
8	96	288	40	248

When the price of beef is increased to $3/lb, the physical production function shown in the first two columns of table 4.5 remains unchanged. The Total Revenue Product (TRP), however, is increased by a factor of three, since TRP = TPP*P_Y. To find the profit-maximizing (optimal) level of input use, we calculate the profit level (B = TRP – TFC) for each level of input use. The highest profit level is $259, when seven bushels of feed are used by the feedlot.

This result indicates that when the output price increases, a business firm will increase the amount of input that it uses. Intuitively, this makes perfect sense, since a business firm will earn higher levels of profits at higher output prices, because the firm will increase the production of output in response to a higher output price. Higher levels of production require higher levels of input use [recall the production function: $Y = f(X)$]. Therefore, a major result of this analysis is that when output prices increase, more inputs will be purchased by profit-maximizing firms.

(Quick Quiz 4.12: if the price of wheat increases, do wheat producers purchase more inputs? Explain why.)

4.2.7 Graphs of Optimal Input Use.

We have seen that a firm will choose the optimal level of input use by purchasing inputs one unit at a time. The firm will purchase inputs as long as the benefits (the increase in revenues brought about by using one more unit of input in the production process) are larger than the costs (the payment required to purchase the input). We can show this result graphically by graphing the TRP and TFC functions on the same graph, as can be seen in figure 4.3.

The profit-maximizing level of input use for a firm can be found where the vertical distance between Total Revenue Product (TRP) and Total Factor Cost (TFC) is the largest. This optimal point is where the slope of the TRP function equals the slope of the TFC function. To see this, draw a line that is parallel (of equal slope) to the TFC line and just tangent (barely touching) the TRP line, as shown in figure 4.3 at X*. At the point X*, the profit level is the highest. By moving either to the right or the left, the distance between TRP and TFC is decreased, reflecting lower levels of profits at any point other than X*.

Figure 4.3

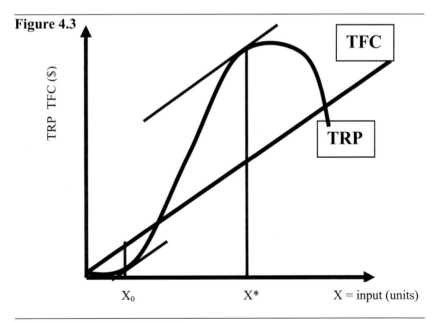

There are two points where the slopes of the two functions are equal, so we must take care to select the correct profit-maximizing point. At point X_0, the slopes of the two functions are equal to each other, but this is not a desirable point for the firm to locate. Why? Because TFC > TRP, which means that the costs of production are greater than the revenues of the firm: at point X_0, the firm is maximizing its losses!

The optimal level of input use can be found using marginal analysis as well as the total functions in figure 4.3, since the information contained in the marginal cost and revenue functions was derived from the total functions. It is helpful to recall the definitions of Marginal Revenue Product (MRP) and Marginal Factor Cost (MFC):

$$MRP = MPP* P_Y = \Delta TRP/\Delta X$$

$$MFC = \Delta TFC/\Delta X.$$

The definitions show that the MRP is the slope of TRP, and the MFC is the slope of TFC. The profit-maximizing rule of input use is to continue buying inputs until MRP = MFC, or when the slopes of TRP and TFC are equal, as in figure 4.3. The marginal analysis is shown in figure 4.4, where the profit-maximizing point of input use ($X*$) is found where MRP = MFC.

Figure 4.4

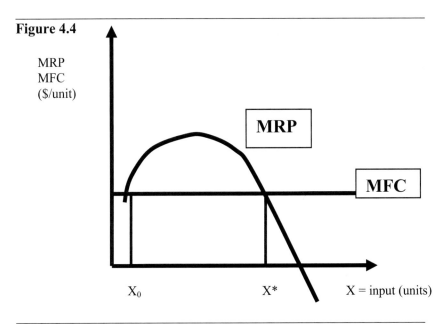

The intuition of the marginal graph can be found by using the definitions of MRP and MFC to understand why the optimal point occurs when MRP = MFC for the Jetmore feedlot.

MRP = ΔTRP/ΔX = rate of change in TRP = slope of TRP = additional value of feeding one bushel of feed

MFC = ΔTFC/ΔX = rate of change in TFC = slope of TFC = additional cost of feeding one bushel of feed.

The feedlot will earn higher levels of profits as it increases input use as long as MRP > MFC, as shown in figure 4.4. When the level of input use reaches X*, where MRP = MFC, then the addition to revenues from using one more unit of input is exactly equal to the addition to costs of purchasing one more unit of input. To increase input use beyond X* would increase production, but lower profits. This is due to diminishing returns: the last unit of input is less productive, so the addition to the revenues of a firm is lower than the cost of the input.

(Quick Quiz 4.13: why does the feedlot not locate at point X_0, where MRP = MFC?)

4.2.8 Tax on the Agrochemical Atrazine.

Our study of input use can be very useful in predicting how firms will respond to changes in input and output prices. One timely and important application of this analysis is to study public policies for agrochemicals. Atrazine was discussed in the introductory chapter, where we learned that it is a herbicide that is used to kill weeds in corn production. Chemical residues of Atrazine that appear in water supplies where the chemical is used have been shown to have an adverse impact on human health.

The chemical is used extensively in Northeast Kansas, and the level of Atrazine has been found to be higher then the Environmental Protection Agency (EPA) recommended level in the Delaware River Valley north of Topeka. The Kansas State Board of Agriculture, together with K-State Research and Extension, has been working on a solution to this problem by asking corn farmers in the area to voluntarily reduce the level of Atrazine used, to lower the residues that appear in Lake Perry, on the Delaware River.

So far, the voluntary reduction appears to have worked well in reducing the measured levels of Atrazine in the lake. However, a second solution to the use of agrochemicals that is often proposed is a tax on

114

Atrazine. The tax would make the chemical more expensive to farmers, who would reduce their use of the input, which would have the desired result of lowering the residue levels in the drinking water.

Suppose that the Kansas State Board of Agriculture asks an economist (you!) to predict the impact of the tax on Atrazine. We know that profit-maximizing producers will use the profit-maximizing level of Atrazine, found where MRP = MFC. The per-unit tax (t) would increase the cost of each additional ounce of Atrazine by t dollars:

$$MFC = P_X + t.$$

The impact of the tax can be found in figure 4.5. The tax increases the cost of purchasing the input from P_X to $(P_X + t)$. This raises the MFC by the amount of the tax, and would reduce to the profit-maximizing level of Atrazine from X_0^* to X_1^*.

Figure 4.5

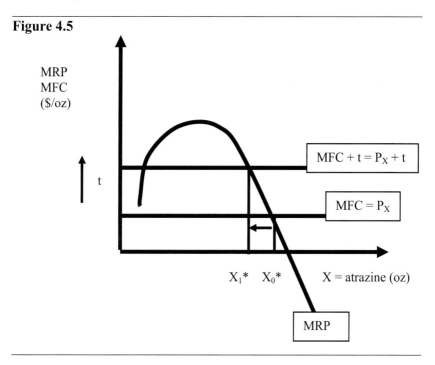

Through the imposition of the tax, the government has made it more costly to use an undesirable input. The level of Atrazine residues that appear in water supplies could be targeted to an optimal rate. This environmentally safe level of Atrazine could be reached by adjusting the tax level up or down. Many goods that are considered to have adverse effects are taxed in a similar manner to this: cigarettes, gasoline, lottery tickets, alcohol, etc.

(Quick Quiz 4.14: use graphical analysis to show the impact of a gasoline tax on agricultural production in Kansas. Will consumers of agricultural products be affected by such a tax? Explain why or why not.)

3. The Profit-Maximizing Level of Output.

This section is the heart of all economics: we will find the optimal, profit-maximizing level of output for a business firm! The concepts and ideas presented in this section can be usefully applied to a diversity of business decisions, career choices, and personal issues. The punch line of our course continues to be:

CONTINUE ANY ACTIVITY AS LONG AS BENEFITS OUTWEIGH COSTS!

We now switch our attention away from the input decision of the firm to the output decision. The questions, "How much wheat should I produce this year?" and "What is the optimal herd size for my dairy?" are examples of situations where economics analysis can be useful and consequential, as we will discover below.

4.3.1 Profit-Maximization Using Total Revenue and Total Cost Curves.

We will continue to assume that the goal of the firm is to maximize profits. In economics, we focus our attention on the bottom line (profits), defined as **Total Revenues** (TR) minus **Total Costs** (TC):

$\pi = TR - TC$, where

Total Costs (TC) = The sum of Fixed Costs and Variable Costs. TC = TFC + TVC.

Total Revenues (TR) = The amount of money received when the producer sells the product. Also called gross income or total sales. TR = TPP* P_Y.

Total revenues are just the amount of money earned from the production and sale of a good:

$$TR = TPP*P_Y = Y*P_Y, \text{ where Y is output, and } P_Y = \text{price of}$$
output ($/unit).

Total costs are the costs of production, including both fixed and variable costs. All units are in dollars for profits, total revenues and total costs.

(Quick Quiz 4.15: are the costs in TC economic costs or accounting costs? Are the profits economic profits or accounting profits? Are opportunity costs included?)

What are the costs facing this firm? We know that the firm will have both fixed and variable costs, and that the total costs will increase with output.

$$\pi = TR - TC$$

$$\pi = P_Y*Y - TC(Y)$$
(TC are a function of Y)

The equation above shows that both TR and TC are a function of how much is produced (Y). The intuition of profit-maximization, or marginal decision-making, is to continue any activity as long as additional, or marginal, benefits outweigh additional, or marginal, costs. Therefore, the firm will continue to produce output as long as the additional revenues brought in from the production and sale of the good are greater than the additional costs of production incurred when an additional unit of output is produced.

We are now ready to maximize profits with the use of a graph of total costs and total revenues. **Total Revenues** (TR) will be a straight line, since the price of output, P_Y, is fixed and constant. When we multiply a constant by the variable, Y, we get a straight line as shown in figure 4.6. The **Total Cost** (TC) curve has the "standard" shape of costs increasing at a decreasing rate, then increasing at an increasing rate. This shape reflects the Law of Diminishing Returns.

Figure 4.6

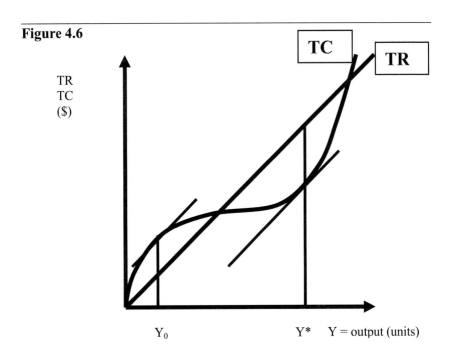

TR
TC
($)

TC

TR

Y_0 Y^* Y = output (units)

In the graph, profits are found as the vertical distance between the TR and TC functions, since π = TR – TC. The firm's objective is to maximize the distance, or gap, between TR and TC. To do this, we draw a line parallel to TR and tangent to (just touching) the TC curve. The point of tangency is the output level of maximum profit, and occurs at output level Y^*. Geometrically, this is the point where the slope of TR is equal to the slope TC (or MR = MC). Any movement to the right or left of Y^* will result in a decrease in the vertical distance between TR and TC, or a reduction in profits.

Note that there are two points in figure 4.6 where the slope of TR is equal to the slope of TC. The firm must be sure to maximize profit, rather than minimize profit. The point Y^* is profit maximizing, since MR = MC and TR > TC. The first condition for profit-maximization occurs at point Y_0, but this point is a cost-maximization point, since at Y_0, TR < TC.

4.3.2 Profit-Maximization Using Marginal Revenue and Marginal Cost Curves.

We can summarize marginal decision making by defining **Marginal Revenues (MR)** and **Marginal Costs (MC)**:

118

Marginal Revenues (MR) = The addition to Total Revenue from selling one more unit of output. $MR = \Delta TR/\Delta Y$.

Marginal Cost (MC) = The addition to Total Cost of producing one more unit of output. $MC = \Delta TC/\Delta Y$.

These terms are analogous to the marginal terms we used when studying a firm's business decision: **Marginal Revenue Product (MRP)** and **Marginal Factor Cost (MFC)**. To conduct marginal analysis, we can plot the same information that was used in the total analysis on a second graph.

Figure 4.7

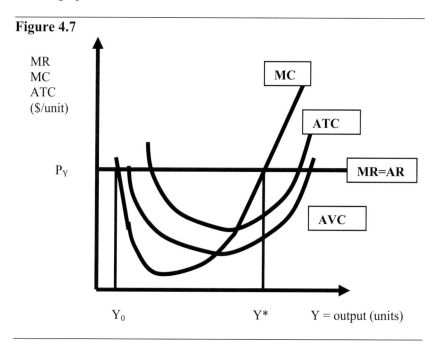

Marginal Revenue is the slope, or rate of change, in Total Revenue: $MR = \Delta TR/\Delta Y$. We can see in figure 4.6 that the slope of TR is constant. Therefore, MR is constant for every level of output. We can also see this in the formula for Total Revenue: $TR = P_Y*Y$. Since the output price is constant, is does not change. Therefore, any change in TR comes from a change in output, Y.

$$\Delta TR = \Delta(P_Y*Y) = P_Y(\Delta Y)$$

We can substitute this into the definition of marginal revenue.

$MR = \Delta TR/\Delta Y = [P_Y(\Delta Y)]/\Delta Y = P_Y$

This is why the MR line in figure 4.7 is labeled, P_Y.

Average Revenues (AR) are the per-unit revenues that the firm earns from the production and sales of a good.

Average Revenues (AR) = The average dollar amount received per unit of output sold. $AR = TR/Y$.

Average Revenues are constant at the output price, since $AR = TR/Y = (P_Y*Y)/Y = P_Y$.
Since MR and AR are constant, then $MR = AR$.

(Quick Quiz 4.16: what is the relationship between average and marginal? Does the relationship hold in this case?)

To find the profit-maximizing level of output, the firm sets $MR = MC$, or $P_Y = MC$. This condition is met at two points in figure 4.7: Y_0 and Y^*. These two points in figure 4.7 are identical to the points with the same labels in figure 4.6. Remember that the information contained in both graphs is identical. The optimal, profit-maximizing point is Y^*, since at that point $TR > TC$. Because of this, the Profit-maximizing condition has two parts.

PROFIT MAXIMIZING CONDITION:

1. MR = MC

2. MC must cut MR from below

This condition is so important to economics that it is the "theme" of this book. It succinctly summarizes what a manager needs to do to make good decisions, and "think like an economist." He or she must continue any activity as long as the benefits exceed the costs. The two conditions given above guarantee this.

4.3.3 The Intuition of Profit Maximization.

Economists argue that individuals should continue with any activity as long as the benefits outweigh the costs. This is the same as saying that $MR = MC$. This is the optimal point for any activity, whether

120

it be eating pizza, feeding hogs, studying, producing wheat, or exercising.

Let's look at a specific activity: the production of a good. How does a firm decide how much to produce?

Figure 4.8

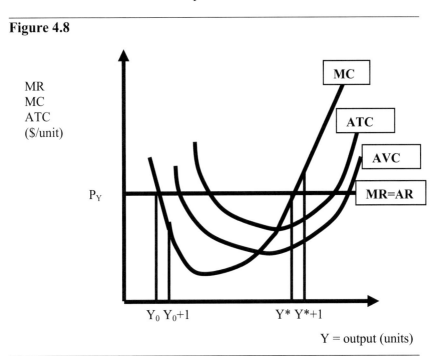

To demonstrate how a business manager can use marginal decision making, suppose that the manager collects data on the costs of production and the output price. From the cost data, the manager can derive the ATC, AVC, and MC curves as shown in figure 4.8. The marginal revenue is exactly equal to the output price, P_Y. Suppose that the manager begins production at a low level, say Y_0. Thinking like an economist, the manager asks the question, "Should this firm produce one more unit?" If the benefits of producing one more unit outweigh the costs, then the manager should produce one more unit of a good.

At Y_0, the benefits of producing one more unit of output are equal to ΔTR. By rearranging the definition of MR, we can see these benefits in the graph above. Rearrange:

$MR = \Delta TR/\Delta Y$ to get:

$\Delta TR = MR*\Delta Y$.

The last term ($MR*\Delta Y$) is equal to the area under the marginal revenue curve between the two points Y_0 and Y_0+1. Why? Because the base of this area is equal to)Y (=$Y_0+1 - Y_0 = 1$), and the height of the area under the MR curve is equal to MR. So, the change in revenues associated with a single unit increase in output (ΔTR) is equal to the area under the MR curve. Since MR equals the output price, this area is equal to P_Y. So, for every unit of production, the addition to revenues is the price of the good. This makes perfect sense, because we have assumed a competitive industry, with a constant price.

(Quick Quiz 4.17: list the four characteristics of a perfectly competitive industry.)

Using similar logic, we can show that the change in costs associated with a one-unit increase in output is equal to the area under the MC curve. First, we rearrange the definition of MC. Rearrange:

$MC = \Delta TC/\Delta Y$ to get:

$\Delta TC = MC*\Delta Y$.

The last equation shows that the change in costs is equal to the area under the MC curve, which represents what the firm must pay to produce one more unit. The base of this area equals one ($\Delta Y = Y_0+1 - Y_0 = 1$), and the height is equal to MC.

The manager knows that as long as benefits outweigh costs, production should be continued. At point Y_0, the manager asks, "Is it profitable to continue activity?" Or, "Should the firm produce Y_0+1 units?" The manager then looks at the benefits and costs. In this case, the benefits outweigh the costs. This can be seen in figure 4.8: the price line (MR) is higher than the MC curve at point Y_0+1. Therefore, the revenues received from producing and selling one more unit (MR) are greater than the costs of producing one more unit. The manager continues to think incrementally, and by using marginal analysis, continues to expand production until the point Y^* is reached.

At Y^*, the manager asks again, "Should I produce one more unit?" And, for the first time, the answer is, "No." This is because at point Y^*+1, the MC curve is higher than the price line (=MR), so the costs of production are greater than the price received for the output. Therefore, the manager makes a good economic decision by continuing to produce more output until Y* is reached. Then, the manager stops because the costs begin to outweigh the benefits at that point. Should a firm produce one more unit? It should continue as long as the marginal benefits exceed the marginal costs. This is why a firm sets MR=MC at point Y*. All of the additional benefits of increasing profits are exhausted at that point.

To recap the intuition of profit-maximization, economists study the behavior of business firms that are assumed to produce goods and sell them for profits. The objective of these firms is to maximize profits by purchasing inputs (factors, resources) and combining them into outputs that are sold to consumers. Producing goods is not costless: it requires resources to pay for the production of a good. The good must be sold to earn revenues to pay for the scarce resources that were used in the production of the good.

(Quick Quiz 4.18: what is scarcity?)

The firm will continue to purchase inputs as long as the benefits (MRP) are greater than the costs of inputs (MFC). Once the profit-maximizing point (MRP = MFC) has been reached, profits are maximized. The firm will also continue to produce output as long as the benefits (MR) exceed the costs (MC). When the optimal point (MR = MC) is reached, the firm is at the point of maximum profit, which means that it has reached its objective.

4. Profits and Losses; Break-Even and Shut Down Points.

How do we know if the firm is earning profits or losses? Remember that in all of our graphs, we are looking at economic profits, not accounting profits.

(Quick Quiz 4.19: what is the difference between economic profits and accounting profits?)

The cost curves depicted here include opportunity costs. Therefore, the cost curves include both explicit and opportunity costs. In this section, we will calculate profit levels, both algebraically and graphically. We will start by defining profits explicitly.

π = TR – TC, where

$$TR = TPP*P_Y = Y*P_Y = Y*MR, \text{ and}$$

$$TC = Y*ATC$$

(from the definition of Average Total Costs, $ATC = TC/Y$).

Total Revenues (TR) are simply the level of output (Y) times the output price (P_Y). In a perfectly competitive industry, we know that the output price is constant, so $P_Y = MR = AR$, as can be seen in figure 4.9. In figure 4.9, the firm maximizes profits by setting $MR = MC$, where MC cuts MR from below. Graphically, Total Revenues are the rectangular area defined by the horizontal distance $0Y^*$, and the vertical distance $0P_Y$. This rectangle represents the dollar value of revenues that the firm earns from the sales of its product ($TR = Y*P_Y$).

Total costs are found in a similar manner: total costs are the per-unit costs (ATC) times the level of output (Y). Graphically, this is the smaller rectangle defined by the horizontal distance $0Y^*$ and the vertical distance $0ATC^*$. This rectangle represents the total costs of the firm ($TC = ATC*Y$).

Profits are defined as total revenues minus total costs ($\pi = TR - TC$), which is the shaded rectangle in figure 4.9. In the case shown below, profits are positive ($\pi > 0$) because the price line ($P_Y = MR = AR$) is above the Average Total Cost curve ($P_Y > ATC$). The firm will earn positive profits when this condition holds. If the price falls below the ATC curve, the firm will earn negative profits, a case that we turn to next.

In figure 4.10, the price has fallen below the ATC curve ($P_Y < ATC$). The firm continues to maximize profits by setting $MR = MC$, where MC cuts MR from below. However, in this case, profits are negative ($\pi < 0$), and the firm is earning less than the opportunity costs of all of its inputs. Total Revenues (TR) are the rectangle defined by the horizontal distance ($0Y^*$) and the vertical distance ($0P_Y$). Total Costs (TC) are the larger rectangle defined by a base of ($0Y^*$) and a height of ($0ATC^*$).

Figure 4.9

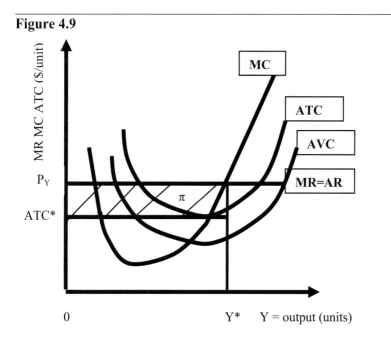

Profits are negative and are the shaded rectangle ($\pi = $ TR – TC). If the firm were to maximize profits, it would use its productive inputs in their next-best alternative use, which would earn a higher level of profits.

The results above show that a firm could quickly determine if profits are positive or negative by noting the following rule:

If P_Y > ATC, then profits are positive

If P_Y < ATC, then profits are negative.

When the output price is exactly equal to the per-unit costs, we say that the firm is just "breaking even," meaning that TR equals TC, and economic profits are equal to zero.

(Quick Quiz 4.20: when economic profits equal zero, is this good or bad for the firm?)

Figure 4.10

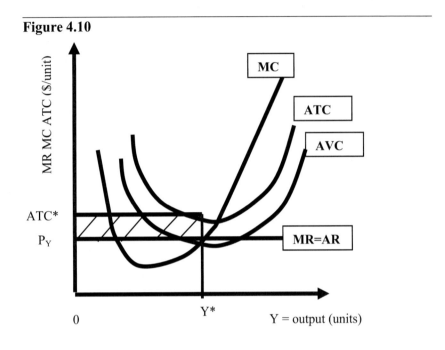

4.4.1 The Break-Even Point.

The **Break-Even Point** occurs when $P_Y = MC$ at the minimum ATC point. At the break-even point, there are no economic profits or losses, as in figure 4.11.

Break-Even Point = The point on a graph that shows the condition that Total Revenue (TR) is equal to Total Cost (TC).

It may seem as if a firm should shut down, since profits are equal to zero. However, this is the difference between accounting profits and economic profits. The owners of a firm are still earning salaries, which are taken into account in cost curves. Even though profits equal zero, the returns to the owners are as high as what they could be earning in their next-best alternative use.

One interesting feature of the break-even point is that the following condition holds:

$$P_Y = ATC = MC = AR = MR.$$

126

Since the firm's revenues are exactly equal to the firm's costs, profits equal zero (B = 0). If the price falls below the ATC curve, economic profits become negative. A firm will remain in business, even though it is receiving negative economic profits, under certain conditions, as is explained in the next section.

Figure 4.11

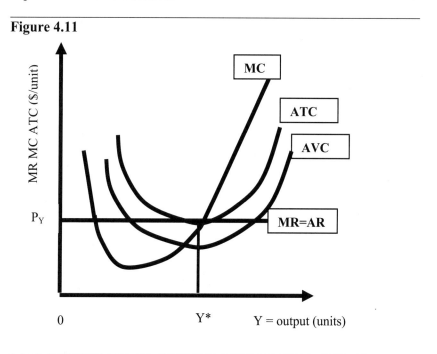

4.4.2 The Shut-Down Point.

It seems as if a firm should shut down if profits were negative, but there is a good reason why the firm will still produce when the price falls below the ATC curve. In the short run, some of the inputs are fixed, and the firm must pay the fixed costs no matter how much they produce. If the output price falls below per-unit costs, the firm's total costs will not be covered. Since the firm is not earning enough to pay its costs of production, it might shut down. If it does shut down, it must continue to pay all of the fixed costs. For example, even if a business in Aggieville closes its doors, it will still have to pay the rent. The firm might be better off remaining in business and paying off at least part of its fixed costs than not earning any revenue and still having to pay fixed costs.

The discussion will be clearer if we keep the definition of total costs in mind:

$$TC = TFC + TVC$$

If we divide all three terms by the level of output, we get:

$$ATC = AFC + AVC$$

In the short run, a firm will have both fixed and variable costs. Fixed costs do not vary with the level of output, so must be paid no matter what the level of output is. In figure 4.11 above, the vertical difference between the ATC and AVC curves is equal to the level of fixed costs ($AFC = ATC - AVC$). In the long run, all of the fixed costs become variable.

(Quick Quiz 4.21: why do the fixed costs become variable in the long run?)

In the long run, $ATC = AVC$, and $AFC = 0$. When all fixed costs become variable in the long run, the ATC curve is the same as the AVC curve, and fixed costs disappear.

If the output price lies between average total costs and average variable costs ($ATC > P_Y > AVC$), then the firm is covering all of its variable costs, and part of the fixed costs. Remaining in business is a better situation than closing down and owing all of the fixed costs. So, the firm remains in business with negative profits in order to minimize costs. This is the optimal, profit-maximizing (cost-minimizing) solution.

If the output price falls below the average variable cost curve ($P_Y < AVC$), then the firm will shut down. Since the firm can not meet even its variable costs of production, it is losing money on each unit of output that it produces. We can clarify the concept of the **Shut Down Point** with figure 4.12.

Shut Down Point = The point on a graph where Marginal Revenue (MR) is equal to Average Variable Costs (AVC).

Figure 4.12

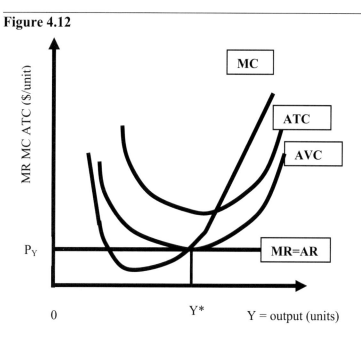

At any point above the shut down point (P_Y > AVC), the firm will remain in business. This is because the firm can meet all of its variable costs and at least part of its fixed costs.

At any point below the shut down point (P_Y < AVC), the firm will shut down. This is because the firm can not meet its variable costs of production.

The firm minimizes losses by producing where MR = MC, which is where the price line intersects the MC curve, and the MC curve cuts the price line from below. At this point, total costs exceed total revenues, but as long as firm is covering its variable costs, the firm will set MR = MC and continue producing.

4.4.3 Example: Profit Maximization for a Catfish Producer in Garden City, Kansas.

In the 1980s, several large packing plants were built in Southwest Kansas. These plants employ a large number of recent immigrants to the United States from Mexico, Central American, and Southeast Asia (Vietnam, Laos, and Cambodia). The Asian population has increased the demand for fish. Several entrepreneurs in the region

129

have started new business firms that produce fish to market to the new populations that have moved to the area to work in the packing plants.

Let's consider a catfish producer as an example of a profit-maximizing firm, to review what we have learned. In the short run, the catfish producer will have both fixed and variable inputs: suppose that the fixed input is the land and buildings where the fish tanks are located. Variable costs might include fish, water, electricity, feed, and labor.

$$TC = TFC + TVC$$

Dividing these three terms by the level of output (Y), we convert the total costs into average, or per-unit, costs.

$$ATC = AFC + AVC$$

Recall that fixed costs are payments to inputs that do not vary with output. Restated, the land and building inputs remain at the same level whether the catfish produced equal zero or one million. The rent must be paid no matter what the output level is. Fixed costs represent the vertical distance between the ATC and AVC curves in figure 4.13.

Figure 4.13

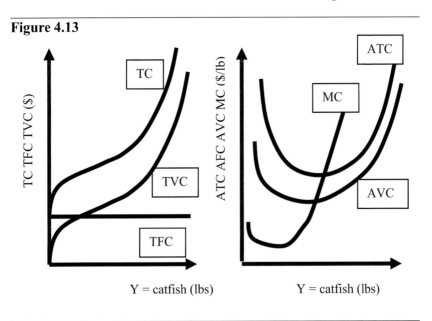

In the long run, all of the fixed inputs become variable: TC = TVC, and TFC =0. Graphically, the long run curves reflect the variability of all inputs, as in figure 4.14.

To find the profit-maximizing level of catfish to produce, the firm can use either the total or the marginal graphs. On the total graph (figure 4.15), the catfish firm will find the number of catfish (Y*) that will maximize the vertical difference between the TR and TC curves (π = TR – TC). The firm must make sure that the second condition of profit-maximization holds (TR > TC). At point Y_0, costs are maximized. On the marginal graph, the firm will find the optimal, profit-maximizing point (Y*) by finding the point where (1) MR = MC, and (2) MC cuts MR from below. The profit-maximizing point is identical in both graphs, because the functions in the marginal graph reflect the same information that appears in the total graph.

Figure 4.14

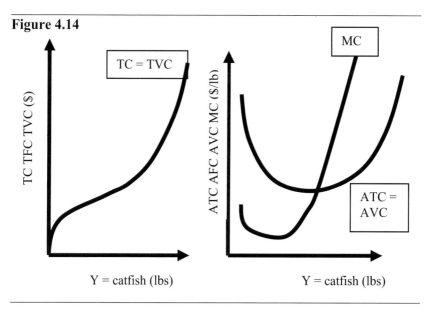

We have assumed a perfectly competitive industry in catfish, so the price of output (P_Y) is constant. This is why the TR function is a straight line in figure 4.15 (TR = P_Y*Y), and the MR function is constant (P_Y = MR = AR). Marginal analysis (the "economic way of thinking!") for a catfish producer involves starting at a low level of output, and asking the question, "Should I produce one more unit of output?" The answer is "yes" as long as the marginal revenues (benefits) are greater than the marginal costs (costs).

Figure 4.15

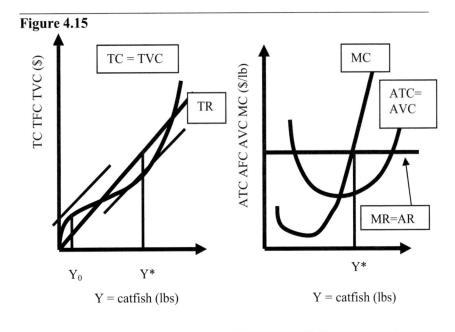

The catfish producer will continue to produce more catfish until he reaches point Y*. At that point, one more unit would raise production costs higher than the price of catfish. Any point to the left or right of the optimal, profit-maximizing point of Y* will result in lower profits for the catfish firm. This chapter has demonstrated how to find the profit-maximizing point of both input and output use. In the next chapter, we will see the optimal combination of inputs to maximize profits.

Chapter Four Summary

1. The economic way of thinking, or marginal analysis, compares the benefits and costs of every activity, one unit at a time.
2. An industry is a group of firms that produce and sell the same product.
3. Perfect competition is defined by: (1) a large number of buyers and sellers, (2) a homogeneous product, (3) freedom of entry and exit, and (4) perfect information.
4. In a perfectly competitive industry, the output price is fixed and given to a firm.
5. Total Revenue Product (TRP) is the dollar value of output produced from alternative levels of variable input (TRP = TPP*P_Y).
6. Total Factor Cost (TFC) is the total cost of an input (TFC = P_X*X).
7. Marginal Revenue Product (MRP) is the additional value of output obtained from each additional unit of a variable input.
8. Marginal Factor Cost (MFC) is the cost of an additional unit of input.
9. Marginal analysis suggests that an individual should continue any activity as long as the marginal (incremental) benefits are greater than the marginal (incremental) costs.
10. The profit-maximizing level of input use can be found by setting MRP = MFC.
11. When the price of an input increases, the quantity demanded of that input will decrease.
12. When the output price increases, a business firm will increase the amount of input that it uses.
13. A tax placed on an input will cause a business firm to purchase less of that input.
14. The profit-maximizing level of output can be found where MR = MC.
15. When the output price is greater than average total costs, profits are positive. When the output price is below the average total costs, profits are negative. When the output price is equal to the average total costs, then the firm is breaking even, and earning zero economic profits.
16. The break-even point occurs where P_Y=MC at the minimum ATC point. Economic profits are equal to zero at the break-even point.

17. The shut-down point occurs where MR equals minimum AVC. At output prices above the shut-down point, the firm will remain in production. At output prices below the shut down point, the firm will shut down.
18. Graphically, the profit-maximizing level of output can be found by locating the maximum vertical distance between the TR and TC curves. The profit-maximizing level of output can also be found by locating the point where (1) MR = MC, and (2) MC cuts MR from below.

Chapter Four Glossary

Average Revenues (AR). The average dollar amount received per unit of output sold. $AR = TR/Y$.

Average Revenue Product (ARP). The average value of output per unit of input at each input use level. $ARP = APP*P_Y$.

Break-Even Point. The point on a graph that shows the condition that Total Revenue (TR) is equal to Total Cost (TC).

Factor Demand. The firm's demand for the variable input used in production: MRP in Stage II of Production. Also, the relationship between the price and quantity demanded of a variable input.

Homogeneous Product. A product that is the same no matter which producer produces it. The producer of a good can not be identified by the consumer.

Industry. A group of firms that all produce and sell the same product.

Marginal Cost (MC). The additional cost of producing one more unit of output. $MC = \Delta TC/\Delta Y$.

Marginal Factor Cost (MFC). The cost of an additional (marginal) unit of input; the amount added to total cost of using one more unit of input. $MFC = \Delta TC/\Delta X$.

Marginal Revenues (MR). The addition to Total Revenue from selling one more unit of output. $MR = \Delta TR/\Delta Y$.

Marginal Revenue Product (MRP). The additional (marginal) value of output obtained from each additional unit of the variable input. $MRP = MPP* P_Y$.

Perfect Competition. A market or industry with four characteristics: (1) large number of buyers and sellers, (2) homogeneous product, (3) freedom of entry and exit, and (4) perfect information.

Perfect Information. A situation where all buyers and sellers in a
    market have complete access to technological information and
    market information (all input and output prices, and all quantities
    bought and sold).

Price maker. A non-competitive firm that can influence the price of a
    good.

Price taker. A competitive firm that can not influence the price of a
    good.

Shut Down Point. The point on a graph where Marginal Revenue (MR)
    is equal to Average Variable Costs (AVC).

Total Costs (TC). The sum of Fixed Costs and Variable Costs. TC =
    TFC + TVC.

Total Factor Cost (TFC). The total cost of a factor, or input. TFC =
    P_X*X.

Total Revenues (TR). The amount of money received when the
    producer sells the product. Also called gross income or total
    sales. TR = TPP* P_Y.

Total Revenue Product (TRP). The dollar value of the output produced
    from alternative levels of variable input. TRP = TPP* P_Y.

Chapter Four Review Questions

1. A large number of buyers and sellers results in:
    a. a homogeneous product
    b. a fixed and constant price
    c. freedom of entry and exit
    d. perfect information

2. All of the following have freedom of entry and exit except:
    a. Gas station
    b. Copy store
    c. Cable television
    d. Clothing store

3. Which physical product curves can be graphed on the same graph?
    a. TPP and APP
    b. APP and MPP
    c. TPP and MPP
    d. TPP, APP, and MPP

4. The cost of an additional unit of input is:
    a. Total Revenue Product
    b. Marginal Factor Cost
    c. Marginal Revenue Product
    d. Total Factor Cost

5. A firm will continue to purchase more input until:
    a. $MPP = MFC$
    b. $MRP = P_Y$
    c. $TRP = TFC$
    d. $MRP = MFC$

6. When the price of corn increases, feedlots will:
    a. Purchase more corn
    b. Purchase less corn
    c. Purchase same corn amount
    d. Can not tell

7. When the price of automobiles increases, Ford Motor Company will purchase:
   a. More glass, steel, and rubber
   b. Less glass, steel, and rubber
   c. The same amount of glass, steel, and rubber
   d. Can not tell from the information given

8. If a tax is placed on gasoline, then a wheat producer will produce:
   a. More wheat
   b. Less wheat
   c. The same amount of wheat
   d. Can not tell from the information given

9. The profit-maximizing level of output can be found where:
   a. MR=MC, and MC cuts MR from below
   b. MR=MC, and MC cuts MR from above
   c. TR = TC
   d. The horizontal distance between TR and TC is largest

10. The shut down point occurs where:
   a. P = min ATC
   b. P = min AVC
   c. ATC = AVC
   d. MR = MC

11. The break-even point occurs where:
   a. P = MR =MC = ATC
   b. P = min AVC
   c. AVC = ATC
   d. P = MC

CHAPTER FIVE
OPTIMAL INPUT SELECTION

So far in this course, we have studied the physical production process (Chapter Two), the costs of production (Chapter Three), and how to select the profit-maximizing level of inputs and outputs (Chapter Four). We continue by investigating how inputs are related to each other in the production process. There are many different combinations of inputs that can be used to produce output. For example, farm equipment can be built with a labor-intensive production process (skilled workers), or a capital-intensive production process (robots).

In this chapter, we will see how a firm selects the optimal, profit-maximizing combination of inputs. The take-home message from this chapter is that a firm will select inputs based on **Relative Prices**. In low-income nations where labor is inexpensive, business firms most often employ a labor-intensive production process, whereas in high-income nations, labor is often expensive, and capital-intensive production processes are used.

Think of the comparison of agricultural production practices in Kansas compared to Africa. In Kansas, we use large, expensive machines to till the soil, plant the crop, harvest the crop, and transport it to market. In Africa, labor is used for these same activities. In this chapter, we will explore why firms in both Kansas and Africa are making rational economic decisions when employing vastly different production processes.

1. The Relationship between Inputs.

To study how different combinations of inputs can be used to produce output, we recall the production function:

$$Y = f(A, L, K, M).$$

(Quick Quiz 5.1: define a production function, and explain what the letters Y, f, A, L, K, and M stand for.)

We devoted Chapter Two to the analysis of the relationship between one input and one output, by using the assumption of *ceteris paribus*, or holding all else constant. We allowed one input (here, labor) to vary, while all other inputs were held constant:

$$Y = f(L \mid A, K, M).$$

(Quick Quiz 5.2: is the firm represented by this production function in the short or long run? Explain.)

The production function captures the physical relationship between inputs (X) and output (Y). The physical product functions (TPP, APP, and MPP) were all derived from the production function.

(Quick Quiz 5.3: define the physical product terms TPP, APP, and MPP. Graph each function.)

We will now change our emphasis to focus on the relationship between two variable inputs and output. We can do this by shifting our *ceteris paribus* line in the production function to now include two variable inputs, rather than one:

$$Y = f(L, K \mid A, M).$$

In this equation, the firm has allowed labor (L) and capital (K) to vary, holding all of the other productive inputs constant. This is to focus on the relationship between labor and capital in the production process. One of the five major trends affecting agriculture in Kansas and the Great Plains as described in the first chapter is the huge substitution of capital for labor. Over the past several decades, the agricultural sector of the United States has replaced literally millions of agricultural laborers with highly productive and expensive machinery. Our analysis in this chapter will allow us to find the determinants of the substitution of machines for labor over time.

Let's take a look at a flour mill to give us an idea of how we can determine the best combination of inputs to use. Recall that the term, "capital" in economics refers to *physical* capital, and includes (1) machines, (2) buildings, (3) tools, and (4) equipment. Capital (machines) is often used as a substitute for labor, or workers.

Suppose that the flour mill can use several different combinations of machines and labor to produce the flour. The mill can use four workers and one machine (4 L, 1 K), or two workers and two machines (2 L, 2 K) to produce 100 five-pound bags of flour using the physical production relationship:

$$Y=f(L, K \mid A, M).$$

Notice that the mill manager must hire both workers and a mill to produce flour from wheat. The key idea here is that there are many different possible production processes for flour. We can graph these different production practices by plotting capital (K) and labor (L) on the same graph.

Notice that figure 5.1 has altered our perspective on the production process from 1-output, 1-input to 1-output, 2-inputs. Each axis in figure 5.1 represents an input, rather than one input on the horizontal axis and the output on the vertical axis, as has been common in previous chapters. This changes the way that we look at production, as we are now trying to answer a different question about production. Here, we are interested in selecting the profit-maximizing *combination* of two inputs, rather than the optimal *level* of one input.

Figure 5.1

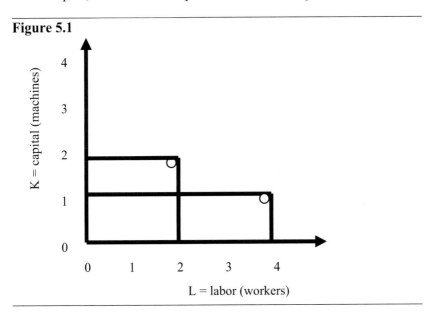

2. Isoquants.

The two points shown in figure 5.1 define an **Isoquant**, which relates two variable inputs to a given level of output.

Isoquant = A line indicating all combinations of two variable inputs that will produce a given level of output.

For the flour mill in figure 5.1, there were two possible production methods. Now suppose that there are several combinations of labor and capital that could be used to produce the same level of output, as shown

141

in figure 5.2.

Figure 5.2

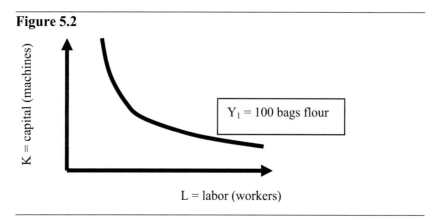

L = labor (workers)

Every point on the isoquant, or the curved line in figure 5.2, will produce a constant level of output, Y^* (100 5-lb bags of flour). The isoquant shows that capital and labor are substitutable: a flour mill could use any combination of K and L on the isoquant to produce the same quantity of flour.

Efficient firm managers will recognize the potential for substitution among inputs, and will select the profit-maximizing combination of inputs.

5.2.1 Isoquant Examples.

There are numerous combinations of inputs that can produce agricultural products. For example, farmers in Kansas can use different quantities of machinery, chemicals, and labor to produce field crops. Wheat producers make choices of technology when selecting the appropriate amount of machinery to use in their wheat production practices, as shown in figure 5.3. We can draw several isoquants, each one representing a different level of output.

Figure 5.3

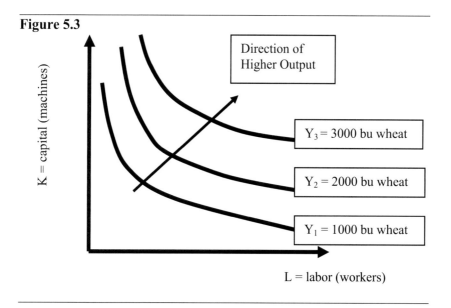

Output increases as we move to the Northeast in the graphs with an input on each axis. This is because more inputs result in more outputs [Y = f(X)].

3. Relative Prices.

As mentioned above, there are numerous combinations of inputs that can produce the same level of agricultural products, since there are many different ways to produce food. Some obvious differences in agricultural production techniques are different levels of technology: the level of mechanization is vastly different across regions and nations. Farmers can select between (1) labor-intensive methods, or (2) capital-intensive technology, as shown in figure 5.4.

The production technology represented by point A in figure 5.4 is characterized by a relatively large amount of labor and small amount of capital (L_A, K_A). This labor-intensive technology is currently used in many low-income nations. High-income nations typically use a capital-intensive production process in agriculture (L_B, K_B), shown in figure 5.4 at point B. Why do different nations use drastically different levels of technology? The answer is *relative prices*: in regions where labor is cheap relative to capital, more labor is used. In areas where labor is expensive, machines are used because they can produce agricultural output in a less expensive manner than labor.

Figure 5.4

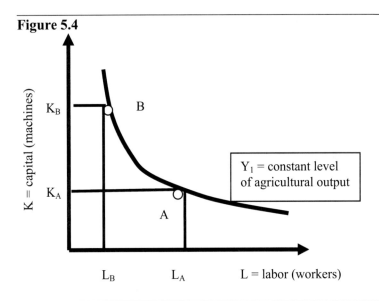

Agricultural policy in the United States has subsidized farmers since 1933, with a major goal of maintaining family farms. The outcome of this policy is to keep American agriculture closer to a labor-intensive technology than it would be without the subsidies. Why? Because large subsidies keep small family farms in business, which prevents more labor from migrating out of agriculture and into other pursuits. The government of the USA is supporting labor-intensive agriculture through subsidies.

Interestingly, research at land-grant universities such as Kansas State University results in new technology, which leads to more capital-intensive production. Public money is used to try to move agriculture toward the capital input through the development of new machinery in the Biological and Agricultural Engineering Department, and new agrochemicals and seeds in the Agronomy Department.

So, we have several forces pushing in different directions on the isoquant. Where we end up on the isoquant is determined by relative prices, together with the available technology. Agricultural producers ask themselves, "How much does it cost to buy labor and capital?" and then select the optimal combination of inputs based on these costs.

In the United States, labor is relatively expensive. Highly educated and skilled workers can do many productive things with their time. This is the same as saying that American labor has a very high opportunity cost: the next-best alternative is pretty good! Capital, on the other hand, is relatively cheap and getting cheaper every day due to the information revolution. American agricultural firms are therefore likely to use capital-intensive production techniques such as GIS (Geographical Information Systems, a satellite system) and computerized combines.

In Africa, labor is relatively inexpensive. The opportunity cost of labor in many Sub-Saharan African nations is quite low. Job opportunities are not high for a relatively unskilled and uneducated workforce. Therefore, low-income nations typically use labor-intensive techniques such as hand plowing, hoeing, and harvesting. Although this sounds inefficient to American producers, these labor-intensive techniques can still be optimal, since the decision is based on relative prices, as shown in figure 5.5.

Figure 5.5

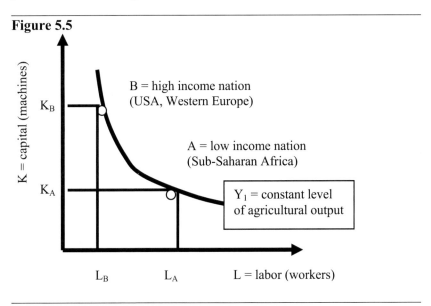

Figure 5.5 can be used to explain the huge migration of labor out of agriculture over the past several decades. As labor has become more expensive over time due to increases in productivity and education levels, farmers have shifted out of labor and into machinery. This is the major result of our analysis so far: ***THE CHOICE OF TECHNIQUES DEPENDS ON RELATIVE PRICES.*** Agribusiness firms will choose combinations of inputs that minimize their costs of production!

5.3.1 Examples of Choice of Production Techniques.

Have you ever noticed differences in car washes in different areas? In rural areas and small towns like Manhattan, car washes use capital-intensive production techniques. There are no workers, and the car washes are fully automated. In urban areas such as Kansas City or Chicago, when you get your car washed, it is by hand. This is due to relative prices. Urban areas have larger numbers of people with low levels of education, and as a result, lower opportunity costs. Labor is cheaper and more abundant in urban areas, so much of the car washes are powered by hand. In areas where labor is scarce (and relatively expensive), machines do the car washing.

If the price of labor increases over time, we would expect car wash owners to use more machines and less labor. Why? Relative prices!

Another good example of the choice of technique is the fast food industry. McDonalds can hire either workers or machines to produce burgers, fries, cokes, shakes, etc.

(Quick Quiz 5.4: do you ever order chicken nuggets?)

If the minimum wage increases, McDonalds must pay a higher price for labor, and the burger company will substitute out of labor and use more machines. Can they really do this? Yes, the decision depends on relative prices. The French fry machines are virtually fully automated, and many features of the fast food production process could be easily mechanized when machines and computers become cheaper than labor.

(Quick Quiz 5.5: have you ever seen an automatic drink dispenser at a fast food restaurant? Very cool... and due to relative prices!)

Another example of the choice of techniques is the degree of mechanization of Kansas farms. In Western Kansas, farming is practiced on a very large scale, with huge machines (tractors, combines) on a lot of acres. Wallace County, Kansas is located on the Colorado border. Contrast this with agriculture near Manhattan, which is conducted on a much smaller scale, as can be seen in table 5.1. Manhattan is in Riley County.

Table 5.1 Farm Number & Size in Riley and Wallace Counties, Kansas.

County	Farms (number)	Farm Size (acres)
Riley	550 farms	460 acres
Wallace	330 farms	1621 acres

Why does this pattern exist? Agriculture in Wallace County is characterized by land-intensive production. In Western Kansas, land is cheap and labor is scarce relative to Eastern Kansas, where Riley County is located. Therefore, farmers there employ larger quantities of land and have fewer farms (and hence less farm labor).

4. Isoquant Types.

The production processes of firms are highly diverse: contrast the lemonade stands run by my children when they were young with the production of a good as complex as a John Deere combines. The relationships between inputs and output are varied and complex. In this section, we discuss several possible types of isoquants, which reflect the variety of ways that inputs can be combined into output.

5.4.1 Perfect Substitutes.

Perfect Substitutes are inputs that can be interchanged completely, without changes in output. An example of perfect substitutes is High Fructose Corn Syrup (HFCS) and sucrose (sugar) in soda. Soda producers such as Coca-Cola and Pepsi can use either type of sweetener without any effect on the product. Thus, HFCS and sugar are perfect substitutes.

Perfect Substitutes = Inputs that are completely substitutable in the production process.

The graph of perfect substitutes is shown in figure 5.6. The isoquant is a straight line, since the two inputs can be substituted without impact. The slope of the isoquant is constant.

Figure 5.6

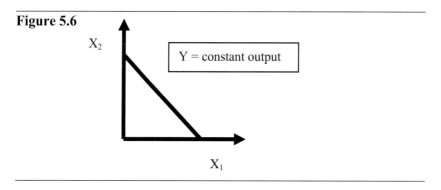

X_2

Y = constant output

X_1

Other examples of perfect substitutes include: (1) cane sugar and beet sugar (no difference in the chemical composition), (2) bag seed and bulk seed, (3) 5-lb. bags of flour and 10-lb. bags of flour.

(Quick Quiz 5.6: are John Deere combines and CASE-IH combines perfect substitutes?)

5.4.2 Perfect Complements.

Perfect Complements are inputs that must be used together. Think of a tractor and a plow: one input without the other is worthless! A farmer needs both the tractor (power source) and the plow (implement) to get the field cultivated. Another example is right shoes and left shoes. One without the other is not productive.

Perfect Complements = Inputs that must be used together in a fixed ratio. The proportion of each input is fixed in the production process.

The graph of perfect complements is a right angle, showing that extra units of one input are not useful if there is only one of the other input.

Figure 5.7

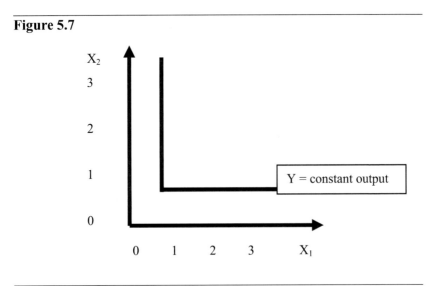

All points on isoquant represent the same level of output. If a farmer has only one tractor, it doesn't matter how many plows she has over one: only one could be used at a time. Similarly, if there were only one plow, additional tractors over one would be wasted.

148

5.4.3 Imperfect Substitutes.

The case of **Imperfect Substitutes** is the "typical" case: inputs can be substituted with each other, but not perfectly. Think of skilled and unskilled labor. These two inputs can in many situations be used in a production process, but are not perfect substitutes.

Imperfect Substitutes = Inputs that substitute for each other incompletely in the production process.

Due to the Law of Diminishing Marginal Returns, it takes larger and larger amounts of one input to replace equal reductions of the other inputs. This gives the isoquant a shape that is convex to the origin.

Figure 5.8

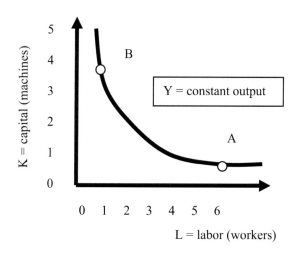

At point A in figure 5.8: a firm has a lot of workers, and only one machine. At this point, the firm could replace a lot of workers by purchasing one additional machine. Output would remain constant if the firm purchased one more machine and used three fewer workers.

At point B in figure 5.8: a firm has a lot of machines, but only one worker. The firm could replace several machines with the hire of an additional worker. At B, there are many machines and only one worker to operate all of them. Labor is scarce, so the addition of one more worker would replace several machines, and output would be unchanged.

Imperfect substitutes mean the ability to substitute between inputs. Because there are many different ways of producing goods, firm

149

managers can select the optimal combination based on relative prices of the inputs.

5.4.4 Imperfect Substitutes Example.

An example of imperfect substitutes from Kansas agriculture is the substitution between two inputs used in crop production: soil and chemicals. Many individuals believe that soil is a prerequisite for growing food and fiber commercially. The truth of the matter is that crops can be grown without soil, using water and chemicals. Soil and agrochemicals are close to perfect substitutes, because farmers can use chemicals to replace soil. Farmers can replace the nutrients necessary for crop production with chemicals.

This should not be surprising to anyone who has visited Epcot Center at Disney World in Florida, where crops are grown hydroponically (in water). It should also not surprise anyone familiar with Kansas agriculture, since a large area of crop production in Southwest Kansas uses sand to grow crops, with very little to no soil. With modern irrigation technology, farmers can drip nutrients into the sand with a center-pivot irrigation system (these are the big circles you can see from an airplane). We can graph the imperfect substitutes of soil and chemicals, as is done in figure 5.9.

Figure 5.9

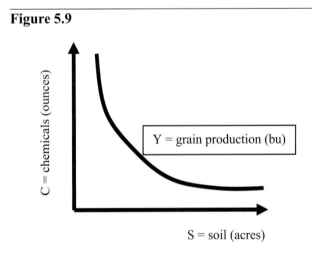

The graph shows the possibilities for substitution between the two inputs of soil and chemicals. There are many forces that cause movements along this isoquant. Soil erosion is considered a big issue in agriculture, since cultivating the soil causes soil loss from wind and water erosion. As more soil is lost, we have seen a movement out of soil and into chemicals, such as in Southwestern Kansas. However, new technologies have been developed to minimize soil loss, such as "low-till" and "no-till" planting systems that allow grain to be planted without having to plow the soil. These new technologies allow for the use of more soil, but often require high chemical use.

The federal government has taken millions of productive acres out of agricultural production through the Conservation Reserve Program (CRP). This program has taken many highly erodible acres out of production, which was the intended goal of the program. However, when fewer acres are in production, farmers substitute out of soil and into chemicals by applying higher levels of agrochemicals to the acres remaining in production.

5. Optimal Input Decisions.

Now that we have set the stage for choosing the optimal combination of inputs, we will get down to work to find the cost-minimizing set of inputs to purchase for use in the production process. Cost-minimization is identical to profit-maximization, since lowering costs is the same as increasing profits ($\pi = TR - TC$). We will see that **Relative Prices** drive the decision of what inputs to use, and changes in relative prices result in shifts out of the relatively expensive input into the relatively inexpensive input.

5.5.1 The Marginal Rate of Technical Substitution.

The slope of an isoquant is called the **Marginal Rate of Technical Substitution (MRTS)**. The MRTS reflects how well one input can be substituted for another.

Marginal Rate of Technical Substitution (MRTS) = The rate that one input can be decreased as the use of another input increases. The slope of the isoquant. $MRTS = \Delta X_2 / \Delta X_1$

The best way to get a feel for what the MRTS is all about is with a graph.

Figure 5.10

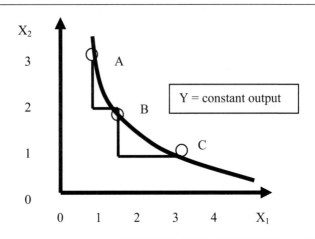

In figure 5.10, we can measure the slope of the isoquant, or MRTS between inputs X_1 and X_2. The slope of a line is the "rise over the run," or $\Delta Y/\Delta X$. In this graph, X_2 is on the y-axis, and X_1 is on the x-axis, so the slope of the isoquant equals $\Delta Y/\Delta X = \Delta X_2/\Delta X_1$. In the case of imperfect substitutes, as in figure 5.10, the slope changes from steep to less steep as we move from left to right. Therefore, the MRTS changes values as we move along the isoquant, reflecting the technical possibilities for substitution between inputs.

As we move from point A to point B, the firm can keep output constant by reducing X_2 by one unit (from 3 to 2 on the vertical scale) and increasing X_1 by one input (from 1 to 2 on the horizontal scale). This results in a calculated MRTS of negative one:

$$\text{MRTS(AB)} = \Delta X_2/\Delta X_1 = (2 - 3)/(2 - 1) = -1$$

We know that the MRTS must always be a negative number, since isoquants must always be downward-sloping. What does it mean for the firm to move from A to B? It simply means that the firm can select a wide variety of input combinations that will yield the same level of output. In fact, any point on the isoquant will, by definition, result in the same level of output. So, the movement from A to B represents a movement out of input X_2 and into input X_1.

When we look at the movement from point B to C, we expect that the MRTS will be a smaller negative number, because the slope of the isoquant becomes more gradual as we move from left to right. Let's calculate the MRTS from points B to C.

152

MRTS(BC) = slope of isoquant = $\Delta X_2/\Delta X_1$ = (1-2)/(4-2) = -1/2 = -0.5

The slope of the isoquant, or MRTS, is crucial to determining at which point a firm will locate on the isoquant. The isoquant describes input combinations that are technically feasible. We need to add economic information to this technical information to determine the cost-minimizing levels of input use. We switch now to the input prices, which allow the firm manager to determine the optimal combination of inputs to use in the production process.

5.5.2 The Isocost Line.

How will a profit-maximizing producer determine how many pounds of fertilizer to apply, or whether to use a labor-intensive, or capital-intensive production technique? The producer does so by combining the technical information contained in the isoquant with cost information that is summarized by the **Isocost Line**. The prefix "iso" refers to "same, or equal," and cost refers to the value that is placed on inputs. So, the term isocost means "equal costs," and an isocost line is a line with every point on the line having equal costs.

Isocost Line = A line indicating all combinations of two variable inputs that can be purchased for a given, or same, level of expenditure.

Consider an agricultural implement dealer that faces a price of labor equal to $10/hour, a price of capital of $100/machine, and total expenditures equal to $1000. We can derive an algebraic equation for an isocost line, by using the definition of total costs:

$TC = P_1X_1 + P_2X_2.$

In our example, the equation becomes:

$TC = (\$10/hour)*X_1 + (\$100/machine)*X_2$
$\qquad = 10L + 100K$

where X_1 is labor (L) and X_2 is capital (K). We can rearrange this equation to find the equation of a line: y = b + mx, where b is the y-intercept and m is the slope. To do this, we use simple algebra to isolate the term on the vertical axis (in our example, K) on the left-hand side of the equation. We know that total expenditures (TC) equal $1000, so:

$TC = 10L + 100K$

153

$$1000 = 10L + 100K$$

Subtract 10L from both sides:

$$1000 - 10L = 100K$$

Reverse sides to isolate the expression for K on the left-hand side:

$$100K = 1000 - 10L$$

Lastly, divide both sides by 100 to get:

$$K = 10 - 0.1L.$$

Now, we have an equation of our isocost line. Careful scrutiny shows that this line is graphically correct with figure 5.11: the y-intercept is equal to 10 and the slope is equal to 0.1 (=10/100). Simple algebra was used to find the equation of the isocost line. We can do this for any isocost line, as shown here:

$$TC = P_1X_1 + P_2X_2$$

$$P_2X_2 = TC - P_1X_1$$

$$X_2 = TC/P_2 + (-P_1/P_2)*X_1$$

Here, we see that the slope of the isocost line equals $(-P_1/P_2)$, and the y-intercept equals TC/P_2). We will use this equation to find the optimal, cost-minimizing combination of inputs for a business firm. Next, we will combine the technical production information contained in the isoquant with the economic information contained in the isocost line to make a good economic decision on inputs!

5.5.3 Equilibrium: Isoquant and Isocost Together.

Let's use our example of the agricultural implement dealer to find the optimal combination of machines and workers for the firm to employ. We do this by combining the isoquant and the isocost line in the same graph, as in figure 5.11.

Figure 5.11

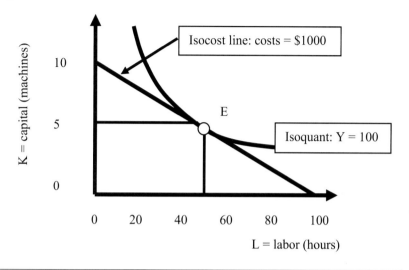

To find the optimal combination of inputs, the firm will locate at the tangency point of the isoquant and the isocost line (the point where the two lines are just barely touching). In figure 5.11, this occurs at the point (50, 5), where the firm purchases 50 hours of labor and 5 machines.

Note that this point is exactly "in the middle" of the isocost line, where exactly one-half of the expenditures are spent on each input. This is due solely to the location of the isoquant, and is not always the point where the firm will locate. The actual point depends on the *technology* (represented by the isoquant) and *relative prices* (represented by the isocost line).

The firm's objective is to minimize costs. It can meet this objective by finding an **Equilibrium** point at the tangency, where the slope of the isoquant = the slope of the isocost line. **Equilibrium** is a point where the firm is doing as well as it possibly can, given the situation, and does not desire to change.

Equilibrium = A point or situation from which there is no tendency to change.

The equilibrium condition can be shown algebraically to be where the slope of the isoquant (= MRTS = $\Delta X_2/\Delta X_1$) is equal to the slope of the isocost line (= $-P_1/P_2$).

$$\Delta X_2/\Delta X_1 = -P_1/P_2$$

155

We can rearrange this equation to find the equilibrium condition for optimal input use:

$$P_2 \Delta X_2 = -P_1 \Delta X_1.$$

This equation shows that in equilibrium, the changes in expenditures on each input are equal to each other. The relationship states that a firm manager will continue to substitute inputs until the cost of the input added is equal to the cost of the input being taken out of the production process. To make this idea more clear, consider the case when the equality in the equilibrium condition above does not hold:

If $P_2 \Delta X_2 > -P_1 \Delta X_1$, then more X_1 should be used because the cost of adding one more unit of X_2 is greater than the cost savings of decreasing the use of X_1.

If $P_2 \Delta X_2 < -P_1 \Delta X_1$, then more X_2 should be used because the cost of adding one more unit of X_1 is greater than the cost savings of decreasing the use of X_2.

This equilibrium condition indicates that the optimal, cost-minimizing, combination of inputs occurs when the physical rate of substitution (MRTS) is equal to the economic rate of substitution (the price ratio). Graphically, the equilibrium condition can be demonstrated to be the least-cost solution for the firm.

Figure 5.12

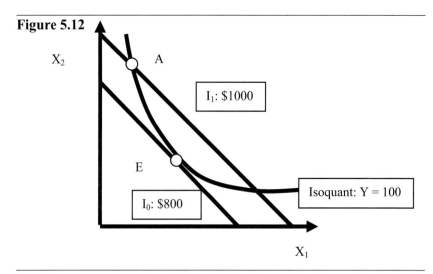

At point A, the firm is not in equilibrium, since the slope of the isoquant (MRTS) is greater (steeper) than the price ratio:

$$P_2 \Delta X_2 > -P_1 \Delta X_1$$

This inequality signals to the manager to substitute out of the expensive input (X_2) and into the less expensive input (X_1). This substitution will continue until point E is reached, where $\Delta X_2 / \Delta X_1 = -P_1/P_2$. At point E, the firm is in equilibrium.

(Quick Quiz 5.7: what is the definition of equilibrium? Why is point E an equilibrium point?)

As can be seen in figure 5.12, through the process of input substitution, the firm relocated on a lower isocost line (I_0), with a cost savings of $200 ($1000 - $800). Next, we will take a look at a wheat producer's input combination selection decision.

5.5.4 Example: Wheat Producer in Marysville, Kansas.

Suppose that the goal of a wheat producer in Marysville, Kansas (the City of Black Squirrels) is to minimize costs. The producer's objective is to produce 100 bushels of wheat at the lowest possible cost. Suppose that the production of wheat requires N inputs (X_1, X_2, X_3, ... , X_N), and the two most expensive inputs are land (X_1) and fertilizer (X_2). To focus on these two major inputs, we will hold all of the other inputs constant. The wheat producer's production function is given by:

$$Y = f(X_1, X_2 \mid X_3...X_N), \text{ where}$$

$$X_1 = \text{land (acres)}$$

$$X_2 = \text{fertilizer (lbs)}.$$

We will look at two inputs and one output to find the optimal combination of land and fertilizer to use in the production of wheat in North central Kansas. Figure 5.13 shows an isoquant, which reflects all combinations of inputs (land and fertilizer) that produce the same level of output (wheat).

The slope of the isoquant (Y) is the Marginal Rate of Technical Substitution = MRTS = $\Delta X_2 / \Delta X_1$. The question that the wheat grower would like to answer is: how many acres of land and pounds of fertilizer to use to produce 100 bushels of wheat? Since land and fertilizer are substitutes, there are numerous combinations of the two inputs that would produce 100 bushels. These combinations are the points on the isoquant, which reflects the physical relationship between inputs and outputs (the production function).

Figure 5.13

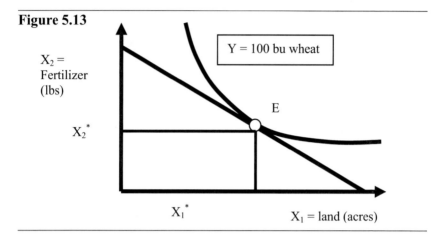

(Quick Quiz 5.8: explain why fertilizer and land are substitutes in the production of wheat. Are the perfect or imperfect substitutes? Explain why.)

Since the goal is to minimize costs, the producer will want to locate the cost-minimizing combination of inputs to produce the 100 bushels. She can do this with the use of the isocost line, a line with points of equal costs. Recall that the algebraic equation for the isocost line is derived from total costs:

$$TC = P_1X_1 + P_2X_2$$

$$P_2X_2 = TC - P_1X_1$$

$$X_2 = TC/P_2 + (-P_1/P_2)X_1$$

To minimize the costs of producing 100 bushels, the wheat producer locates the tangency point of the isoquant and isocost lines: the point where the slope of the isoquant = slope of the isocost line (MRTS = price ratio):

$$\Delta X_2/\Delta X_1 = -P_1/P_2.$$

158

The equilibrium point is where the changes in expenditures from substituting land and fertilizer along the isoquant are equalized.

$$-P_2\Delta X_2 = P_1\Delta X_1$$

If the change in expenditure for one input were greater than the change in the other input, the producer could lower costs by moving toward the equilibrium point.

Interestingly, the equilibrium condition for selecting the optimal combination of inputs follows the same logic as the profit-maximizing condition of input use. Recall that the profit-maximizing rule for input use it to set the marginal revenue product (MRP = MPP*P_Y) equal to the marginal factor cost (MFC = P_X):

MRP   = MFC

MPP*P_Y = P_X

$(\Delta Y/\Delta X)$*P_Y = P_X

ΔY*P_Y = ΔX*P_X

The final line shows that the profit-maximizing condition results in equilibrium where the incremental increase in revenues (ΔY*P_Y) is equal to the incremental increase in input costs (ΔX*P_X). In the next section, we will use our analysis of input combination selection to see how producers react to input price changes.

6. Optimal Responses to Price Changes.

We have seen that relative prices drive the economic decisions of producers in their quest to maximize profits and/or minimize costs. We will now consider a change in the price of an input, to see how producers will respond. Our economic intuition tells us that when it is possible to substitute between inputs, producers will shift out of expensive inputs, and into less expensive inputs. For example, a current choice that must be made by Kansas farmers is what combination of agrochemcals and land to use in the production process.

Our discussion of isoquants and isocost lines has focused on setting the MRTS equal to the slope of the isocost line, or the price ratio (P_1/P_2). The equilibrium condition highlights the importance of relative prices in the economy: if the price of one input changes, it changes the price ratio, and results in a new equilibrium combination of inputs for producers.

5.6.1 Price Change for the Farm Implement Manufacturer.

To see how input price changes affect input combination selection, let's return to the farm implement manufacturer example from above. This firm used labor (L = workers), and capital (K = machines) to produce implements. The price of labor is $10/hour, and the price of machines is $100/hour, and total expenditures are $1000, as can be seen in figure 5.14.

Figure 5.14

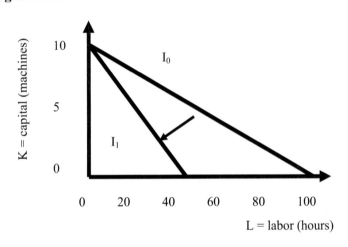

Suppose that the wage rate increases from $10/hour to $20/hour. This will shift the isocost line from I_0 to I_1. We can focus our attention on the shift in isocost lines by recalling the algebraic equation (y = b + mx) of the isocost lines:

$$X_2 = TC/P_2 + (-P_1/P_2)X_1$$

The y-intercept of the isocost line (TC/ P_2) remains unchanged, because the total expenditures and the price of machines have remained unaltered. The slope (-P_1/P_2), however, becomes steeper due to the increase in the price of labor. The slope of I_0 is equal to the price ratio prior to the price change: -P_1/P_2 = -10/100 = -0.1. After the wage increase, the price ratio increases (in absolute value) to: -P_1/P_2 = -20/100 = -0.2. This is reflected in figure 5.14: the "rise over the run" is equal to

160

-10/50 = -0.2. By adding isoquants to the graph, we can see that the firm's choice of inputs will change when the relative prices change.

Figure 5.15

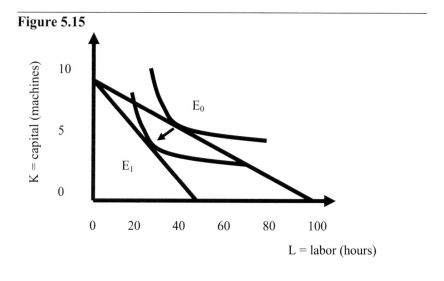

If the total expenditures of the firm remain constant at $1000, the firm ends up on a lower isoquant, showing that production is lowered due to the increase in input price. This reflects the discussion in the previous chapter: if the price of an input increases, production costs increase, and the firm lowers the level of output. The price change also alters relative prices (the slope of the isocost line) and results in a substitution out of labor and into capital.

The wheat producer's goal was to produce 100 bushels of wheat at the lowest cost. If the price of land increases, the slope of the isocost will change, but this firm manager will desire to remain on the same isoquant, to remain at the production goal of 100 bushels. The price change will cause a shift in the cost-minimizing combination of inputs, as can be seen in figure 5.16.

The increase in the price of land causes the slope of the isocost line to become steeper. To remain on the same isoquant, the producer will shift out of the more expensive input (land) and into the less expensive input (fertilizer) until a new equilibrium is reached (E_1). At the new equilibrium, fewer acres of land are employed, and more fertilizer. We will now use these principles to explore the impact of gambling casinos in Northeast Kansas on the optimal selection of inputs to use in agriculture.

Figure 5.16

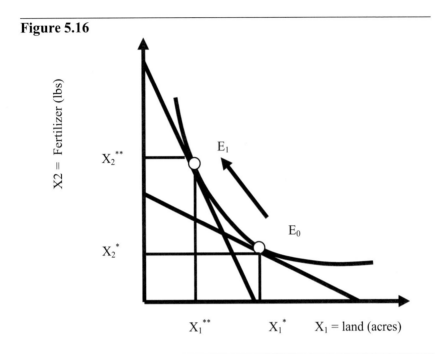

5.6.2 Example: The Impact of Gambling on Input Selection in Northeast Kansas.

Over the past few years, several large gambling casinos have located in Northeast Kansas. These casinos have been built on agricultural land, making the number of acres available for agricultural production scarcer in this area. The casinos employ several hundred persons, who have moved to the area and purchased houses. The increase in visitors has also increased the demand for hotel rooms, restaurants, gasoline stations, and convenience stores. So, the business climate has improved dramatically with the excitement (Wahoo!) over casino gambling. One impact of the casinos is an increase in the price of land due to the increase in the population of the area. We can use graphical analysis to understand how gambling has affected the use of chemicals in Northeast Kansas.

Figure 5.17

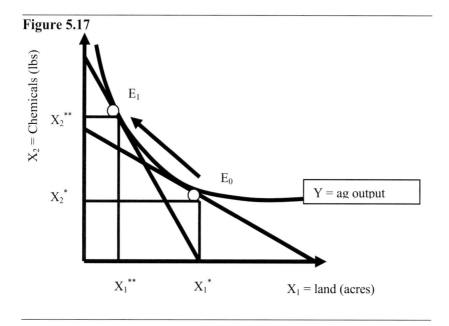

If the price of land (P_1) increases, then the price ratio increases, and the slope of the isocost line becomes steeper. To produce the same amount of agricultural output, or remain on the same isoquant, the farmers in the area must use more chemicals and less land. Therefore, the introduction of gambling casinos into the area results in a substitution out of land and into chemicals.

5.6.3 Relative Prices Rule!

We can now conclude that: ***RELATIVE PRICES RULE!*** So far in this course, we have seen that relative prices determine the optimal level of output (Chapter 3), the optimal level of inputs to use (Chapter 4), and the cost-minimizing combination of inputs to use (Chapter 5). In Chapter 6, we will see how relative prices also determine the most profitable combination of outputs to produce. Relative prices run the entire economy, since the decisions of business firms are all determined by the relative prices of scarce resources.

Chapter Five Summary

1. A firm will select inputs based on relative prices.
2. There are many different combinations of inputs that can produce the same level of output.
3. An isoquant is a line that represents all combinations of two variable inputs that will produce a given level of output.
4. Different nations use drastically different production practices, based on relative prices. When labor is cheap relative to capital, a labor-intensive production practice will be used.
5. Agribusiness firms will choose combinations of inputs that minimize their costs of production.
6. Perfect substitutes are inputs that can be interchanged completely. The isoquant for perfect substitutes is a straight line.
7. Perfect complements are inputs that must be used together in a fixed ratio. The isoquant for perfect complements has an "L" shape.
8. Imperfect substitutes are inputs that substitute for each other incompletely in the production process. The isoquant for imperfect substitutes is convex to the origin.
9. The Marginal Rate of Substitution (MRTS) is the rate one input can be decreased as the use of another input increases. The MRTS is the slope of the isoquant.
10. The isocost line indicates all combinations of two variable inputs that can be purchased at the same level of expenditure.
11. To find the optimal combination of inputs, the firm will locate at the point where the isoquant is tangent to the isocost line. At this point, the marginal rate of technical substitution equals the relative price ratio.
12. An equilibrium is a point from which there is no tendency to change.
13. Changes in relative prices result in shifts in the isocost line, and changes in the equilibrium combination of inputs. Firms will substitute out of relatively expensive inputs and into relatively less expensive inputs.
14. Relative prices rule: relative prices determine the optimal level of output, the optimal level of inputs, and the cost-minimizing combination of inputs to use.

Chapter Five Glossary

Complements in Production. Inputs that are used together to produce output.

Equilibrium. A point or situation from which there is no tendency to change.

Imperfect Substitutes. Inputs that substitute for each other incompletely in the production process.

Isocost Line. A line indicating all combinations of two variable inputs that can be purchased for a given, or same, level of expenditure.

Isoquant. A line indicating all combinations of two variable inputs that will produce a given level of output.

Marginal Rate of Technical Substitution (MRTS). The rate that one input can be decreased as the use of another input increases. The slope of the isoquant. $MRTS = \Delta X_2 / \Delta X_1$.

Perfect Complements. Inputs that must be used together in a fixed ratio. The proportion of each input is fixed in the production process.

Perfect Substitutes. Inputs that are completely substitutable in the production process.

Relative Price. The price of a good relative to prices of other goods. (Also see **Absolute Price**).

Substitutes in Production. Inputs that can be used in place of each other in the production process.

Chapter Five Review Questions

1. To draw an isoquant, the graph must show:
    a. One input on each axis
    b. One input and one output
    c. One output on each axis
    d. Cost of production on the vertical axis

2. Each point on the isoquant shows:
    a. The same level of output
    b. The same level of profit
    c. The same level of inputs
    d. The same level of expenditures

3. Relative prices are captured in the:
    a. Equilibrium point
    b. Isoquant
    c. Isocost line
    d. Vertical axis

4. The optimal combination of inputs depends on:
    a. Land grant University recommendations
    b. Tradition
    c. Resource availability
    d. Relative prices

5. In Western Kansas, farms are likely to be:
    a. Larger than in Eastern Kansas
    b. Smaller than in Eastern Kansas
    c. The same size as in Eastern Kansas
    d. Can not determine from the information given

6. Sugar and High Fructose Corn Syrup (HFCS) are:
    a. Perfect substitutes
    b. Perfect complements
    c. Imperfect complements
    d. Imperfect substitutes

7. A pen and a pencil are:
   a. Substitutes
   b. Complements
   c. Unrelated
   d. Irreplaceable

8. Capital and labor are:
   a. Perfect complements
   b. Perfect substitutes
   c. Imperfect substitutes
   d. Unrelated

9. If the price of the input on the x-axis decreases, then the slope of the isocost line will:
   a. Become steeper
   b. Become less steep
   c. Shift out parallel
   d. Shift in parallel

10. Labor-intensive agricultural production practices are most likely to occur in:
    a. Florida
    b. Kansas
    c. Texas
    d. Sub-Saharan Africa

CHAPTER SIX
OPTIMAL OUTPUT SELECTION

The agricultural economy is changing rapidly, as new technologies such as no-till production, Global Positioning Systems (GPS, a satellite technology), and biotechnology have been developed and introduced to farmers. With constant change, producers will seek out the most profitable goods to produce. In Kansas, we have seen a large increase in soybean acres over the past several years, as the price of soybeans has increased relative to other crops.

Agribusinesses are also changing rapidly. As mergers and consolidations take place, large agribusiness corporations are shifting into new product lines and out of old ones. The decisions about which products to produce are made by combining technological and economic information. This chapter is devoted to understanding how firms make decisions about which outputs to produce and sell.

1. Production Possibilities Frontier (PPF).

Most firms can produce more than one output. For example, a Kansas farm is often in a situation where it must choose between several competing crops: wheat, corn, milo, soybeans, and hay. Packing plants can grind all of their meat into hamburger, or slice it into steaks. Since most business firms have the ability to produce multiple outputs, guidance is needed as to which outputs would benefit the firm the most.

A Production Possibilities Frontier (PPF) describes the potential output levels of two products that a firm could produce.

Production Possibilities Frontier (PPF) = A curve depicting all of the combinations of two outputs that can be produced using a constant level of inputs.

The Kansas farmer-stockman provides an example of how managers make decisions on the optimal combination of outputs to produce. A farmer-stockman is a term used to describe the family farms in the Great Plains which produce both grain and cattle, a common type of farm located throughout the Sunflower State. Suppose that the farmer-stockmen can allocate their resources to the production of two outputs: wheat (Y_1) or cattle (Y_2). The production function, or the technical relationship between inputs (X) and outputs (Y) can be expanded to include multiple outputs:

$$Y_1, Y_2 = f(X_1, X_2, X_3, \ldots, X_N)$$

When we study the firm's selection of outputs, the inputs are all held constant. We are considering a firm that has a fixed plant, with a given level of resources (K, L, A, and M).

(Quick Quiz 6.1: what are the four inputs K, L, A, and M? Name the four items that comprise capital.)

These resources can be allocated between the two outputs: the inputs can be used either to raise cattle or to grow wheat. If all of the resources are allocated to cattle, then the farmer-stockman produces all cattle and no wheat. If, on the other hand, all of the resources are allocated to wheat, then the firm produces all wheat and no cattle. The firm can also select an intermediary point where some resources are devoted to both outputs. All of the possible combinations of outputs that can be produced with a fixed level of inputs are graphed in figure 6.1. The units for cattle are hundredweight (cwt, representing one hundred pounds), and the units for wheat are bushels (bu).

Point A represents complete specialization in beef, and point C is the situation when all of the productive resources are committed to wheat. Point B is when some resources are devoted to each output. Point D is attainable by the firm, but inefficient, since it does not lie on the PPF. Interior points are physically possible to achieve, but can be improved upon by moving to points located on the PPF. Point E is not physically attainable, given the fixed level of resource use, as it lies outside of the PPF.

Figure 6.1

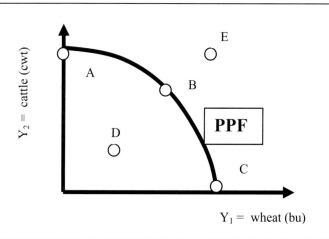

6.1.1 The Shape of the Production Possibilities Frontier.

The production possibilities frontier is concave to the origin (bowed out). This is due to the Law of Diminishing Returns: the first unit of input used is the most productive. As more units of inputs are added, the productivity level decreases. Therefore, if the firm specializes the resources that are most productive in the production of a given output, it will achieve higher levels of production.

Specialization of resources into what they do best allows the firm to use the best grazing acres for the production of cattle, and the best farm ground for the production of wheat. By utilizing the land in this fashion, the farmer-stockman can get more than just the average production rate of the two outputs. The PPF curves out, or is concave to the origin, due to the ability to specialize the inputs in their most productive use.

When increasing returns are present, the PPF would be convex to the origin (bowed in), and constant returns would result in a straight line PPF, as can be seen in figure 6.2.

Figure 6.2

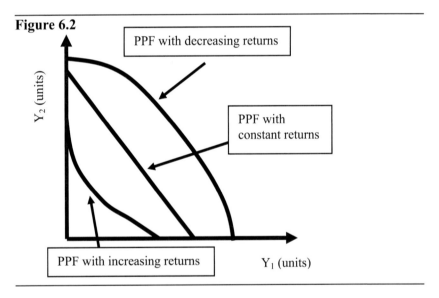

The PPF represents the physical relationship between inputs and outputs (the production function). To find the optimal, or profit-maximizing combination of outputs, we will combine the information contained in the PPF with information on the economic value of the two outputs, otherwise known as relative prices.

(Quick Quiz 6.2: explain why economists say that, "Relative prices rule!")

If the fixed level of inputs changes, or technological change occurs, the PPF will shift. For example, if the farmer-stockman increased the number of acres farmed, then the PPF would shift out and to the right, as shown in figure 6.3.
Technological change will also result in an outward shift of the PPF. Recall that technological change is a change in the relationship between inputs and outputs. Technological change results in more output produced with the same level of inputs.

(Quick Quiz 6.3: what is another way of stating the impact of technological change?)

Technological change in both cattle and wheat would result in an outward shift in the PPF like the one shown in figure 6.3.

Figure 6.3

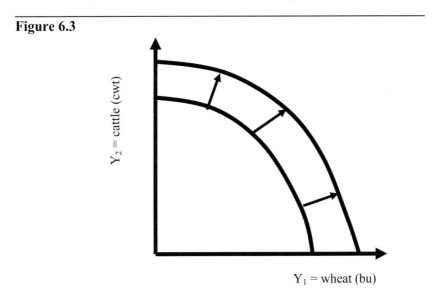

If technological change occurs only in one output, but not in the other, then the shift in the PPF will reflect the change. For example, if a new variety of wheat is developed at Kansas State University, the PPF will shift out for wheat as shown in figure 6.4.

Figure 6.4

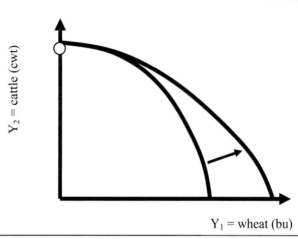

Y₂ = cattle (cwt)

Y₁ = wheat (bu)

With this type of technological change, the y-intercept remains the same before and after the technological change. This is because if all of the firm's resources are devoted to the production of cattle, the total quantity produced will remain the same. If the resources are all devoted to wheat, however, more bushels of output will result from the same level of inputs, and the PPF will shift to the right to reflect this. The firm will be able to produce more of both outputs, since resources that were previously devoted to wheat will now become available for beef production.

We have now seen the large number of possible output combinations that a firm could choose to produce. Next, we turn to how the firm will select the optimal, profit-maximizing combination of outputs. This is accomplished by looking at the rate of change in the PPF.

2. The Marginal Rate of Product Substitution (MRPS).

The slope of the PPF represents the rate of substitution between the two outputs. We call this rate the **Marginal Rate of Product Substitution (MRPS).** This represents the decrease in one output ()Y₁) that must occur if the other output ()Y₂) is to be increased, since the input levels are fixed.

Marginal Rate of Product Substitution (MRPS) = The rate that one output must be decreased as production of the other output is increased.

Also, the slope of the production possibilities frontier (PPF). MRPS = $\Delta Y_2/\Delta Y_1$.

It is easy to see that the slope of production possibilities frontier is simply the "rise over the run," or the change in cattle production divided by the change in wheat production: $\Delta Y_2/\Delta Y_1$. The MRPS represents the physical tradeoff that the farmer-stockman must make when determining the optimal allocation of inputs between the two outputs.

When the production processes for the two outputs are subject to decreasing returns, the PPF will be concave to the origin (bowed out), and the MRPS will be negative and increasing in magnitude. This is one of three possibilities for the MRPS: increasing, constant, and decreasing. The most likely situation is increasing MRPS, since this is the case of a production function that exhibits decreasing returns. We can further investigate the concave shape of the PPF by calculating the MRPS at different points along the PPF for corn and wheat in figure 6.5. Units have been changed to metric tons (mt) to keep the scale somewhat realistic.

Figure 6.5

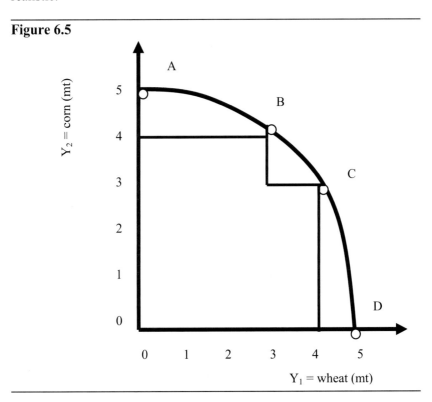

The rate of substitution between outputs (MRPS) changes as we move along the production possibilities frontier (PPF). We will calculate the MRPS along the PPF to show that when the PPF is concave to the origin, the MRPS is increasing in magnitude. Let's start at point A, the point of complete specialization in corn, where 5 metric tons of corn and no wheat are produced. If the firm takes enough resources out of corn production to reduce the output by one unit (from 5 to 4 mt), those resources can be used in the production of wheat. Interestingly, the first units of input in wheat production are the most productive due to the Law of Diminishing Returns. In the example shown in figure 6.5, three metric tons of wheat can be produced with the resources taken out of corn production. The MRPS, or the slope of the PPF, can be calculated to reflect this movement out of corn and into wheat between points A and B.

$$MRPS(AB) = \Delta Y_2 / \Delta Y_1 = (4 - 5)/(3 - 0) = -1/3$$

The first inputs used in wheat production are the most productive. As the firm adds more inputs, productivity declines. This can be seen by calculating the MRPS between points B and C. As corn production is reduced one more unit from 4 metric tons to 3 metric tons, wheat production increases, but not as much as it did between points A and B.

$$MRPS(BC) = \Delta Y_2 / \Delta Y_1 = (3 - 4)/(4 - 3) = -1$$

The absolute value of the MRPS has increased, reflecting decreasing returns: the first units of inputs in the wheat production function are the most productive. As the firm continues to remove resources from corn and put them into wheat production, the productivity continues to decline:

$$MRPS(CD) = \Delta Y_2 / \Delta Y_1 = (0 - 3)/(5 - 4) = -3.$$

We have just seen that the MRPS is increasing when the production functions are subject to decreasing returns. Similarly, the MRPS is constant under constant returns and decreasing when outputs are subject to increasing returns, as seen in figure 6.2 above. In most situations, inputs will be subject to decreasing returns, resulting in a PPF that is concave to the origin. Remember, though, that the PPF is derived from the production functions of the two outputs, so the shape of the PPF and the slope (MRPS) depend on the production function, or the physical relationship between inputs and outputs $[Y = f(X)]$.

Now that the physical production possibilities have been presented, we turn our attention to economic relationships. We will combine relative price information with our knowledge of the production possibilities to determine the profit-maximizing combination of outputs to produce.

3. The Isorevenue Line.

The economic information that will allow a firm to select the optimal output combination is market price information. Relative prices will provide the firm with information about the value of producing a good. In the farmer-stockman example, the firm is interested in the allocation of inputs between cattle and wheat: how much cattle to raise, and how much wheat to grow. The firm can determine this by looking at the revenues accrued from the production and sale of beef and grain. The revenue information can be summarized by the concept of an **Isorevenue Line**, or a line with equal levels of revenue at every point.

Isorevenue Line = A line depicting all combinations of two outputs that will generate a constant level of total revenue.

We can graph an isorevenue line for the farmer-stockman by assuming that the price of wheat (P_1) is \$100/mt, and the price of cattle (P_2) is \$50/cwt. Recall the definition of Total Revenues (TR):

$TR = P_1Y_1 + P_2Y_2$.

$TR = 100*Y_1 + 50*Y_2$.

To illustrate a specific isorevenue line, let TR = \$500. This isorevenue line appears in figure 6.6.

There are an infinite number of isorevenue lines, one for each dollar value of total revenue. We would like to characterize the isorevenue line with math in order to make finding the profit-maximizing level of output easier. The algebraic equation ($y = b + mx$) for the isorevenue line can be derived from the definition of total revenues:

$TR = P_1Y_1 + P_2Y_2$

$P_2Y_2 = TR - P_1Y_1$

Figure 6.6

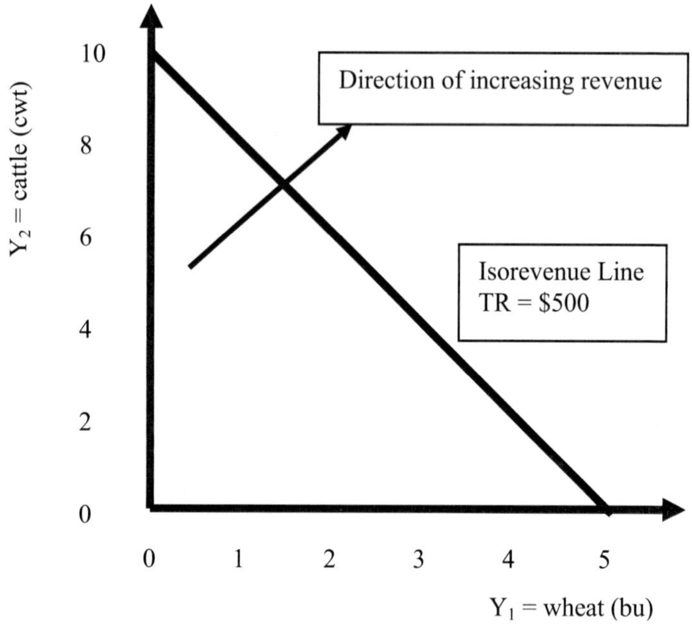

$$Y_2 = TR/P_2 + (-P_1/P_2)*Y_1.$$

This equation shows that the y-intercept is equal to TR/P_2. The y-intercept of an isorevenue line is the situation where all of the revenue is generated by the good on the y-axis (cattle in figure 6.6). In this situation, no wheat is sold, so $Y_1 = 0$, and $TR = P_2Y_2$. From this, we can easily see that the quantity of cattle sold is simply $Y_2 = TR/P_2$. The slope of the isorevenue line represents relative prices, and is equal to the price ratio ($-P_1/P_2$). The slope of the isorevenue line contains all of the economic information that the firm needs to choose the profit-maximizing level of input. Relative prices rule!

(Quick Quiz 6.4: the derivation of the equation of the isorevenue line is similar to the derivation for the isocost line. Derive the algebraic equation for the isocost line (remember?))

To complete the firm's quest to select the profit-maximizing combination of goods to produce and sell is to combine the physical production information contained in the PPF with the economic information contained in relative prices.

176

4. The Optimal Output Combination.

To maximize profits, the firm will want to reach the highest isorevenue line possible, given (1) the technical information given by the PPF, and (2) the relative price information summarized in the isorevenue line. Since higher levels of revenues appear on lines to the Northeast, the firm will locate on the isorevenue line that is tangent (barely touching) to the PPF, represented by point E in figure 6.7.

Figure 6.7

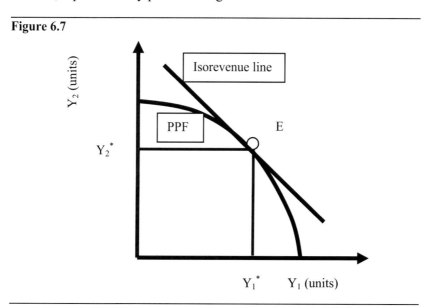

This is the point where the slope of the PPF (the MRPS) is equal to the slope of the isorevenue line (the price ratio). Point E is an equilibrium point for the firm, because it can do no better than E.

(Quick Quiz 6.5: define equilibrium. Why is point E an equilibrium point for the firm?)

The profit-maximizing rule for optimal output selection is to set the MRPS equal to the slope of the isorevenue line, or the output price ratio:

MRPS = slope of isorevenue line

$\Delta Y_2/\Delta Y_1 = -P_1/P_2$

$\Delta Y_2 * P_2 = -\Delta Y_1 * P_1$

This is a familiar result! The firm's manager should shift resources toward the output with the highest revenues. The intuition of this result can be seen from the case when the firm is not in equilibrium. The strategy to maximize profits is to employ resources in the output that will generate the highest returns.

If $\Delta Y_2 * P_2 > -\Delta Y_1 * P_1$, then the firm should move out of Y_1 and into Y_2.

If $\Delta Y_2 * P_2 < -\Delta Y_1 * P_1$, then the firm should move out of Y_2 and into Y_1. This can be seen clearly in a graph.

Figure 6.8

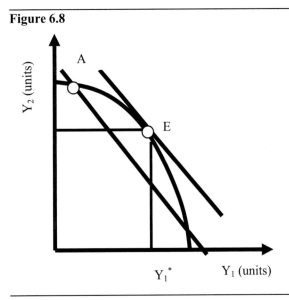

Point A is a feasible point of production, since it lies on the PPF. However, the point is not a profit-maximizing point for the firm, since higher revenues can be achieved at point E. To see this, we note that the magnitude of the slope of the isorevenue line is steeper than the slope of the PPF (the MRPS). Therefore, the following relationship holds at point A:

MRPS(A) < the price ratio

$\Delta Y_2 / \Delta Y_1 < -P_1/P_2$

$\Delta Y_2 * P_2 < -\Delta Y_1 * P_1$

178

The correct strategy for this firm is to reduce the inputs devoted to Y_2, and shift them to the production of Y_1. The reason is simple: at point A, the revenues associated with good Y_1 are higher than the revenues earned from the production and sale of Y_2.

The firm will continue to shift resources out of Y_2 and into Y_1 until the equilibrium point (E) is reached. At that point, the firm cannot earn higher revenues from the production of the two goods: E is an optimal, profit-maximizing point.

If the price of one of the outputs changes, the price ratio will shift, and the isorevenue lines will have a different slope. The firm will shift resources between outputs until the new equilibrium is reached.

5. Price Changes and the Optimal Output Combination.

Relative prices rule! Let's take a look at how relative prices allocate resources in a market economy.

(Quick Quiz 6.6: what are the three types of economic organization? How are resources allocated in each?)

In the past several years, the price of soybeans has increased relative to the price of other grains. This has caused a large shift of agricultural land in Kansas out of wheat, corn, and milo and into soybeans. We can use the Production Possibilities Frontier to understand how grain producers in Kansas have reallocated resources out of wheat and into soybeans. The PPF for grain in Kansas is depicted in figure 6.9.

Initially, at point A, Kansas farmers will produce Y_1* bushels of wheat and Y_2* bushels of soybeans. The initial prices of wheat (P_1) and soybeans (P_2) are reflected in the slope of the isorevenue line ($-P_1/P_2$). When the relative price of soybeans increases, the denominator of the price ration increases, resulting in a decrease in the slope of the isorevenue line. Point A becomes less profitable after the price of soybeans increased.

Kansas grain producers relocate to point B by shifting resources out of wheat and into soybeans. This is exactly what has happened in the past few years as soybean acres in Kansas are at an all-time high, and there has been a reduction in acres planted to wheat! Our economic theory has done a good job of explaining this shift in the outputs that are produced by Kansas farmers.

179

Figure 6.9

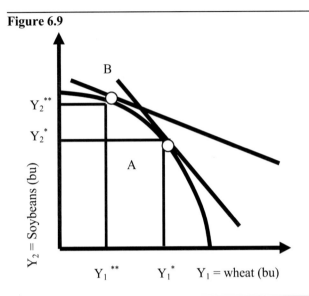

6. Review of Profit-Maximization Rules.

In the first six chapters of this book, we have found profit-maximizing and cost-minimizing rules for optimal input and output use. There is a striking similarity between the profit-maximizing and cost-minimizing rules that we have developed for a business firm. This section will briefly review the profit-maximizing rules that we have developed for:

1. The optimal level of input use (Chapter 4),
2. The optimal level of output production (Chapter 4),
3. The optimal input combination (Chapter 5), and
4. The optimal output combination (Chapter 6).

6.6.1 Rule for Optimal Input Use.

To maximize profits by selecting the level of input use, set the marginal benefits (the Marginal Revenue Product = MRP) equal to the marginal costs (the Marginal Factor Cost = MFC). Next, recall the definitions: MRP = MPP*P_Y, and MPP = $\Delta Y/\Delta X$.

$$MRP = MFC$$
$$MPP*P_Y = P_X$$

$$(\Delta Y/\Delta X)*P_Y = P_X$$
$$\Delta Y*P_Y = \Delta X*P_X$$

The profit-maximizing rule states that the firm manager should continue to use an input until the additional benefits of using the input to produce and sell a good ($\Delta Y*P_Y$) are equal to the additional costs of employing the unit of input ($\Delta X*P_X$).

6.6.2   Rule for Optimal Output Production.

To maximize profits by selecting the level of output to produce, set the marginal benefits (the Marginal Revenue = MR) equal to the Marginal Costs (=MC). Next, recall the definitions: MR = $\Delta TR/\Delta Y$, and MR = P_Y (assuming a competitive industry). Total Costs are the input price times the quantity of input purchased (TC = P_X*X).

$$MR = MC$$
$$P_Y = \Delta TC/\Delta Y$$
$$P_Y = \Delta(P_X*X)/ \Delta Y$$
$$\Delta Y*P_Y = \Delta X*P_X$$

The profit-maximizing rule states that the firm manager should continue to produce output until the additional benefits of production ($\Delta Y*P_Y$) are equal to the additional costs of producing one more output ($\Delta X*P_X$). Compare this result with that for the optimal level of input rule above!

6.6.3   Rule for Optimal Input Combination.

To minimize costs by selecting the optimal combination of inputs, the firm manager will set the slope of the isoquant (MRTS) equal to the slope of the isocost line (the price ratio). Next, recall the definition: MRTS = $\Delta X_2/\Delta X_1$.

$$MRTS = \text{slope of isocost line}$$
$$MRTS = -P_1/P_2$$
$$\Delta X_2/\Delta X_1 = -P_1/P_2$$
$$-\Delta X_2*P_2 = \Delta X_1*P_1$$

The cost-minimizing rule states that the firm manager should purchase inputs until the additional expenditures on each input are equal.

6.6.4 Rule for Optimal Output Combination.

To maximize profits by selecting the optimal combination of outputs, the firm manager will set the slope of the Production Possibility Frontier (MRPS) equal to the slope of the isorevenue line (the price ratio). Next, recall the definition: MRPS = $\Delta X_2/\Delta X_1$.

MRPS = slope of isorevenue line
MRPS = $-P_1/P_2$
$\Delta Y_2/\Delta Y_1 = -P_1/P_2$
$-\Delta Y_2 * P_2 = \Delta Y_1 * P_1$

The profit-maximizing rule states that the firm manager should produce output until the additional revenues from each output are equal.

6.6.5 How to Think Like an Economist.

Relative prices drive all economic decision-making: firms determine what to produce, how to produce, and what quantity to produce based on relative prices. The trick to thinking like an economist is to weigh the benefits and costs of every activity: if the benefits outweigh the costs, then the activity should be undertaken. This holds true for all aspects of production, as we have seen in Chapters 2 through 6. In the next chapter, we will shift our focus from producers to consumers. Consumers will be seen to make economic choices the same way that producers do: a consumer will buy a good if the benefits outweigh the costs! Simple, huh?

Chapter Six Summary

1. The Production Possibilities Frontier (PPF) is a curve that represents all combinations of two outputs that can be produced with a constant level of inputs.
2. The Production Possibilities Frontier is concave to the origin due to the Law of Diminishing Returns.
3. Technological change results in an outward shift in the Production Possibilities Frontier.
4. The Marginal Rate of Product Substitution (MRPS) is the rate that one output must be decreased as production of the other output is increased. It is also the slope of the Production Possibilities Frontier.
5. The isorevenue line depicts all combinations of the two outputs that generate a constant level of total revenue.
6. To find the revenue-maximizing combination of outputs, a firm will reach the highest isorevenue line possible by locating at the tangency between the Production Possibilities Frontier and the isorevenue line.
7. Relative price changes result in shifts in the isorevenue line, and a reallocation of resources.

Chapter Six Glossary

Isorevenue Line. A line depicting all combinations of two outputs that will generate a constant level of total revenue.

Marginal Rate of Product Substitution (MRPS). The rate that one output must be decreased as production of the other output is increased. Also, the slope of the production possibilities frontier (PPF). $MRPS = \Delta Y_2 / \Delta Y_1$.

Production Possibilities Frontier (PPF). A curve depicting all of the combinations of two outputs that can be produced using a constant level of inputs.

Chapter Six Review Questions

1. The production possibilities frontier is:
   a. all combinations of two inputs that can produce a constant level of output
   b. all combinations of two outputs that can be produced with a constant level of inputs
   c. all levels of one output that can be produced with varying levels of inputs.
   d. an isoquant
2. A point located inside the PPF is:
   a. efficient and attainable
   b. efficient but not attainable
   c. not efficient but attainable
   d. neither efficient nor attainable
3. A point located outside of the PPF is:
   a. efficient and attainable
   b. efficient but not attainable
   c. not efficient but attainable
   d. neither efficient nor attainable
4. The Marginal Rate of Product Substitution refers to:
   a. the physical tradeoff between inputs
   b. the physical tradeoff between outputs
   c. the economic tradeoff between inputs
   d. the economic tradeoff between outputs
5. The MRPS is:
   a. constant along the PPF
   b. increasing in absolute value along the PPF
   c. decreasing in absolute value along the PPF
   d. increasing or decreasing, depending on if there is increasing or decreasing returns
6. The slope of the PPF is due to:
   a. the isoquant
   b. relative prices
   c. the production functions of the two outputs
   d. the cost of inputs
7. The isorevenue line is derived from:
   a. the isoquant
   b. relative prices
   c. the production functions of the two outputs
   d. the cost of inputs

8. The profit-maximizing combination of outputs can be found at the tangency of:

      a. the PPF and the isorevenue line

      b. the PPF and the isocost line

      c. the isocost and isoquant lines

      d. the isoquant and isorevenue lines

CHAPTER SEVEN
CONSUMER CHOICES

We saw in the circular flow diagram in Chapter 1 that the economy is composed of two groups: producers and consumers. We have devoted the first several chapters of this book to the profit-maximizing behavior of producers. Now we turn to the behavior of the other major economic group: consumers. Consumers spend their income on the goods and services that are produced by producers. After a close examination of consumer behavior, we will turn to the interaction of producers and consumers in markets in the next chapter. We will learn a lot about the behavior of individuals, groups, and society through our study of markets.

1. Rationality.

In economics, we assume that all human behavior is purposeful and consistent. The term, "**Rational**" in economics is different from the dictionary definition of the term. The dictionary definition of rational states that an individual's behavior is "fully competent, or sane." In economics, rational simply means that individuals do the best that they can, given the constraints that they face. Rational behavior is *purposeful* and *consistent*.

Rational Behavior = Individuals do the best that they can given the constraints that they face. Rational behavior is *purposeful* and *consistent*.

For example, suppose that a person were to drive his car across his Professor's yard and into a stonewall. Is this rational? Using the dictionary definition of the word, we would be hard pressed to claim that this was rational behavior. However, according to the economic definition, this behavior would be considered to be rational. As long as the benefits of the activity outweigh the costs, then this behavior is considered to be rational by an economist. Any behavior is considered to be rational as long as the benefits outweigh the costs.

Another way to think about rational behavior is that individuals do the best that they can, given the constraints that they face. Consumers maximize their own happiness given a budget. For example, a college Professor gets a paycheck twice a month, and uses the income to purchase food, clothes, rent, water, electricity, toothpaste, etc. So, consumers are said to maximize their satisfaction given a budget constraint. As we have seen, producers maximize profits given input and output prices, and technology. In the "economic way of thinking," all individuals do the best that they can by maximizing something, given the constraints that they face: income, prices, and technology.

To introduce our study of consumer behavior, we will see that consumers have preferences for some goods over others. Examples include preferences for the following goods:

Pizza Shuttle or Godfathers Pizza?
Wranglers or Levis?
McDonalds or Burger King?
Grass fed beef or Grain fed beef?
White bread or Wheat bread?

Consumer choices about what goods to buy depend on consumer preferences and the relative prices of goods and services. The benefits of consuming a good come from the satisfaction that is gained from consuming the good, or the consumers' preferences for the good. The costs of consuming a good are the monetary cost of the good (the price), and any time costs associated with the purchase of the good (for example, having to drive to Wal-Mart, locate the good, and then stand in line to pay for it). A consumer will purchase a good if the benefits, or gain in satisfaction, is greater than the costs of buying the good.

This economic way of thinking provides economists with simple advice to firms that desire to maximize profits. For example, agricultural economists use the idea that consumers maximize their satisfaction given a budget in order to give some rather simple advice to the National Cattlemen's Beef Association (NCBA):

1. Pay attention to what consumers want: consumer preferences determine what they buy.

2. Lower costs: lower the price of beef to compete with other products such as chicken and pork.

We will be taking a close look at this advice to the beef industry in our study of consumer behavior. One question that we will try to understand is whether or not advertising for beef increases consumer purchases of beef. Our study of consumer choices will provide us with a solid foundation of how consumers make purchasing decisions, and how firms can profitably sell their goods and services to consumers. In the next section, we will investigate consumer preferences.

188

2. Utility.

Economists use the word "**Utility**" to mean satisfaction, or happiness.

Utility = The consumer's satisfaction derived from consuming a good.

Note that the economic definition of the term "utility" does not necessarily mean "useful" or "practical," as the dictionary definition might suggest. For a good to increase the level of utility, the good brings satisfaction to the consumer. Utility is a concept that can be applied to all economic goods, whether they are bought and sold in markets or not. Consumers can receive utility by purchasing new CDs, clothes, trucks, etc. They can also receive utility from nonmarket goods: babies, love, or watching the sunset. Interestingly, all of the major religions of the world emphasize nonmarket goods (love, faith, good works) more than market goods! Next, we will look into how economists have thought about utility over the decades.

7.2.1 Cardinal and Ordinal Utility.

At the turn of the century, economists desired to measure utility. In their attempt to quantify a consumer's level of satisfaction, they tried to assign an actual numerical value to the satisfaction of each good consumed. These economists developed a new unit, called the "util" to measure consumers' levels of happiness.

Utils = Imaginary units of satisfaction derived from the consumption of goods or services.

Assigning quantitative measures to satisfaction levels is called **Cardinal Utility**.

Cardinal utility = Assigns specific values, or numbers, to the level of satisfaction gained from the consumption of a specific good. The unit of measurement is the util.

For example, these social scientists tried to assign a number of utils to each good:

Apple = 20 utils
Oranges = 10 utils

Copenhagen = 50 utils
Eminem CD = 100 utils
New clothes = 200 utils

These economists soon found out that this was impossible!
People can not assign a value to the level of satisfaction: it differs for
everyone, and is not observable. Since science is based on observation,
these economists concluded that they could not quantify an individual's
feelings. A new concept of utility was needed, and so **Ordinal Utility**, or
ranking goods in order of preference, came to replace the notion of
Cardinal Utility.

Once economists realized that they could not actually measure
utility, they introduced a new concept:

Ordinal Utility = A concept of consumer satisfaction in which goods are
ranked in order of preference: first, second, third, etc.

Using ordinal preferences, goods are not assigned specific
numbers, but ranked according to the satisfaction they provide relative to
other goods. This concept of ranking goods allows modern economists
to observe consumers and develop principles of human behavior to
understand consumer choices.

7.2.2 Positive and Normative Economics.

Recall from Chapter 1 that economists must not make value
judgments about the utility that consumers derive from goods. Whatever
it is that consumers desire, economists take as factual and given, without
bringing their own preferences and opinions to bear on the situation.
Economists make no normative statements about what consumers desire
to buy.

(Quick Quiz 7.1: define and explain positive and normative economics:
kind of fun to remember this, isn't it?)

7.2.3 Total Utility and Marginal Utility.

To continue our study of consumer behavior, we will define the
concept of **Total Utility (TU)**, which represents that total amount of
satisfaction that a consumer receives from the consumption of a good.
Marginal Utility (MU), is the additional amount of satisfaction that is
gained from the consumption of one more unit of a good.

Total Utility (TU) = The total level of satisfaction derived from consuming a given bundle of goods and services.

Marginal Utility (MU) = The change in the level of utility as consumption of a good is increased by one unit. $MU = \Delta TU/\Delta Y$.

We will apply these two new concepts to an example of consumer behavior: drinking your favorite beverage after a long, hot day of work. One of the major predictions of our study of consumers will be: first is best. The first time that you consume something yields the most satisfaction, and the second time is less exciting. We get additional satisfaction, or utility, out of each unit consumed, but typically in a diminishing amount.

To demonstrate this idea, let's look at the relationship between the quantity of a good consumed (Y) and the satisfaction derived from the consumption of the good. Think of wheat harvest in Rawlins County, Kansas. Suppose that you have been working all day on a combine, and you are hot, tired, and thirsty. Your little sister brings you a cooler filled with your favorite beverage. Table 7.1 summarizes the satisfaction that you receive from drinking the beverage at the end of the day. We will use cardinal utility in this example to demonstrate the concepts.

(Quick Quiz 7.2: define and explain the concepts of cardinal and ordinal utility).

Table 7.1 Total and Marginal Utility Derived from Drinking Beverages on a Hot Day.

Y = Quantity Consumed (bottles)	TU = Total Utility (utils)	MU = Marginal Utility (utils/bottle)
0	0	--
1	10	10
2	16	6
3	19	3
4	20	1
5	20	0
6	18	-2

The first bottle of drink brings a lot of satisfaction: 10 utils. The second bottle brings additional satisfaction, since the total utility increased to 16 utils. Notice, however, that the additional satisfaction gained from the second bottle is lower: the marginal utility is 6 additional utils of happiness that were gained from the consumption of the second bottle. This makes perfect sense: the first bottle is the most satisfying!

We can calculate the marginal utility by looking at the rate of change in total utility ($MU = \Delta TU / \Delta Y$). As we move from zero bottles to one bottle, the change in TU equals 10 ($\Delta TU = (10 - 0) = 10$), and the change in quantity consumed is equal to one ($\Delta Y = (1 - 0) = 1$). Thus, the marginal utility is equal to ten: $MU = \Delta TU / \Delta Y = 10/1 = 10$.

As more bottles are consumed, utility increases, but at a decreasing rate. This is due to the consumer's increasing level of satisfaction. The fifth bottle does not provide any additional level of happiness: the consumer is indifferent between drinking the bottle or not.

(Quick Quiz 7.3: have you ever been in the situation where your friends say, would you like one more beverage, and you say, "I could take it or leave it."?)

Something really interesting occurs with the consumption of the sixth bottle. The consumer has moved past the point of indifference, to one of dissatisfaction. We can see this in table 7.1, where the marginal, or additional, satisfaction is negative! The sixth bottle actually makes the consumer feel worse than if he or she didn't drink it at all! Remember that a rational consumer would never undertake any activity in which the costs outweighed the benefits, so our rational consumer would not drink the sixth bottle.

(Quick Quiz 7.4: would anyone ever be irrational enough to drink more than the utility-maximizing level of bottles?)

Next, we will graph the TU and MU functions. Since the MU represents the rate of change in TU, it also represents the slope of the TU function (recall that the slope of any function is $m = \Delta y / \Delta x$).

(Quick Quiz 7.5: Explain why we draw TU and MU on separate graphs.)

192

Figure 7.1

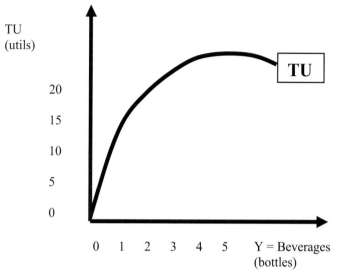

Figure 7.2

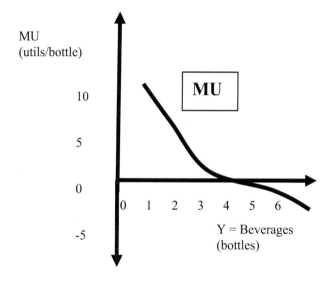

In figure 7.1, we can see that as consumption of the beverage increases, the level of utility (satisfaction) increases, but at a diminishing rate. In our example, the consumer becomes completely satiated at 5 bottles: any additional consumption of soda will result in a decrease in total utility! Too much of a good thing can be a bad thing! The marginal utility graph shows the additional utility gained from the consumption of one more unit of beverage. Marginal utility decreases as more of the good is consumed. This is the topic of the next section: the decreasing rate of marginal utility.

3. The Law of Diminishing Marginal Utility.

We saw from the example in the previous section that as the consumption of beverages increases, marginal utility decreases. Each additional unit consumed gives the consumer less marginal utility. Notice that this does not mean that total utility declines: four is preferred to three; more is better than less. However, more is better than less at a declining rate. At some point, the consumer can consume too much of a good: beverages become noneconomic goods at the point where the marginal utility becomes negative. This pattern of consumer utility is pervasive. Therefore, we define a "law:"

Law of Diminishing Marginal Utility = Marginal utility declines as more of a good or service is consumed during a specified period of time.

An example of the law of diminishing marginal utility is a family's purchase of television sets. If a family did not have a TV, the first set would provide a large increase in satisfaction. The family could watch educational and entertaining shows together. A second set would increase the total level of satisfaction in the family, since there are times when one family member prefers to watch NFL Football, and another wishes to watch a nature show on public television. So, total utility increases with the purchase of the second set, but the increase (or rate of change) in the total utility is not as great as it was with the first set.

A third set will bring some additional satisfaction to the family, but not much more utility than the second. Television watching in the kitchen, as meals are prepared, will result in greater levels of happiness for the family, but the use of televisions is nearing its peak. The first unit of a good consumed yields more satisfaction (or utility) than the next unit consumed, as can be seen in figure 7.3.

Figure 7.3

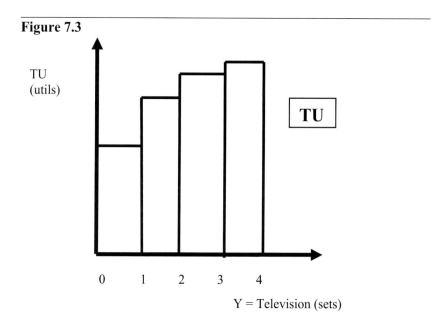

TU
(utils)

TU

0   1   2   3   4

Y = Television (sets)

Figure 7.4

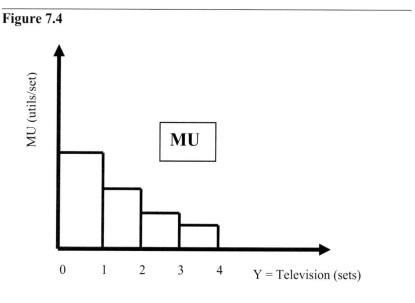

MU (utils/set)

MU

0   1   2   3   4   Y = Television (sets)

Each additional unit consumed gives you less utility. A curious example of the law of diminishing marginal utility is money. Many economists assert that the first dollar earned is worth more than the next. Some evidence for this idea comes from the observation that the poor value money more than the rich. One dollar is worth more to a poor person than a rich person.

Marginal utility declines as more of any good is consumed. There is no actual proof of this, it is just intuition that appears to be so pervasive that economists call it a "law." This law is very powerful: it helps to explain a lot of consumer behavior! Next, we list several common sayings that are related to the law of diminishing marginal utility.

1. *"Variety is the spice of life."*
We will not spend all of our income on one good, because the marginal utility of continuing to buy the same good declines. Instead, we will buy a *variety* of goods.

2. *"Been there, done that."*
In many situations, we will try something once, and that is enough! For many goods such as eating in certain restaurants, attending football games, or traveling to Disney World, the first time is a big thrill, the next time is not.

3. *"The first time is the best."*
We often hear of students turning 21, going drinking in Aggieville, and finding that one night of legal drinking is enough.

Economics can be used to explain all kinds of things, not just dollars and cents. Our law of diminishing marginal utility can be used as a theory of marriage and divorce. Economic theory suggests that an individual will continue to stay married as long as the benefits outweigh the costs. A person such as Elizabeth Taylor will consume numerous spouses, due to diminishing marginal utility!

4. Indifference Curves.

Consumer behavior can be better understood through careful consideration of the properties of consumer preferences. We will investigate three properties of consumer behavior.

7.4.1 Assumptions about Consumer Behavior.

1. Preferences are complete.
When given any two goods, a consumer can determine if he or she prefers A to B, B to A, or is indifferent between A and B. Let the

symbol, ">" mean "is preferred to," and the symbol, "π" mean, "is not preferred to," and the symbol, "~" mean, "is indifferent to."
Completeness of preferences means that for any two goods, A and B, the consumer can tell if:

1. A > B, (A is preferred to B),
2. B > A (B is preferred to A), or
3. A ~ B (the consumer is indifferent between A and B).

Complete preferences allow economists to study all goods, since the consumer is able to rank how a good compares to all other goods in the generation of utility.

2. Consumers are consistent.

Using the same notation as above, consistency of preferences means that:

If A > B and B > C, then A > C.

This can also be called, "transitive preferences," and simply means that consumers don't change their preferences haphazardly. Economists assume that consumer behavior is purposeful and consistent, so purchases must be consistent. This can be an unrealistic assumption in the real world, since consumer behavior is very complicated.

3. Nonsatiation: More is preferred to less.

This property states that more is always preferred to less (2A >A). Consumers can never have enough! This assumption states that a consumer will always want more of a good. When we make this assumption, we are assuming that the consumer is rational, and will not consume "too much" of a good, to the point where marginal utility becomes negative. These three assumptions are used to build models about the world. The objective of applying economic principles to consumer behavior is to *explain* and *predict* consumer behavior. We have seen that relative prices drive a market economy. Therefore, when we study consumer behavior, we are asking the question, "what happens when prices change?"

7.4.2 Consumer Responses to Relative Price Changes.

Suppose, for example, that there is a frost in Florida, where a large fraction of the citrus fruit production takes place in the United States. This frost will result in scarce citrus fruit, and the price of oranges, grapefruit, and lemons increases. How will consumers respond to the increase in the price of citrus fruit?

When the K-State football team becomes better, and an increase in the competitive level of the football program occurs, the price of season tickets for football increases. Also, when the quality of the KSU basketball team increases, with new coaches (Martin) and players (Walker, Beasley), then the price of season tickets for the hoop team skyrockets. Consumers respond to the change in relative prices between the two sports by shifting out of high price tickets.

In Manhattan, there is a debate about the appropriate wage level to pay workers. Many in the community argue for an increase in the minimum wage. If the minimum wage were increased, how do employers (the consumers of workers) respond to this wage hike?

We are studying consumer behavior in order to answer this type of question. Consumers are seen to maximize utility, subject to a budget constraint. When relative prices change, consumers will shift their purchases into the less expensive goods and out of the more expensive goods. We will introduce the concept of **Indifference Curves** to show this movement between goods.

7.4.3 Indifference Curves.

The word, "indifferent" means that an individual does not have a preference between two outcomes; it doesn't matter one way or the other. An indifference curve is a function in a graph that shows all of the points that a consumer is indifferent between. For example, if a friend asks you, "What would you like to do tonight?" and you respond, "I don't care," then you are indifferent.

An indifference curve is used to show a consumer's willingness to trade one good for another. For example, if a consumer has a case of Pepsi, how many bottles is she willing to trade to get one hamburger? Similarly, if I raise cattle and have a freezer full of meat, how many pounds of beef would I trade for two pounds of fruit and vegetables? The indifference curve shows exactly how a consumer is willing to trade one good against another. The formal definition of an **Indifference Curve** is:

198

Indifference Curve = A line showing all of the combinations of two goods that provide the same level of utility.

Since every point on an indifference curve has the same level of utility, we could also call an indifference curve an "isoutility" curve. Next, we provide an example of an indifference curve.

7.4.4 Indifference Curve Example: Pizza and Coke.

Let's look at combinations of Pizza and Coke that a consumer is indifferent between. The indifference curve I_0 in figure 7.5 is a group of points representing combinations of the two goods pizza and Coke between which the consumer is indifferent. The indifference curve represents consumer preferences for two goods. The shape of the indifference curve can be explained with the concept of scarcity.

(Quick Quiz 7.6: define the concept of scarcity and explain why it is the foundation of economics).

Figure 7.5

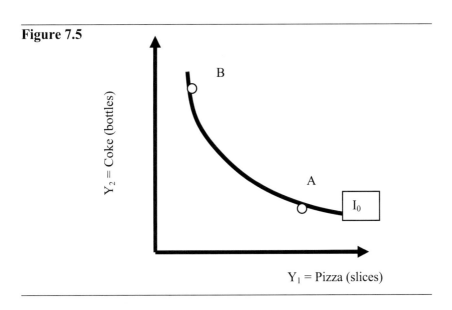

To see why scarcity dictates the shape of the indifference curve, we can look at point A, where Coke is scarce. At this point, the consumer has a lot of pizza and no Coke. Therefore, he is willing to give up several slices of pizza in exchange for one Coke. Likewise, at point B, where Coke is more plentiful and pizza is scarce, the consumer is willing to give up several Cokes to receive the first unit of pizza.

Therefore, indifference curves are convex to the origin, reflecting the Law of Diminishing Utility: the first unit of consumption of a good is the most highly valued.

7.4.5 Four Properties of Indifference Curves.

Convexity to the origin is one of four properties that all indifference curves have:

1. Downward Sloping,
2. Everywhere Dense,
3. Can't Intersect, and
4. Convex to Origin.

We will consider these four properties one at a time.

1. **Downward Sloping.** This must be true, since more is preferred to less. If an indifference curve were upward sloping, then a point such as B, that has more of both goods than point A, would produce the same level of utility (I_0) as point A, which has lower amounts of both goods, as in figure 7.6.

Figure 7.6

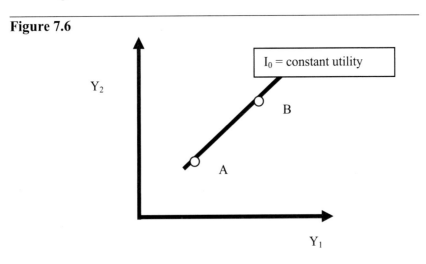

In figure 7.6, if the indifference curve were upward sloping, we would have a contradiction. Point B shows more of both goods, but since it lies on the same indifference curve as point A, it produces the same level of utility. This cannot be true. Thus, all real-world indifference curves are downward sloping. Therefore, due to the property of nonsatiation (more is preferred to less), indifference curves must be downward sloping. A consumer must give up some of one good in order to get the other good. The slope of the indifference curve represents the consumer's willingness to trade one good for another.

2. **Everywhere Dense.** This property comes from the assumption of complete preferences, and means that there is an indifference curve through every single point in the positive quadrant. Every combination of the two goods produces a given level of output. Although the term, "everywhere dense" may sound as if the indifference curves are not so bright, what it really means is that there are an infinite number of isoquants in the plane.

3. **Can't Intersect.** Indifference curves cannot intersect, since that would mean that two different levels of utility were equal to each other! To untangle this problem in logic, we will show that indifference curves can not intersect by contradiction: assume that two indifference curves intersect, as in figure 7.7.

Figure 7.7

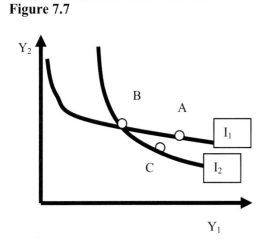

This is a cool proof! First, we notice that points A and B are on the same indifference curve (I_1). Therefore, points A and B have the same level of utility. Next, notice that points B and C are on the same indifference curve (I_2), so they represent the same level of utility. If A and B have equal levels of utility, and B and C have equal levels of utility, then if follows that A and C must have equal levels of utility [A = B and B = C,

201

so A = C]. But we can see in figure 7.7 that combination A produces a higher level of utility than combination C.

Therefore, indifference curves can not intersect because there is a contradiction if they did: A ~ C, but A > C can not both be true simultaneously. So, all indifference curves must not touch, since they each represent a different level of utility.

4. **Convex to Origin.** This property states that the indifference curves must bend toward the origin, or are convex to the origin. This is due to the Law of Diminishing Marginal Utility: the first unit of a good is the most satisfying! This can be shown in a graph, figure 7.8.

Figure 7.8

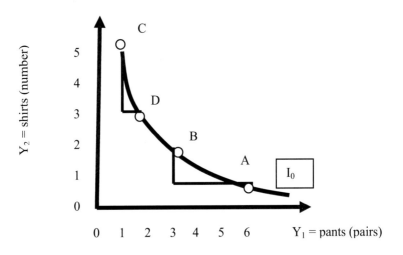

Due to law of diminishing utility, if a consumer has a lot of pants (point A: 6 pairs of pants, one shirt), she is willing to give up 3 pairs of pants for one additional shirt (point B: 3 pairs of pants, 2 shirts). On the other hand, if the consumer had 5 shirts and only one pair of pants (point C), she would be willing to give up two shirts for the second pair of pants (point D: 2 pairs of pants and 3 shirts). So, a consumer's willingness to trade one good for another depends on how much of each good that he or she has: the first unit of consumption of a good is the most valuable.

7.4.6 Indifference Curves for Substitutes and Complements.

Consider the case of two goods being **Perfect Substitutes**, meaning that the consumer is indifferent between consumption of either

202

good. For example, suppose that a consumer is purchasing shirts that are identical in every aspect other than color. If the consumer is indifferent between blue shirts and green shirts, then these two goods are considered perfect substitutes in consumption, and are shown in figure 7.9.

Perfect Substitutes = Goods that are completely substitutable, or that the consumer is indifferent between the two goods. (Also see **Substitutes**).

Figure 7.9

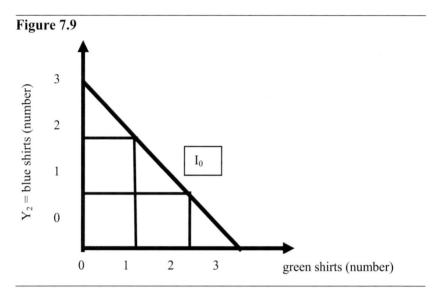

The indifference curve for perfect substitutes is a straight line, with a constant slope. Notice that in our example in figure 7.9, the consumer is indifferent between any combination of blue and green shirts that add up to a total of three shirts. This indifference curve is a special case, since it is not convex to the origin. The consumer is willing to trade one good for the other at a constant rate, so the goods are, in a way, the same good, "shirts."

The opposite case of perfect substitutes are **Perfect Complements**.

Perfect Complements = Goods that must be purchased together in a fixed ratio. (Also see **Complements**).

Here, the two goods are consumed together, for example, left and right shoes, as in figure 7.10. Here, it can be seen that the level of utility along indifference curve I_0 does not increase as more right shoes are added to a pair of shoes. This reflects the fact that left and right shoes must be consumed together to be valuable. Similarly, as left shoes are added, the utility level stays constant. Utility does increase when one of each good is added to achieve two pairs of shoes. This is also a special case of an indifference curve, since the curve is not convex to the origin. Almost all goods are "imperfect substitutes," meaning that they can be substituted with each other, but not perfectly. These goods are characterized by indifference curves that are convex to the origin.

Figure 7.10

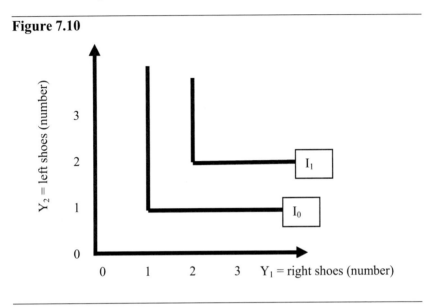

5. The Marginal Rate of Substitution.

The rate of change between goods is captured by the slope of the indifference curve, and is called the **Marginal Rate of Substitution (MRS)**.

Marginal Rate of Substitution (MRS) = The rate of exchange of one good for another that leaves utility unchanged. The slope of an indifference curve. $MRS = \Delta Y_2/\Delta Y_1$.

Recall that the term, "marginal" refers to a small change. The term, "substitution" refers to the trade-off between goods. Thus, the MRS is the number of units of good Y_2 that must be given up per unit of good Y_1 if the consumer is to remain indifferent, or retain the same level of satisfaction.

204

7.5.1 The Diamond-Water Paradox.

A famous economic example will be used to show the Marginal Rate of Substitution (MRS): the "Diamond/Water Paradox." Water is a necessity, we can't live without it, but it is inexpensive to purchase. In fact, water is nearly free, and is free in many situations, such as a drinking fountain. In contrast, diamonds are a luxury; we don't really need them, but they are extremely expensive. The "paradox" is that a good that is crucial to our existence is inexpensive, and a good that is used only for decoration is extremely valuable.

(Quick Quiz 7.7: can you use simple economics to explain the diamond/water paradox?)

The economic answer to the paradox is scarcity. Diamonds are valuable because they are scarce, whereas water is cheap because it is relatively plentiful. Would you ever give up diamonds for water? It sounds unlikely, but you would if you had only diamonds and no water! Would you give up water for diamonds? Certainly, if you had enough water to meet your needs. We can see this in a graph.

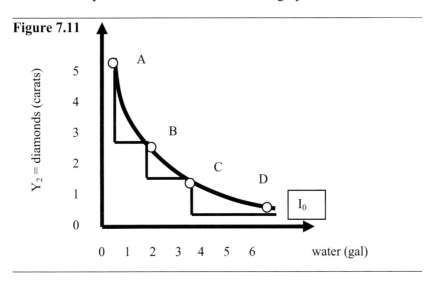

Figure 7.11

The marginal rate of substitution (MRS) is defined as the slope of the indifference curve. The MRS between points A and B shows the willingness of a consumer to trade diamonds for water.

$$MRS(AB) = \Delta Y_2/\Delta Y_1 = (3 - 5)/(2 - 1) = -2.$$

At point A, diamonds are relatively plentiful, so the consumer is willing to give up two diamonds for the one more gallon of water. Let's investigate what happens to the Marginal Rate of Substitution when the consumer trades for one more unit of water:

$$MRS(BC) = \Delta Y_2/\Delta Y_1 = (2-3)/(3-2) = -1.$$

The absolute value of the rate of substitution has declined, as can be seen in figure 7.11, where the slope has decreased in magnitude. This reflects the fact that as water becomes more plentiful (less scarce), the consumer is willing to give up fewer diamonds to acquire more water. The calculation of the MRS for the next gallon of water is:

$$MRS(CD) = \Delta Y_2/\Delta Y_1 = (1-2)/(6-3) = -1/3.$$

The MRS continues to fall in absolute value as more units of water are consumed. The connection between the Law of Diminishing Marginal Utility and the convexity of the indifference curve has been demonstrated graphically. Another example of the tradeoffs that occur between goods is the time allocation of a college student. Suppose that there are two ways for a college student to spend time: (1) studying, and (2) relaxing. In economics, this is called the labor/leisure tradeoff. If a student has been working all of the time (all work and no play), he is willing to give up a lot of work to get the first unit of play in. As a student increases the amount of relaxation, it becomes less valuable, as can be seen in figure 7.12.

Figure 7.12

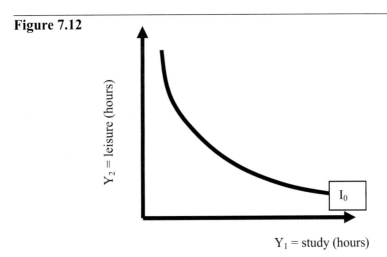

Y_2 = leisure (hours)

I_0

Y_1 = study (hours)

From the indifference curve in figure 7.12, we can see that it is likely that most students will end up somewhere in the middle of the graph. The notion of "balance," suggests that a student will want to consume some of each good: all work and no play results in no fun, and partying all the time can be hazardous to one's future career (and health!). Two additional sayings that are reflected here are: "Everything in moderation," and "Variety is the spice of life." The student will probably end up somewhere in the middle, reflecting the Law of Diminishing Marginal Utility: consumers will receive more utility by consuming a variety of goods, rather than just one good. The sayings "Don't spend all of your money in one place!" and "Don't put all of your eggs in one basket" reflect the idea of diverse consumer desires.

The indifference curve reflects consumer preferences, or what the consumer desires. It is now time for a reality check! Consumers must only spend within their limits, or comply with a budget constraint. In the next section, we will investigate the budget constraint, then we will combine what consumers want (represented by indifference curves) with what they can afford (represented by the budget constraint) to find a utility-maximizing equilibrium point.

(Quick Quiz 7.8: what is an equilibrium?)

We can show that the Marginal Rate of Substitution (MRS) is equal to the ratio of marginal utilities of each good. This makes intuitive sense because the MRS reflects how much of one good the consumer is willing to trade to get an additional unit of the other good, which is the marginal value of the good, or the marginal utility (MU). We can see this mathematically by starting with the definition of the MRS: $MRS = \Delta Y_2/\Delta Y_1$.

Next, divide both the numerator and the denominator by (ΔTU) to get:

$MRS = (\Delta Y_2/\Delta TU)/(\Delta Y_1/\Delta TU) = (1/MU_1)/(1/MU_2) = MU_1/MU_2$.

Simplifying, we get the relationship:

$MRS = MU_1/MU_2$.

Thus, the slope of the indifference curve reflects the marginal valuation of the two goods.

6. The Budget Constraint.

We know that indifference curves are everywhere in a graph of two goods. Economists call the collection of indifference curves in figure 7.13 an indifference curve map.

Figure 7.13

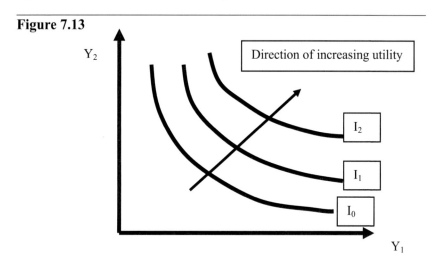

The indifference curves shown in figure 7.13 each depict a group of points representing two goods between which a consumer is indifferent. Each indifference curve represents consumer preferences. Due to the assumption of nonsatiation, more is preferred to less, so the level of utility increases as we move to the Northeast. What is stopping a consumer from going to the highest indifference curve possible? The consumer is constrained by a budget.

Consumers maximize utility, subject to a budget constraint. Utility, or consumer preferences, is represented by the indifference curves, and the budget is represented by the **Budget Constraint**:

Budget Constraint = A limit on consumption caused by the size of the budget, and the prices of goods.

Consumer choices depend on the interaction of (1) preferences, and (2) relative prices. Remember our goal of studying consumer behavior is to find out how consumers respond to changes in prices and income. We are in the process of developing a simple theory of consumer behavior to see how consumers respond to price changes and income changes. We will define the budget constraint for a graphical

208

model of two goods, since we have only two dimensions on the page of this book. Assume that a consumer spends all of his income on only food and clothing.

First, we will define the variables of a budget constraint.

M = income (\$)
Y_1 = food (calories)
P_1 = price of food (\$/calorie)
Y_2 = clothes (outfits)
P_2 = price of clothes (\$/outfit)

We will combine these ingredients into a budget equation. Remember that economics uses graphs to simplify or to represent the real world. This model will assume that the consumer spends all of his income on food and clothes. The budget equation states that income must be greater or equal to the expenditures on food (Y_1) and clothing (Y_2).

$$M \geq P_1 Y_1 + P_2 Y_2$$

If we assume that we spend all of our income, this changes the inequality in the equation above into an equality:

$$M = P_1 Y_1 + P_2 Y_2$$

The budget constraint shows that the amount of money that we earn (M = income) is exactly equal to how much we spend on food and clothing. Let's use some specific numbers to illustrate a budget constraint.

$M = \$100$/month; $P_1 = \$1$/calorie; $P_2 = \$20$/outfit

Let's include this information on our graph of consumer behavior to find out what we can afford to buy.

We can graph the budget line by finding the y-intercept and x-intercept. We do this by asking the question, how much of a good could the consumer purchase if she spent all of here money on the good? For example, to find the x-intercept, we calculate how many calories of food could be purchased at an income level of \$100/month, and a price of food equal to \$1/calorie: [$M/P_1 = \$100/(\$1$/calorie$) = 100$ calories].

Figure 7.14

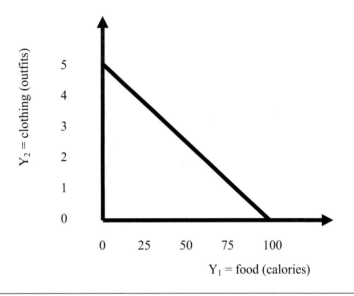

Similarly, we can find the y-intercept by calculating how many outfits of clothing could be purchased if all of the income were spent on clothing: [$M/P_2 = \$100/(\$20/\text{outfit}) = 5$ outfits]. By finding these two intercepts on the graph, and connecting them with a straight line, we are able to locate the budget constraint. The slope of this **Budget Line** is the "rise over the run," or $\Delta y/\Delta x = \Delta Y_2/\Delta Y_1 = -5/100 = -0.05$.

Budget Line = A line indicating all the combinations of two goods that can be purchased using the consumer's entire budget.

The equation of a line is given by: $y = b + mx$, where b is the y-intercept and m is the slope. We can use the equation of a budget constraint to derive the equation for the budget line. This derivation should look very familiar! It is identical to what we have previously done for the isocost and isorevenue lines for producers.

$$M = P_1Y_1 + P_2Y_2$$
$$P_2Y_2 = M - P_1Y_1$$
$$Y_2 = (M/P_2) + (-P_1/P_2)\ Y_1$$

The y-intercept (b) is equal to M/P_2, equal to $\$100/(\$20/\text{outfit}) =$ 5 outfits (this confirms our calculation above). To confirm our calculation of the slope of the budget line, we find that $m = \Delta y/\Delta x = -P_1/P_2 =$ relative prices. The slope of the budget constraint represents relative prices of the 2 goods.

The **Opportunity Set** is the triangle formed by the budget line.

Opportunity Set = The collection of all combinations of goods that is within the budget constraint of the consumer.

The area between the axes and the budget line is called the opportunity set because we can consume at any point in the opportunity set within our budget. Any point outside of the opportunity set is not feasible: the consumer does not have enough money to afford it. The opportunity set is defined by the budget line: any point in the triangle formed by the budget line and the axes is affordable to the consumer. Points to the Northeast are not affordable.

Figure 7.15

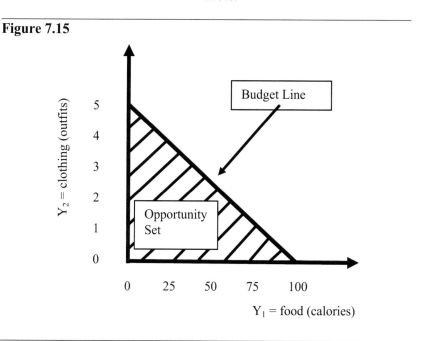

The consumer will desire to maximize utility, subject to the budget constraint shown in figure 7.15. The consumer will desire to locate as far to the Northeast as possible, staying within the opportunity set. We will see in the next section how a consumer will select the

211

utility-maximizing point by combining the preference information contained in the indifference curves with budget information contained in the budget line.

7. Consumer Equilibrium.

Recall that economists use the term "equilibrium" to describe a situation, or point, where there is no tendency to change. At an equilibrium point, producers and consumers are doing the best that they can. In equilibrium producers are maximizing profits subject to technology and prices, and consumers are maximizing utility, subject to a budget constraint. An equilibrium is an "optimal" point: the individual is doing the best that he or she can, given the constraints that they face. If something is optimal, then a person does not want to change from it.

We noted that consumer preferences can be summarized by a "map" of indifference curves. These curves represent the tradeoffs between food (Y_1) and clothes (Y_2). The slope of an indifference curve is the Marginal Rate of Substitution (MRS), which represents consumer preferences for the two goods, Y_1 and Y_2: how many units of Y_1 must be given up to get an additional unit of good Y_2? This will depend on the consumer's preferences of each good. Specifically, the MRS reflects the Marginal Utility for each good, or how much additional satisfaction that a consumer receives from each unit of the good consumed.

$$MRS = \Delta Y_2 / \Delta Y_1 = MU_1 / MU_2$$

We also noted that a consumer's budget constraint represents what he or she is able to purchase. A consumer will want to reach the highest level of satisfaction possible. This optimal, or highest utility level will be the highest indifference curve that is still within the opportunity set, or the indifference curve that is tangent to the budget line (point E in figure 7.15).

Point E represents the consumer's optimum, or equilibrium point. In this example, the equilibrium is 50 calories of food and 2.5 outfits (I suppose that a single shirt with no pants is one-half of an outfit). This equilibrium point happens to be at the "half-way" mark between the vertical and horizontal axes. However, there are numerous possible equilibria, depending upon the preferences of the consumer (the location of the indifference curve).

So, the optimal, or equilibrium point, from which there is no tendency to change, is found at the tangency of the indifference curve and the budget line.

Figure 7.16

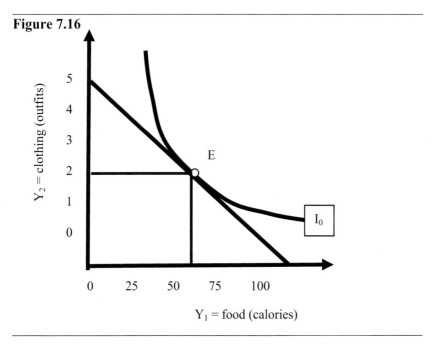

Y_1 = food (calories)

The slope of the budget line represents relative prices, as it is equal to the price ratio ($-P_1/P_2$). The budget line represents what you can buy. The slope of the indifference curve represents the consumer's preferences, or what the consumer wants. The graphical analysis is just like a story about going shopping. Each time we go to the store, we are matching up two things:

1. What you can afford (the budget constraint), and

2. What you want to consume (the indifference curve).

The mathematical equation for the equilibrium reflects this story:

Slope of the indifference curve = slope of the budget line

$$MRS = \text{price ratio}$$

$$\Delta Y_2/\Delta Y_1 = -P_1/P_2$$

$$MU_1/MU_2 = -P_1/P_2$$

213

$-MU_1/P_1 = MU_2/P_2$

This equilibrium condition states that a consumer should equalize the additional utility gained from the consumption of a good (MU) per price of the good for all goods. If a consumer was able to gain more satisfaction from a good per unit of cost than another good, then the consumer should shift her consumption into that good and out of other goods. This allows the consumer to reach the highest indifference curve possible, within the budget constraint.

8. The Demand for Meat in Hutchinson, Kansas.

We are learning about consumer behavior in order to better understand real-world issues in the agricultural economy. Currently, there is a big issue in the red meat industry: the per-capita consumption of beef in the USA has declined for several years. Economists argue about whether this decrease in beef consumption is due to:

1. Changes in the relative price of meats, or
2. Changes in consumers' knowledge of the impacts of red meat on health.

7.8.1 Consumer Equilibrium for the Hutchinson Consumer.

We will use our simple model of consumer behavior to analyze this issue. Let's take a look at a consumer in Hutchinson, Kansas (Home of the Cosmosphere!) Assume that the budget for weekly expenditures on meat is twenty dollars (M = $20), the price of beef is four dollars per pound (P_1 = $4/lb), and the price of chicken is two dollars per pound (P_2 = $2/lb). Figure 7.17 shows the budget line for the Hutchinson consumer.

(Quick Quiz 7.9: locate the opportunity set in figure 7.17).

The opportunity set for meat is found by finding how much beef and chicken could be purchased if all of the consumer's income were spent on one good. If the entire budget was spent on beef, the consumer could purchase 5 pounds of meat (x-intercept, M/P_1 = $20/$4/lb = 5 lbs).

214

Figure 7.17

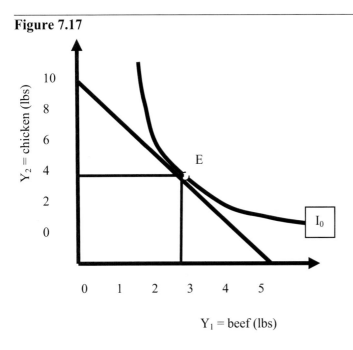

Y_2 = chicken (lbs)

Y_1 = beef (lbs)

If, on the other hand, the consumer spent all of the income on chicken, 10 pounds of chicken could be purchased (y-intercept, M/P_2 = $20/$2/lb = 10 lbs). The opportunity set reflects what is possible for the consumer to purchase.

The indifference curves represent the consumer's preferences. The slope of the indifference curve is the Marginal Rate of Substitution (MRS = MU_1/MU_2).

Marginal utility is defined as the additional satisfaction gained from consuming one more unit of a good.

The slope of the budget line reflects relative prices, and is equal to $-P_1/P_2$. The equilibrium for purchases of meat is found where the MRS is equal to the relative price ratio, as shown in figure 7.17. At the equilibrium point, the Hutchinson meat eater consumes 2.5 pounds of beef and 5 pounds of chicken (point E).

7.8.2 An Increase in Income for the Hutchinson Consumer.

Now suppose that the local economy in Hutchinson expands due to an increase in the demand for salt, since one of Hutchinson's biggest products is salt. Alternatively, the economic growth could be a result of a really big year at the Kansas State Fair. Regardless of the source of growth, the economic expansion results in an increase in the wages and salaries paid to the workers in Hutchinson. This, in turn, allows consumers in Hutchinson to spend more money on meat. Suppose that total meat expenditures rise from $M_0 = \$20$/week to $M_1 = \$40$/week.

We will show that the increase in income is a good thing for the beef industry, and a good thing for beef producers in Kansas. Figure 7.18 shows the impact of the increase in income on the consumer's meat purchases.

Figure 7.18

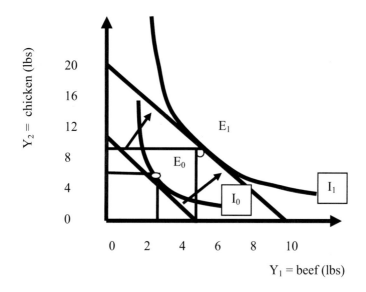

The original consumer equilibrium for the meat eater in Hutchinson (E_0) is 2.5 pounds of beef and 5 pounds of chicken. After the income increase, the equilibrium shifts to 5 pounds of beef and 10 pounds of chicken (E_1).

(Quick Quiz 7.10: what determines the location of the equilibrium point on the budget line?)

An increase in income will have an impact on the beef industry in Kansas: when income levels increase, consumers typically spend more money on "luxury" goods such as beef. Many agricultural economists believe that economic growth in China will result in a huge increase in the demand for both meat products and grain products from the USA. We noted in the introduction that Japan had a very large increase in meat consumption after World War II, due in large part to a huge increase in the standard of living. If China follows the same pattern, it is likely that meat consumption will increase enormously. This would increase the consumption of meat and grain products, since meat production requires seven pounds of grain to produce one pound of meat. Thus, Kansas agricultural producers are very interested in the economic development of China. Changes in income have a large impact on consumption!

(Quick Quiz 7.11: can you think of any goods that would have a decrease in consumption when income levels increase?)

7.8.3 The Impact of General Inflation on the Hutchinson Consumer.

General inflation can be defined as an increase in all prices in an economy. We argued in Chapter 1 that inflation of this type would not impact the economy at all, since the price of labor (wages and salaries) would increase at the same rate as the prices of all other goods and services. If all of the prices in the economy double, for example, including wages and salaries, then the consumption and production of goods and services would remain unchanged.

Let's use our simple model of consumer behavior to investigate the intuition behind this proposition. The price and income data below reflect a general inflation where all prices double, where the subscript refers to the good (1=beef ; 2=chicken) and the superscript refers to time periods zero and one.

Before:	After:
$M^0 = \$20/week$	$M^1 = \$40/week$
$P_1^0 = \$4/lb$	$P_1^1 = \$8/lb$
$P_2^0 = \$2/lb$	$P_2^1 = \$4/lb$

The budget line ($M = P_1Y_1 + P_2Y_2$) will be identical both before and after the inflation!

Before:	After:
$20 = 4Y_1 + 2Y_2$	$40 = 8Y_1 + 4Y_2$
$2Y_2 = 20 - 4Y_1$	$4Y_2 = 40 - 8Y_1$
$Y_2 = 10 - 2Y_1$	$Y_2 = 10 - 2Y_1$

Since the budget line remains unchanged, the equilibrium does not change, and the general inflation has no effect whatsoever on the economy! Relative prices have not changed, so nothing happens. Interesting, don't you think?

217

7.8.4 The Impact of A Change in Beef Prices on the Hutchinson Consumer.

Suppose that beef production costs decease due to technological change in packing plants: prior to the introduction of the technological change, $P_1^0 = \$4/\text{lb}$ and after the technological change, $P_1^1 = \$2/\text{lb}$. The price and income data are as follows, where the subscript refers to the good (1=beef; 2=chicken) and the superscript refers to time periods zero and one.

$$M^0 = \$20/\text{week} \quad P_1^0 = \$4/\text{lb} \qquad P_2^0 = \$2/\text{lb}$$
$$M^1 = \$20/\text{week} \quad P_1^1 = \$2/\text{lb} \qquad P_2^1 = \$2/\text{lb}$$

The budget constraint changes, since the relative prices of beef and chicken change. Recall that the slope of the budget line is the relative price ratio.

Before:	After:
$20 = 4Y_1 + 2Y_2$	$20 = 2Y_1 + 2Y_2$
$Y_2 = 10 - 2Y_1$	$Y_2 = 10 - Y_1$

In figure 7.19 below, the original consumer equilibrium (E_0) before the price change is 2.5 pounds of beef and 5 pounds of chicken. After the price changes, the budget line shifts to reflect an increase in purchasing power, since the price of beef is lowered. The y-intercept remains at 10, since both income (M) and the price of chicken (P_2) have remained unchanged. The x-intercept shifts from 5 pounds ($M^0/P_1^0 = \$20/\$4/\text{lb} = 5$ lbs) to 10 pounds ($M^1/P_1^1 = \$20/\$2/\text{lb} = 10$ lbs).

The consumer equilibrium after the technological change (E_1) moves to four pounds of beef and 6 pounds of chicken, determined by the tangency of the indifference curve and the budget line (MRS = the price ratio). Notice that the consumer can expand the consumption of *both* goods, although the price of chicken remained constant. This is because of the increase in purchasing power associated with a price decrease. Interestingly, the price of beef has a strong affect on consumer purchases of both beef and chicken.

The technological change increased the amount of beef sold in Hutchinson, and we can predict that any factor that causes a relative price decrease will result in more of the good being sold. Kansas cattlemen are better off, since more beef is sold. (Note that the price of cattle does not decrease, just the price of meat in the grocery store).

218

Conversely, any factor that increases the relative price of beef in the grocery store will have an adverse effect on the cattle producers.

Figure 7.19

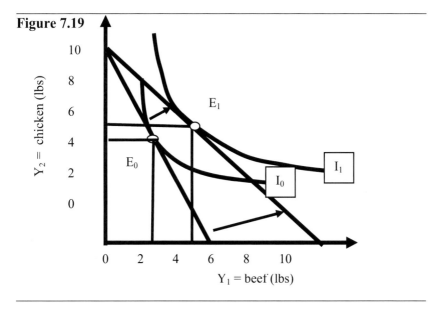

7.8.5 The Impact of A Change in Chicken Prices on the Hutchinson Consumer.

Does a change in the price of chicken really affect the beef market? Definitely yes! Just as the beef price decline caused an increase in the consumption of both beef and chicken, a chicken price change will affect the market of both beef and chicken. Suppose that there is an decrease in the relative price of chicken from $2/lb to $1/lb:

$M^0 = \$20/\text{week}$ $P_1^0 = \$4/\text{lb}$ $\qquad$ $P_2^0 = \$2/\text{lb}$
$M^1 = \$20/\text{week}$ $P_1^1 = \$4/\text{lb}$ $\qquad$ $P_2^1 = \$1/\text{lb}$

The budget line shifts due to the price change.

Before:	After:
$20 = 4Y_1 + 2Y_2$	$20 = 4Y_1 + Y_2$
$Y_2 = 10 - 2Y_1$	$Y_2 = 20 - 4Y_1$

Figure 7.20 shows that the x-intercept does not change, but that the budget line pivots upward and outward. The original equilibrium (E_0: 2.5 lbs beef; 5 lbs chicken) and the new equilibrium after the price change (E_1: 2 lbs beef; 12 lbs chicken). With the price decrease of

chicken, the consumer substitutes out of the more expensive product (beef) and into the cheaper product (chicken). Beef and chicken are substitutes: consumers will shift their purchases toward the least expensive product.

Relative prices rule! We have seen that any change in the relative price of beef will affect the quantity of beef purchased, whether the change is a change in the price of beef or a change in the price of chicken.

7.8.6 Conclusions of Beef Consumption of the Hutchinson Consumer.

Given the example of the meat eater in Hutchinson, what can we conclude about the demand for beef? Let the quantity of beef purchased by consumers be the demand for beef, Q^d_{beef}. We have seen that the demand for beef is a function of the prices of beef and chicken and income: $Q^d_{beef} = f(P_1, P_2, M)$. We have greatly simplified consumer behavior, by looking at the most important determinants of consumer purchases: prices and income. The results of our study are summarized below:

Figure 7.20

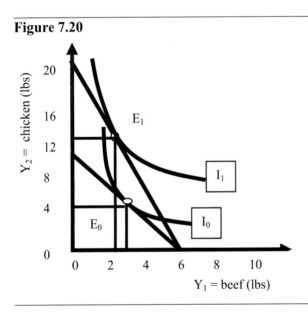

$Y_1 = $ beef (lbs)

1. $P_1\downarrow$: The price of beef decreases:
   $P_1\downarrow$: Q^d_{beef} increases
2. $P_2\downarrow$: The price of chicken decreases:
   $P_2\downarrow$: Q^d_{beef} decreases
3. $M\uparrow$: Income increases:

220

M ↑: Q^d_{beef} increases

Given our knowledge of the demand for beef, we can summarize an economist's advice to the beef industry:

1. Lower production costs in every way possible: P_1 decreases.

2. Pay attention to consumer preferences: pay attention to the prices of chicken and pork.

3. Look to consumer groups with growing income for new markets: low-income nations.

We have identified the optimal, utility-maximizing point for the consumer. The model of consumer behavior yielded the major determinants of consumer demand: relative prices and income. In the next chapter, we will investigate how markets work by deriving supply and demand curves, then studying the interaction of supply and demand, or markets!

Chapter Seven Summary

1. In economics, we assume that individuals are rational. Rational behavior indicates that individuals do the best that they can, given the constraints that they face. Rational behavior is purposeful and consistent.
2. Utility is the satisfaction derived from consuming a good.
3. Cardinal utility assigns specific values to the level of satisfaction gained from the consumption of a good.
4. Ordinal utility ranks consumer satisfaction from the consumption of a good.
5. Total utility is the level of satisfaction derived from consuming a given bundle of goods and services. Marginal utility is the change in the level of utility as consumption of a good is increased by one unit.
6. The Law of Diminishing Marginal Utility states that MU declines as more of a good is consumed.
7. Three assumptions about consumer behavior are: (1) preferences are complete, (2) consumers are consistent, and (3) more is preferred to less (nonsatiation).
8. An indifference curve is a line showing all of the combinations of two goods that provide the same level of utility.
9. Indifference curves have four properties: (1) downward-sloping, (2) everywhere dense, (3) can't intersect, and (4) convex to the origin.
10. Perfect substitutes are goods that a consumer is indifferent between. Perfect complements are goods that must be purchased together in a fixed ratio. Most goods are imperfect substitutes, meaning that they can be substituted with each other, but not perfectly.
11. The Marginal Rate of Substitution (MRS) is the rate of exchange of one good for another that leaves utility unaffected. Also, the slope of the indifference curve. The slope of the indifference curve is equal to the marginal valuation of the two goods.
12. The budget constraint is the limit imposed on consumption by the size of the budget and the prices of the two goods.
13. A consumer maximizes utility by locating at the tangency of the indifference curve and the budget line.
14. The opportunity set is the collection of all combinations of goods that is within the budget constraint of the consumer.

Chapter Seven Glossary

Budget Constraint. A limit on consumption caused by the prices of goods and the size of the budget.

Budget Line. A line indicating all the combinations of two goods that can be purchased using the consumer's entire budget.

Cardinal Utility. Assigns specific values, or numbers, to the level of satisfaction gained from the consumption of a specific good. The unit of measurement is the util. (See also **Ordinal Utility**).

Complements in Consumption. Goods that are consumed together (e.g. peanut butter and jelly). (Also see **Substitutes in Consumption**).

Complements in Production. Goods that are produced together (e.g. beef and leather). (Also see **Substitutes in Production**).

Indifference Curve. A line showing all of the combinations of two goods that provide the same level of utility.

Law of Diminishing Marginal Utility. Marginal utility declines as more of a good or service is consumed during a specified period of time.

Marginal Rate of Substitution (MRS). The rate of exchange of one good for another that leaves utility unchanged. The slope of an indifference curve. $MRS = \Delta Y_2 / \Delta Y_1$.

Marginal Utility. The change in the level of utility as consumption of a good is increased by one unit. $MU = \Delta TU / \Delta Y$.

Opportunity Set. The collection of all combinations of goods that is within the budget constraint of the consumer.

Ordinal Utility. A concept of consumer satisfaction in which goods are ranked in order of preference: first, second, third, etc. (See also **Cardinal Utility**).

Perfect Complements. Goods that must be purchased together in a fixed ratio. (Also see **Complements**).

Perfect Substitutes. Goods that are completely substitutable, or that the consumer is indifferent between the two goods. (Also see **Substitutes**).

Rational Behavior. Individuals do the best that they can given the constraints that they face. Rational behavior is *purposeful* and *consistent.*

Substitutes in Consumption. Goods that are consumed either/or. (e.g. wheat bread and white bread.) (Also see **Complements in Consumption**).

Substitutes in Production. Goods that compete for the same resources in production. (e.g. wheat and barley). (Also see **Complements in Production**).

Total Utility. The total level of satisfaction derived from consuming a given bundle of goods and services.

Utility. The consumer's satisfaction derived from consuming a good.

Utils. Imaginary units of satisfaction derived from consumption of goods or services.

Chapter Seven Review Questions

1. An individual who stays up so late that they feel sick the next day is:
   a. rational
   b. irrational
   c. not an economic individual
   d. can not tell from the information given

2. Placing a numerical value on the consumption of a piece of apple pie is an example of:
   a. normative economics
   b. cardinal utility
   c. ordinal utility
   d. positive economics

3. Modern economics uses which type of consumer theory:
   a. cardinal utility
   b. ordinal utility
   c. total utility
   d. public utility

4. Marginal utility refers to:
   a. the extra level of electricity from a public utility
   b. the level of satisfaction from consuming a good
   c. utility derived from consuming a good
   d. a change in utility when consumption is increased by one unit

5. When a consumer is indifferent between consuming an additional unit of a good:
   a. TU is negative
   b. MU is equal to zero
   c. TU is equal to zero
   d. MY is negative

6. All of the following are assumptions about consumer behavior except:
   a. complete preferences
   b. consistent consumers
   c. nonsatiation
   d. relativity

7. Indifference curves are convex to the origin due to:
   a. the Law of Diminishing Marginal Utility
   b. the Law of Diminishing Returns
   c. relative prices
   d. the Law of Demand

8. A tractor and a plow are:
   a. substitutes
   b. complements
   c. perfect substitutes
   d. not enough information to answer

9. Peanut butter and jelly are:
   a. substitutes
   b. complements
   c. perfect substitutes
   d. not enough information to answer

10. The indifference curve represents:
    a. consumer income
    b. consumer preferences
    c. what consumers can afford
    d. what consumers actually purchase

11. An increase in the price of chicken will affect;
    a. the amount of chicken purchased
    b. the amount of beef purchased
    c. the relative price of beef and chicken
    d. all of the other three answers

12. A general inflation will lead to:
    a. a decrease in the consumption of beef
    b. an increase in the consumption of beef
    c. no change in the consumption of beef
    d. unemployment

13. If income decreases then the consumption of beef will:
    a. increase
    b. decrease
    c. not change
    d. not enough information to answer

CHAPTER EIGHT
SUPPLY AND DEMAND

The first seven chapters of this book have described and explained the behavior of individual economic units: producers and consumers. We have seen how these economic actors locate the optimal point in economic decisions. Producers select the profit-maximizing level of inputs and outputs, and consumers purchase goods to maximize utility.

The overall economy is affected by the decisions of individual producers and consumers. When we aggregate (add up) all of the decisions that producers make, we can see how an entire market is affected by the profit-maximizing decisions made by all of the individual producers in an industry. Similarly, all of the individual consumer decisions can be aggregated to see how entire markets change when consumers shift their purchases due to changes in relative prices and other economic conditions.

In this chapter, we will make the connection between individuals and markets explicit by deriving market supply and demand curves from the behavior of individual producers and consumers. We will also study the determinants of market supply and demand, and introduce the concept of elasticity, or how responsive producers and consumers are to changes in economic variables. In the following chapter, we will see how supply and demand curves interact to determine prices and quantities in markets.

1. Supply.

Supply is the relationship between the available quantity of a good and its price:

Supply = The amount of a good available in a given location or time frame at a given price.
Supply refers to a direct functional relationship between the price and quantity of a good;

$$Q^s = f(P)$$

Where Q^s is the quantity supplied of a good, and P is the price of the good. As we shall see, when the price of a good increases, the quantity supplied of a good increases.

8.1.1 The Individual Firm's Supply Curve.

In previous chapters, we used the symbol Y to denote the production of a firm. In the next several chapters we will use the notation Q^s to denote the market, or aggregate, level of quantity supplied, and q^s to denote a single firm's quantity supplied. This will allow us to easily distinguish between graphs for single firms and for entire markets. We will see that markets are merely the collection of actions of all individual firms.

To derive the supply curve of an individual firm, let's start with a single firm's cost curves, shown in figure 8.1.

Figure 8.1

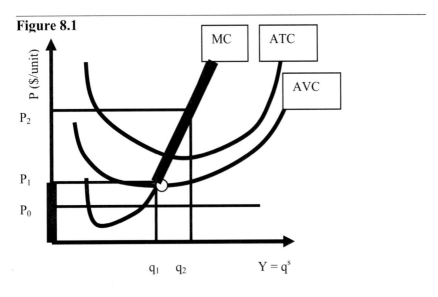

Recall the profit-maximizing behavior of an individual producer: the producer will continue producing a good until $MR = MC$. Since we are assuming a competitive industry, we know that price is fixed and constant and equal to the MR line.

(Quick Quiz 8.1: why does the assumption of competition result in a fixed price? Why is the price equal to the MR?)

At a given market price of P_2 in figure 8.1, this firm will maximize profits by setting $MR = MC$, or $P = MC$ at q_2 units of output. If the firm were to produce one more unit of output, the additional (marginal) costs would increase above the marginal revenue line, and profits would decrease. If the firm produced one fewer unit of output, profits would be reduced since the marginal revenues are higher than the marginal costs at that point.

The individual firm will always set price equal to MC, and the relationship between the price of a good and the quantity supplied is found on the MC curve. Since supply refers to a direct, functional relationship between the price and quantity supplied of a good, the marginal cost curve represents the supply curve of the individual firm. This is true for all prices, as long as the price is above the shut down point.

(Quick Quiz 8.2: define the shut down point for a firm in the short run and the long run.)

In the short run, the firm will continue to produce as long as price is greater or equal to the average variable cost ($P \geq AVC$). At prices below AVC, the firm will shut down. The price P_1 in figure 8.1 is the shut down point. For all prices above price P_1, the individual firm's supply curve is equal to the MC curve, and for all prices below price P_1, the supply curve is equal to zero (the line on the vertical axis below price P_1 in figure 8.2.

Supply Curve = The marginal cost curve above the minimum average variable cost curve.

Figure 8.2

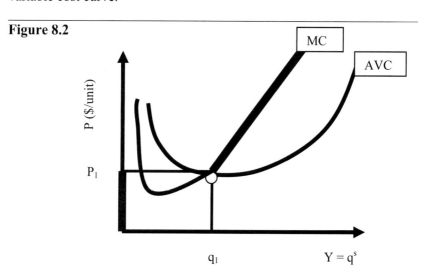

Notice that there are two segments to the individual firm's supply curve (1) above the shut-down point, supply is equal to the marginal cost curve, and (2) below the shut-down point, the supply curve is equal to zero. In the long run, the shut down point is the ATC curve, since ATC = AVC in the long run.

(Quick Quiz 8.3: why does ATC = AVC in the long run? Draw an individual firm's long run supply curve.)

8.1.2 The Market Supply Curve.

The market supply curve (also called the industry, or aggregate supply curve) can be found by the horizontal summation of all of the individual firms' supply curves. This is shown in figure 8.3.

The term, "horizontal summation" refers to the way that the quantity supplied by each firm is aggregated into the market supply curve. In figure 8.3, two firms out of an entire market are represented, to simplify the aggregation procedure. The ellipsis (…) represents the numerous other firms that are also in the market, but are not included in the diagram due to lack of space.

Figure 8.3

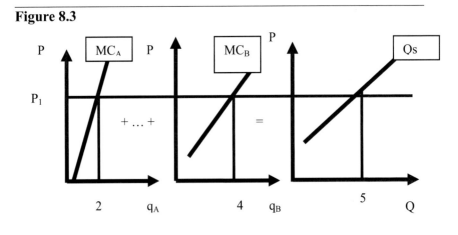

We will add together the MC curve of all firms in the industry to arrive at the market supply curve in the far right graph. Note that the three graphs to the left are all individual firms, represented by the symbol, "q." A "Q" represents the market supply curve, to indicate that the units for the total market are much larger than those for the individual firms.

230

At an initial price of P_1 dollars per unit, firm A sets MR = MC, and produces 2 units of output. Firm B follows the same behavior, and produces 5 units of output. To find the point on the market supply curve for price P1, we simply add up all of the individual firm supply curves:

$$Q_1 = q_A + \ldots + q_B.$$

If this procedure is followed for different price levels, a market supply curve (Q^s) can be derived by the horizontal summation of all individual supply curves. Be sure to keep in mind that only three of the numerous firms appear in the diagram above, and that most of the firms are not shown. The definition of the **Market Supply** curve is:

Market Supply = The horizontal summation of all individual supply curves for all individual producers in the market.

By gathering data on how each individual firm in a market will adjust their production levels to changes in price, we can summarize the market supply information in a supply schedule, as shown in table 8.1.

Table 8.1 The Market Supply of Bread in Phillipsburg, Kansas.

Price (P) ($/loaf)	Quantity supplied (Q^s) (1000 loaves)
1	10
2	20
3	30
4	40
5	50

The definition of the supply schedule is straightforward:

Supply Schedule = A schedule showing the relationship between the price of a good and the quantity of a good supplied.

Next, we will use the information from the supply schedule to graph a market supply curve and summarize the relationship between the price and quantity supplied of a good.

231

8.1.3 The Law of Supply.

The key result of the information provided in the supply schedule is that when the price of a good increases, the quantity supplied increases, due to the profit-maximizing behavior of individual firms. This positive, or direct, relationship between price and quantity supplied is so pervasive in all of the economies of the world that economists call it a "law:"

Law of Supply = The quantity of goods offered to a market varies directly with the price of the good, *ceteris paribus*.

The information contained in the supply schedule can be used to draw a market supply curve, as in figure 8.4.

Figure 8.4

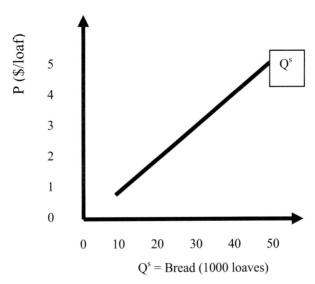

Q^s = Bread (1000 loaves)

There is an unusual feature of this market supply graph that we will discuss next. In economics, we study supply (the behavior of producers) and demand (the behavior of consumers). When we graph a supply curve, we are graphing the relationship between the price and quantity supplied of a good. Price is the *independent variable*, since it causes (determines) the quantity of a good sold: price *causes* quantity supplied.

$$P => Q^s \, (P \text{ causes } Q^s)$$

232

P = independent variable
Q^s = dependent variable

$Q^s = f(P)$

Recall from our study of competitive industries that producers take prices as given and decide how much to sell. Individual firms cannot affect the price of a good, since each individual firm is very small relative to the numerous firms in the market. Therefore, price causes quantity supplied.

In mathematics, we put the independent variable on the x-axis and the dependent variable on the y-axis. For example, the physical relationship between precipitation and the yield of wheat, is shown in figure 8.5.

x => y (x causes y)
y = f(x)
x = fixed = independent variable
y = dependent variable

Figure 8.5

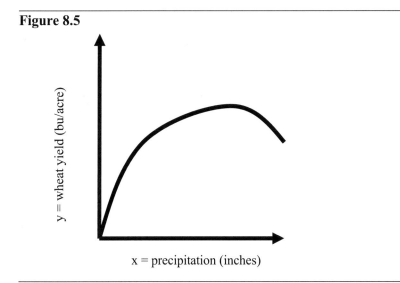

y = wheat yield (bu/acre)

x = precipitation (inches)

In economics, we draw supply and demand curves "backward." This is because of the first economist to draw supply and demand curves: Alfred Marshall. Alfred lived in England at the turn of the century, and was the first economist to study the relationship between price and quantity using graphical analysis. Economists have not changed these graphs ever since, even though it breaks with the mathematical tradition

233

of placing the independent variable on the horizontal axis and the dependent variable on the vertical axis.

In figure 8.4, price is the independent variable, but it is drawn on the vertical axis. Quantity supplied is the dependent variable, but it is drawn on the horizontal axis. Thus, always be aware when we work with graphs of supply and demand that the graphs are "backward," since price is the independent variable.

In conclusion, a market supply curve is the positive relationship between the price and quantity supplied of a good. The Law of Supply states that when the price of a good increases, the quantity supplied will also increase, holding all else constant. Individual firms will produce greater levels of output when prices are higher, to maximize profits! In our graph of market supply (figure 8.4) we are isolating the relationship between price and quantity supplied by holding everything in the economy constant except for the price and quantity supplied of a good. The market supply curve will provide us with an abundance of information about how the economy functions, as we shall see in the remainder of this chapter.

2. The Elasticity of Supply.

So far in this chapter, we have seen that the profit-maximizing behavior of business firms leads to a positive relationship between the price and quantity supplied of a good, or an upward-sloping supply curve. To study the responsiveness of business firms to changes in output price, we introduce the concept of "elasticity," which measures the responsiveness of one variable to a small change in another variable. We can calculate an elasticity for any two variables, as we shall see throughout this chapter, but we will start by calculating the responsiveness of producers to a change in price. First things first, however.

8.2.1 The Definition of Elasticity.

An **Elasticity** is a measure of responsiveness:

Elasticity = The percentage change in one economic variable with respect to a percentage change in another economic variable.

We begin our study of elasticities by defining the "elasticity of supply," which measures how quantity supplied changes when the price of a good increases one percent:

234

Elasticity of Supply = The percentage change in the quantity supplied with respect to a percentage change in price.

Mathematically, the elasticity of supply (ε) is given by:

ε = (% change in Q^s)/(% change in P)
   = %ΔQ^s/%ΔP

8.2.2 Elasticity Classifications.

This formula shows that the elasticity of supply is the responsiveness (measured by the percentage change) in quantity supplied, given a one-percent change in price. The elasticity of supply is measuring the movements along a supply curve such as the supply curve for bread in Phillipsburg shown in figure 8.4. The responsiveness of producers to price changes can be categorized into three degrees of responsiveness: (1) **Inelastic** supply, (2) **Elastic** supply, and (3) **Unitary Elastic** supply.

An **Inelastic** supply curve is one that is relatively unresponsive to changes in price: a one-percent change in price results in a smaller than one-percent change in quantity supplied. Mathematically, this is equivalent to: %ΔQ^s < %ΔP, or ε < 1. In this case, the elasticity of supply is inelastic, or relatively unresponsive to changes in price.

Inelastic = A change in price brings about a relatively smaller change in quantity.

An **Elastic** supply curve is one that is relatively responsive to changes in prices: a one-percent change in price results in a larger than one-percent change in quantity supplied. Mathematically, this is equivalent to: %ΔQ^s > %ΔP, or ε > 1. In this case, the elasticity of supply is elastic, or relatively responsive to changes in price.

Elastic = A change in price brings about a relatively larger change in quantity.

The third category of elasticity is unitary elastic, which takes its name from an elasticity of supply equal to one. This means that the change in quantity supplied is equal to the change in the price of a good (%ΔQ^s = %ΔP, or ε = 1).

Unitary Elastic = The percentage change in price brings about an equal percentage change in quantity.

The percentage change of a variable is just the change in the variable (Δx), divided by the level of the variable ($\Delta x/x$). For example, if a student's test scores improved from 80 to 90 points, the percentage change in tests scores would be: $(t_1 - t_0)/t_0 = (90 - 80)/80 = 10/80 = 0.125$. So, the percentage change in quantity supplied is equal to $\Delta Q^s/Q^s$, and the percentage change in price is equal to $\Delta P/P$.

$$\varepsilon = (\Delta Q^s/Q^s)/(\Delta P/P) = (\Delta Q^s/\Delta P)*(P/Q^s)$$

The degree of responsiveness depends on the ability of a firm to respond to a change in price. A firm will have more flexibility in the long run, as the inputs become variable. Therefore, the elasticity of supply will become more elastic as time passes. In the immediate short run, very little about a firm's production process can be changed, so the elasticity of supply is very inelastic. Over time, the firm has more opportunities for making choices, so supply becomes more elastic.

Let's calculate a supply elasticity to put our new economic tool into operation. Suppose that the price of bread in Phillipsburg increases from \$1/loaf to \$2/loaf: what is the elasticity of supply? We start with the mathematical expression for the supply elasticity:

$$\varepsilon = (\Delta Q^s/Q^s)/(\Delta P/P) = (\Delta Q^s/\Delta P)*(P/Q^s)$$

We can see from table 8.1 that the quantity of bread supplied at a price of \$1/loaf is 10,000 loaves. At a price of \$2/loaf, 20,000 loaves are supplied. So, $\Delta Q^s = 20,000 - 10,000 = 10,000$, and $\Delta P = \$2/loaf - \$1/loaf = \$1/loaf$. We can substitute these numbers into the formula above, but we need to know what numbers to use for "Q^s" and "P." If we used the *initial* values of quantity and price (\$1/loaf and 10,000) we would calculate a different number for the supply elasticity than we would if we used the *ending* values (\$2/loaf and 20,000 loaves). Therefore, it is common practice to use the average values of prices and quantities to calculate the "arc" elasticity of supply between two prices.

Arc Elasticity = A formula that measures responsiveness along a specific section (arc) of a supply or demand curve, and measures the "average" price elasticity between two points on the curve.

To calculate the arc elasticity, we use the average value of price and quantity in the formula for price elasticity. Let Q^s* and $P*$ be the average values of price and quantity:

$$Q^s* = (Q^s_1 + Q^s_0)/2 \qquad\qquad P* = (P_1 + P_0)/2$$

Substitution of these terms in the elasticity equation results in:

$$\varepsilon = (\Delta Q^s/\Delta P)*(P*/Q^{s*}) = (\Delta Q^s/\Delta P)*[(P_1 + P_0)/(Q^s_1 + Q^s_0)]$$

Notice that the twos drop out, since there is a two in both the numerator and the denominator. With this formula, we can calculate the elasticity of supply of bread for a price increase from $1/loaf to $2/loaf:

$$\varepsilon = (\Delta Q^s/\Delta P)*[(P_1 + P_0)/(Q^s_1 + Q^s_0)]$$

= [(20,000 loaves –10,000 loaves) / ($2/loaf – $1/ loaf)]*
  [($2/ loaf + $1/ loaf) / (20,000 loaves + 10,000 loaves)]

= [10,000 loaves /$1/loaf]*[$3/loaf/30,000 loaves] =
  (10,000/30,000)*(3/1) = 1.

The supply elasticity of bread in Phillipsburg, Kansas is **Unitary Elastic**.

(Quick Quiz 8.4: define and explain the terms elastic, inelastic, and unitary elastic).

Interestingly, there are no units for an elasticity: all of the loaves and dollars have cancelled each other out, since they appear in both the numerator and the denominator:

ELASTICITIES ARE UNITLESS!!!

This feature of elasticities is highly desirable: economists can compare elasticities across all goods and services. If we tried to compare the level of apples with the level of oranges, we could not graph them on the same graph or compare them directly, since they are in different units. When elasticities are calculated, however, we are able to compare the responsiveness of any goods, since the units are identical: unitless!

8.2.3 Own-Price and Cross-Price Supply Elasticities.

Elasticities of supply can be calculated for changes in price, but also for changes in any other economic variable. The most common elasticity that is calculated is the own-price elasticity of supply, which reflects the responsiveness of quantity supplied to the price of the same good.

Own-Price Elasticity of Supply = Measures the responsiveness of the quantity supplied of a good to changes in the price of that good.

Another common elasticity that is calculated is the cross-price elasticity of supply, which measures the responsiveness of quantity supplied to a change in the price of a related good. A related good is any good that has an impact on the production of the good under consideration. For example, when cattle are slaughtered, the two major products are beef and hides. If the price of hides increases, this will affect not only the quantity of hides supplied, but also the quantity of beef supplied.

Cross-Price Elasticity of Supply = Measures the responsiveness of the quantity supplied of a good to changes in the price of a related good.

8.2.4 The Relationship between Elasticity and Slope.

To get a better idea about how to calculate supply elasticities, assume that there are only two firms in the carbonated beverage industry: Coke and Pepsi. Price and quantity supplied information are presented in table 8.2.

Table 8.2. Price and Quantity Supplied Data.

Soda Price ($/can)	Coke Q^s (m.cans)	Pepsi Q^s (m.cans)	Soda Market (m.cans)
0.50	25	20	45
0.75	50	25	75

The elasticity of supply for Coke can be calculated:
$\varepsilon_{coke} = (\Delta Q^s/\Delta P)*[(P_1 + P_0)/(Q^s_1 + Q^s_0)] = [(50-25)/(0.75-0.50)]*[(0.75 + 0.50)/(50 + 25)]$

$\varepsilon_{coke} = [25/0.25]*[1.25/75] = 100*0.0167 = 1.67$

The supply of Coke is elastic, meaning that a one percent increase in the price of Coke results in a 1.67 percent increase in the quantity of Coke supplied. This means that Coke has a fairly flexible production function, and is able to respond to changes in price. The elasticity of supply for Pepsi can also be calculated:

$\varepsilon_{pepsi} = (\Delta Q^s/\Delta P)*[(P_1 + P_0)/(Q^s_1 + Q^s_0)] = [(25–20)/(0.75–0.50)]*[(0.75 + 0.50)/(25 +20)]$

$\varepsilon_{pepsi} = [5/0.25]*[1.25/45] = 20*0.0278 = 0.55$

The elasticity of supply of Pepsi is relatively inelastic: a one percent increase in the price of Pepsi results in only a 0.55 percent increase in the quantity of Pepsi supplied. Relative to Coke, Pepsi's production process is less flexible, and is therefore less responsive to changes in price. The market elasticity of supply is calculated in the same manner as the individual firm's supply elasticities. We anticipate the market elasticity of supply to be in between the two individual firm elasticities, since the market is comprised of the two firms alone.

$\varepsilon_{market} = (\Delta Q^s/\Delta P)*[(P_1 + P_0)/(Q^s_1 + Q^s_0)] = [(75-45)/(0.75–0.50)]* [(0.75 + 0.50)/(75+45)]$

$\varepsilon_{market} = [30/0.25]*[1.25/120] = 120*0.0104 = 1.25$

As expected, the soda market supply elasticity is between the individual firm elasticities: $0.55 < 1.25 < 1.67$.

(Quick Quiz 8.5: is the soda market supply elasticity elastic or inelastic? Explain why.)

(Quick Quiz 8.6: what is an arc elasticity?)

Figure 8.6 shows two supply curves with different elasticities. The elasticity of supply reflects how responsive a firm is to a change in price. This is directly related to the slope of the supply function.

In figure 8.6, the firm with the relatively elastic supply (q^s_B) has a flatter slope than the firm with a relatively inelastic supply (q^s_A). This can be seen by the response of the two firms depicted in figure 8.6 to a price increase from P_0 to P_1. Firm A is less responsive, and increases

239

output from q^0_A to q^1_A. Firm B, on the other hand, is more responsive to the change in output price, and increases output from q^0_B to q^1_B. The own-price elasticity of a firm, or the responsiveness of a firm to a change in price, depends on the ability of the firm to adjust inputs and outputs to a change in price.

Figure 8.6

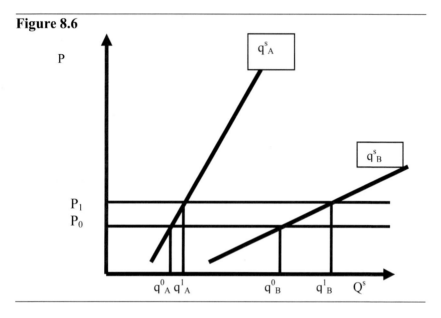

Although the price elasticity of supply is *related* to the slope of the supply curve, it is not equal to the slope, as can be demonstrated easily:

$$\text{Slope} = \Delta y/\Delta x = \Delta P/\Delta Q \qquad \text{Elasticity} = (\Delta Q/\Delta P)*(P/Q)$$

As can be seen in the above equations, the elasticity is the inverse of the slope, and depends on the magnitude of P and Q. When two supply curves are drawn together in the same graph, one can quickly determine which curve is more elastic by the relative slope. However, be careful when trying to assess the elasticity of a supply curve from a graph: the slope depends on the scale of the graph, and a steeply-sloped curve may be elastic. It depends on what scale is used for the graph.

3. Change in Supply; Change in Quantity Supplied.

In this section, we will introduce some new and useful terminology that will allow us to understand supply curves at a more knowledgeable level. The terms, "supply," and "quantity supplied" actually refer to two different things, which can cause confusion when the terms are first introduced. With a little practice, however, the terms become simple, and very useful in ascertaining the impact of economic variables on the supply of a good.

When the price of a good changes, this causes a movement along a supply curve, which is called a **Change in Quantity Supplied**:

Change in Quantity Supplied = When a change in the quantity of a good sold is a result of a change in the price of the good. A movement along the supply curve.

This can be seen by observing the market supply of hamburgers in Colby, Kansas, in figure 8.7.

Figure 8.7

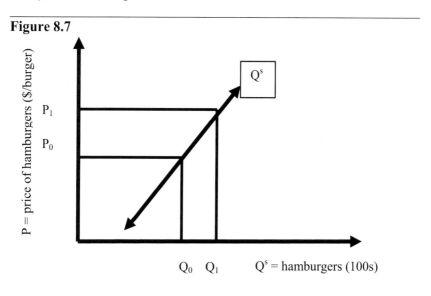

Q^s

P_1

P_0

Q_0 Q_1 Q^s = hamburgers (100s)

P = price of hamburgers ($/burger)

If the price of hamburgers increases, the supply curve shows how many more hamburgers will be supplied to the market in Colby. We know this from the definition of supply: the direct relationship between the price and quantity supplied of a good. In figure 8.7, if the price of hamburgers increases from P_0 to P_1, a movement along the supply curve results in a change in the quantity supplied from Q_0 to Q_1.

The graph of the market supply curve for hamburgers holds everything constant other than the price and quantity supplied. Therefore, if anything other than the price of hamburgers changes, it causes a shift in the entire supply curve, or a **Change in Supply**:

Change in Supply = When a change in the quantity of a good sold is a result of a change in an economic variable other than the price of the good. A shift in the supply curve.

A change in supply is depicted in figure 8.8:

Figure 8.8

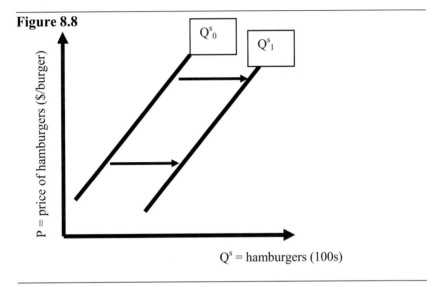

Q^s = hamburgers (100s)

A shift in the supply curve to the right is an increase in supply, since more hamburgers will be supplied at each price level. Likewise, a shift in the supply curve to the left is a decrease in supply. The increase in supply that is shown in figure 8.8 could be the result of an increase in the technology available to the firm. Shifts in the entire supply function are caused by all of the determinants of supply other than price. The economic determinants of supply will be discussed in the next section.

4. Determinants of Supply.

The supply of a good is determined by numerous economic variables. Here, we list the supply determinants that are considered to be the most important influences on the supply of a good: (1) input prices, (2) technology, (3) prices of related goods, and (4) the number of sellers. We can write a supply curve in the following manner:

Q^s = f(own price | input prices, technology, prices of related goods, no. of sellers).

In a graph of a supply curve, we look at the relationship between the quantity supplied of a good (Q^s) and the price of the good (own price), holding all else constant (*ceteris paribus*).

(Quick Quiz 8.7: why do we hold all variables other than the price constant?)

The determinants of supply other than price are often called, "supply shifters." This is because any change in one of the determinants of supply other than the price results in a shift in the entire supply curve (a change in supply). Recall that if the price of a good changes, it results in a movement along the supply curve, or a change in quantity supplied. We will now investigate each of the supply determinants in detail.

8.4.1 Input Prices.

The prices that firms pay to purchase inputs have a direct effect on the cost of production, as we have seen in Chapter 3. The costs that must be paid by a firm are the price of inputs multiplied by the quantity of inputs purchased. Since the individual firm's supply curve is the marginal cost curve above the shut down point, any increase in the price of an input that is used in the production process will increase the costs of production, and hence shift the supply curve upward and to the left.

(Quick Quiz 8.8: how is the shut down point defined? How is the break even point defined?)

Figures 8.9 and 8.10 demonstrate how an increase in input prices shifts the supply curve. We can think of the decrease in supply in two ways. First, figure 8.9 shows that if the price of hamburger meat increases, it shifts the supply of hamburgers up, since the marginal costs curve increases. This is called a "decrease in supply."

(Quick Quiz 8.9: why isn't it a decrease in quantity supplied?)

At a given price of hamburgers of P_0, the firm will decrease its output of hamburgers from Q_0 to Q_1 in response to the increase in the price of hamburger meat. So, an increase in the price of an input is an increase in the cost of production, which results in a decrease in supply: a shift of the supply curve to the left.

Figure 8.9

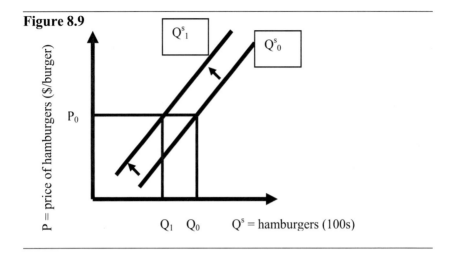

Figure 8.10 shows the same shift in the supply curve of hamburgers, due to the increase in the price of hamburger meat, but it can be interpreted in a different way. Here, we can see that to produce and sell a given quantity of hamburger, the firm must raise the price of hamburgers from P_0 to P_1 to cover the costs of production.

Figure 8.10

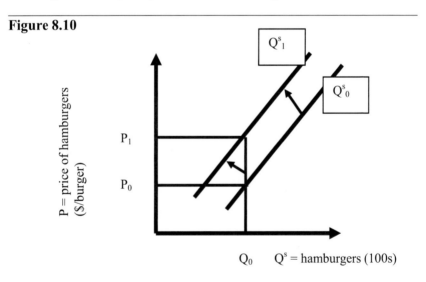

8.4.2 Technology.

The impacts of technology on the production function were described in Chapter 2. Technological change allows more output to be produced with the same level of inputs, (or, the same level of output could be produced with fewer inputs). Technology will therefore lower the cost of production, or shift the entire supply curve to the right.

(Quick Quiz 8.10: is a shift in the supply curve a change in supply or change in quantity supplied?)

As can be seen in figure 8.11, technological change allows the firm to produce a greater quantity at the same cost.

Figure 8.11

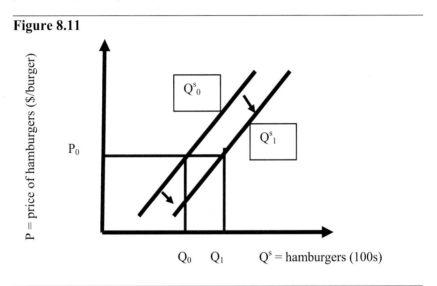

A rightward shift in supply is an increase in supply. More output can be produced at the same price, or the same level of output can be produced at a lower price.

8.4.3 Prices of Related Goods.

Often firms will produce more than one good. Recall from Chapter 6 that a firm will choose which goods to produce based on relative prices.

(Quick Quiz 8.11: graph the firm's optimal output selection).

Goods that are related in the production process will be affected by relative prices. For example, a packing plant produces both beef and leather. If the price of leather increases, it will affect (1) the quantity supplied of leather, and (2) the supply of beef. Test your knowledge of

245

the difference between a change in supply and a change in quantity supplied by explaining to yourself why an increase in the price of beef affects (1) the quantity supplied of beef, and (2) the supply of leather.

Goods that are produced together are called complements in production.

Complements in Production are defined:

Complements in Production = Goods that are produced together (e.g. beef and leather).

The **Cross-Price Elasticity of Supply** (γ_{Y1Y2}) for complements in production is positive: if the price of one complement increases, it results in an increase in the supply of the complementary good:

$$\varepsilon_{Y1Y2} = (\Delta Q^s_{Y1}/\Delta P_{Y2})*[(P_{Y2}{}^0 + P_{Y2}{}^1) / (Q^s_{Y1}{}^0 + Q^s_{Y1}{}^1)] > 0$$

The opposite of complements in production is **Substitutes in Production**. If two goods compete for the same resources, then they are considered to be substitutes in production:

Substitutes in Production = Goods that compete for the same resources in production. (e.g. wheat and barley).

The cross-price elasticity of demand for substitutes in production is negative:

$$\varepsilon_{Y1Y2} = (\Delta Q^s_{Y1}/\Delta P_{Y2})*[(P_{Y2}{}^0 + P_{Y2}{}^1)/(Q^s_{Y1}{}^0 + Q^s_{Y1}{}^1)] < 0.$$

If the price of a substitute increases, this causes an increase in the quantity supplied of the substitute good. It also causes resources to be shifted into the good with the relatively higher price, and out of the good with the relatively lower price. Thus, the increase in the price of a substitute good results in a decrease in the supply of the other substitute good.

8.4.4 Number of Sellers.

The impact of the number of sellers is direct: more sellers results in a larger supply of a good. If new firms enter an industry, the supply curve will shift to the right, resulting in an increase in supply. If firms exit the industry, the supply curve will shift to the left, resulting in a decrease in supply.

There are many other determinants of supply, or "supply shifters." In agriculture, the weather is an important determinant of supply: when weather conditions are favorable, agricultural output increases, resulting in a shift in supply. Government programs can also shift the supply curves of agricultural goods: subsidies result in a shift to the right, and taxes shift supply curves to the left.

We will now shift our attention from the behavior of *producers* to the behavior of *consumers*. Supply curves are the marginal cost curves of individual firms. In the next section, we will show that demand curves are derived from the utility-maximization decisions of consumers.

5. Demand.

We now change our attention from firms, which produce goods and services for sale, to consumers, who purchase the goods and services from the producers. In the previous Chapter, we saw that consumers maximize utility by choosing the goods that yield the greatest level of satisfaction. **Demand** can be defined as what the consumer purchases, or:

Demand = Consumer willingness and ability to pay for a good.

We will investigate the determinants of demand, of which the good's price is the most important. The relationship between the price of a good and the quantity demanded is the **Demand Curve** for that good or service.

Demand Curve = A function connecting all combinations of prices and quantities consumed for a good, *ceteris paribus*.

In this section, we will derive an individual consumer's **Demand Curve**, then find the market demand curve by adding up all individual **Demand Curves**.

8.5.1 The Individual Consumer's Demand Curve.

Our goal is to show how the demand curve for an individual consumer is derived. We will assume that a K-State college student has $40/week to spend on food. The student makes two types of food purchases: macaroni and cheese (Y_1), which initially costs $2/box ($P_{Y1}$ = $2/box), and pizza ($Y_2$), which costs $5/pizza ($P_{Y2}$ = $5/pizza). Suppose that the grocery store lowers the price of macaroni and cheese from the initial price of $2/box to $1/box, and later, all the way to $0.50/box. From these data, we hope to derive the relationship between the price of macaroni and cheese and the quantity demanded (Q^d). We will answer the question, "How do changes in price affect demand?"

We know that $40/week is spent on food, so income (M) equals $40/week. Here are the facts that we need to graph a consumer's equilibrium in figure 8.12.

Y_1 = mac-n-cheese P_{Y1} = $2/box

Y_2 = pizza P_{Y2} = $5/pizza

First, we graph the budget line for the student:

$M = P_{Y1}Y_1 + P_{Y2}Y_2$

$Y_2 = (M/P_{Y2}) + (-P_{Y1}/P_{Y2})*Y_1$

$Y_2 = (40/5) + (-2/5)* Y_1 = 8 - 0.4*Y_1$

Figure 8.12

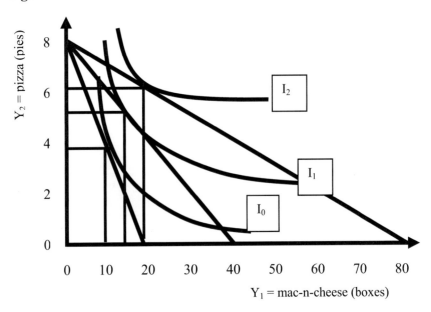

248

The y-intercept (M/P_{Y2}) is equal to 8, and the slope is negative 0.4, as is shown in figure 8.12. Consumer equilibrium is located where the Marginal Rate of Substitution (MRS), or the slope of the indifference curve, is equal to the price ratio, or the slope of the budget line. In figure 8.12, we have drawn this initial equilibrium at the point (10, 4), or ten boxes of macaroni and cheese, and 4 pizzas.

As the price of macaroni and cheese falls, the opportunity set of the consumer increases. In figure 8.12, we can see that the consumer can purchase more of both goods when the price of macaroni and cheese falls, since the purchasing power of the consumer increases. By lowering the price of a good and observing how the quantity purchased of a good changes, the grocery store can derive the relationship between price and quantity demanded, or a demand curve!

(Quick Quiz 8.12: what is the opportunity set in figure 8.12?)

In table 8.2, we have data for a Demand Schedule for the K-State Student.

Demand Schedule = Information on prices and quantities purchased.

Table 8.2. Price and Quantity Data.

Price of Macaroni and Cheese (P_{Y1} = $/box)	Quantity of Macaroni and Cheese (Y_1 = boxes)	Quantity of Pizza Purchased (Y_2 = pies)
2	10	4
1	15	5
0.5	20	6

Recall that a demand curve is the relationship between the price and quantity of a good purchased, or:

$$Q^d_{mac\ cheese} = f(P_{Y1}, P_{Y2}, M)$$

From the consumer's equilibrium points identified in figure 8.12 and table 8.2, we can hold everything constant but the price of macaroni and cheese to derive the demand curve for the K-State student, which is shown in figure 8.13.

Figure 8.13

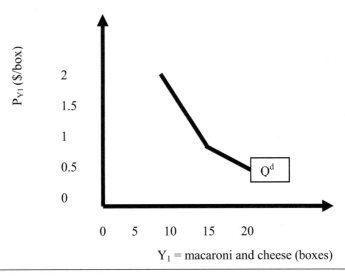

The demand curve in figure 8.13 contains the same information that appears in the consumer equilibrium graph in figure 8.12: we have changed the variable on the y-axis from pizza (Y_2) to the price of macaroni and cheese (P_{Y1}). The demand curve depicted in figure 8.13 is the relationship between the price of macaroni and cheese and the quantity purchased of the good, holding all else constant. Mathematically, this can be expressed as:

$$Q^d_{\text{mac cheese}} = f(P_{Y1} \mid P_{Y2}, M)$$

Demand curves can be derived for all goods in a similar fashion.

(Quick Quiz: graphically derive the demand curve for pizza.)

8.5.2 The Market Demand Curve.

To derive a market demand curve we add up all of the individual demand curves in the market. Just as when we aggregated the individual supply curves, we add the demand curves in a specific way. To add individual consumer demands to achieve the market demand, we "Do it horizontally." So, if we were to add up all individual demands for bread, for example, we would need to look at all of the consumers individual demand for bread, as in figure 8.14.

Figure 8.14

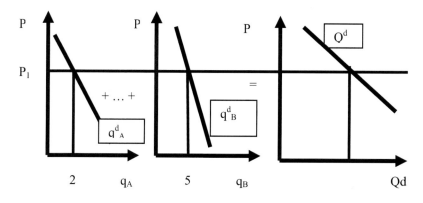

The market demand curve for bread is the horizontal summation of all of the individual demand curves, in this case, consumers A, and B. Note that there are numerous consumers whose demand curve does not explicitly appear in figure 8.14: the ellipsis (...) represents the remaining consumers in the market, for whom there is not enough space on the page to graph! To add up demand curves horizontally, we take a given price such as P_1, and find the quantity demanded for each consumer at that price.

For example, consumer A buys 2 loaves of bread, and B purchases 5. We add these quantities together to get the total quantity of bread purchased ($Q_1 = 2 + ... + 5$). Next, a different price is selected, and the horizontal summation process is repeated. The **Market Demand** curve is the outcome of this procedure, and appears on the right-hand side of figure 8.14.

Market Demand = The horizontal summation of all individual demand curves for all individual consumers in the market.

8.5.3 The Law of Demand.

We have seen that an increase in the price of a good results in a lower quantity of the good purchased. This regularity of consumer behavior is know as the **Law of Demand**:

Law of Demand = The quantity of a good demanded varies inversely with the price of the good, *ceteris paribus*.

Restated, the Law of Demand says that, "Demand Slopes Down." This is true for all individual consumers, as well as all market demand curves. Figure 8.15 shows a demand curve for steak dinners in Manhattan. The downward slope indicates that as a good becomes scarcer as we move from right to left in the graph, the good becomes more valuable. This reflects the Law of Diminishing Marginal Utility: the first steak dinner is the best! As more steaks are consumed, the value decreases.

Figure 8.15

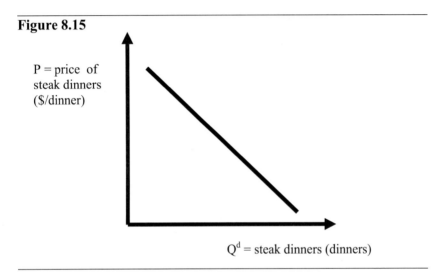

Q^d = steak dinners (dinners)

In economics, supply and demand are of critical importance! We have now learned about both producer behavior (supply) consumer behavior (demand). When we graph a supply curve or a demand curve, we are graphing the relationship between price and quantity. We put price (the independent variable) on the vertical axis, and quantity demanded (the dependent variable) on the horizontal axis.

(Quick Quiz 8.13: why do we draw supply and demand curves backward in economics?)

Price causes quantity demanded.

$P => Q^d$ P = independent

$Q^d = f(P)$ Q^d = dependent

Consumers take prices as given and decide how much to buy. Because of our assumption about competition, each individual consumer cannot affect the price of a good. Therefore, price causes quantity demanded.

(Quick Quiz 8.14: why does the assumption of competition cause prices to be fixed?)

To summarize, the demand curve captures the relationship between the price of a good (P), and the quantity demanded (Q^d), *ceteris paribus*. The Law of Demand states that if the price of a good increases, then the quantity demanded will decrease, *ceteris paribus*. The next section will present the concept of the elasticity of demand, which economists use to indicate how responsive consumers are to changes in prices and other economic variables.

6. The Elasticity of Demand.

As we saw earlier in this chapter, the term, "elasticity" refers to a measure of responsiveness of one variable to another variable. We can calculate an elasticity for any two variables, even if they are not economic variables. The price elasticity of demand tells us how responsive quantity demanded is to a change in price. The price elasticity of demand answers the question, "How much does quantity demanded change when price changes?" We can see this with a graph of a demand curve, as in figure 8.16.

Figure 8.16

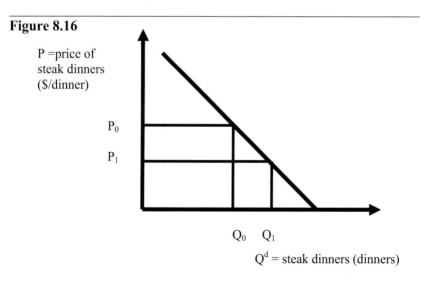

P = price of
steak dinners
($/dinner)

P_0

P_1

Q_0 Q_1

Q^d = steak dinners (dinners)

When the price of steak dinners falls from P_0 to P_1, the Law of Demand tells us that consumers will purchase more steak dinners. How many more steak dinners that will be purchased at a lower price is determined by the price elasticity of demand, which is related to the slope of the demand curve. The major determinant of the elasticity of demand is the availability of substitutes. ***THE ELASTICITY OF DEMAND IS DETERMINED BY THE AVAILABILITY OF SUBSTITUTES.***

If there are very few substitutes for a good, then consumers can not "substitute" out of more expensive goods and into cheaper goods. However, if there are substitutes available, then the consumer's response to a price change will be elastic, as we can see in an example of the demand for cigarettes.

Figure 8.17

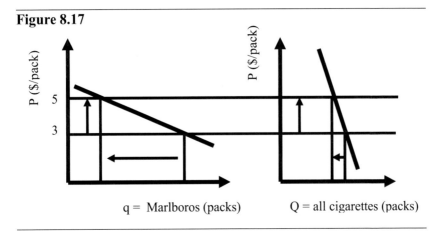

q = Marlboros (packs)   Q = all cigarettes (packs)

Suppose that a K-State student is studying for a final exam, and finds himself in need of some nicotine. The student goes to the convenience store, where cigarettes are sold. Suppose further than the price of Marlboro cigarettes is $5/pack, whereas all other brands are sold for $3/pack. The consumer will be very responsive to this change in price, since there are many substitutes available: if the price of Marlboros is relatively higher, then the student can purchase Lucky Strikes or Camels, for example.

On the other hand, if the price of all cigarettes increases to $5/pack, then the student is likely to purchase a pack anyway, even though the price has increased. Why? Because the demand for goods like cigarettes is very inelastic: when a guy needs a smoke, he needs a smoke! In figure 8.17, we can see in the left panel that if the price of one specific brand of cigarettes increases, then consumer responsiveness is large. In this case, consumers shift out of relatively expensive brands

254

and into cheaper brands. In the right-hand panel, the demand for all cigarettes is shown. There, a price increase does not result in a big substitution out of cigarettes: there are no good substitutes (the student needs nicotine!). In general, the elasticity of demand is determined by the availability of substitutes, or how willing consumers are to switch their purchases to another good.

(Quick Quiz 8.15: which is more elastic to changes in price, oranges or fruit?)

When we define goods narrowly, the elasticity of demand is greater, since there are more substitutes available. For example, if the price of blue shirts increases, consumers will switch into green shirts, but if the price of all shirts increases, consumers have few other options. Therefore, the elasticity of blue shirts is greater than the elasticity of all shirts.

8.6.1 The Definition of The Elasticity of Demand.

The price elasticity of demand is defined as:

Elasticity of Demand = The percentage change in the quantity demanded with respect to a percentage change in price.

The price elasticity of demand at a single point on a demand curve can be defined:

$$\eta = (\Delta Q^d / Q^d)/(\Delta P/P) = (\Delta Q^d / \Delta P)*(P/Q^d)$$

Economists calculate elasticities, rather than slopes of demand functions, because we can't compare the slopes of the demand for apples and oranges. Recall that we cannot graph two variables on the same graph if the units of the two variables are different. In figure 8.18, it appears that apples are more responsive to price than oranges, but we really can't say for sure unless we calculate the responsiveness to price changes explicitly. The reason is that the scale of the graphs are different for apples and oranges.

255

Figure 8.18

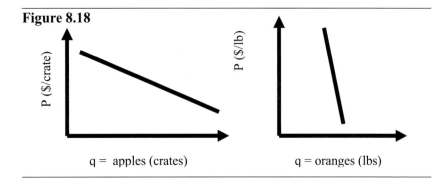

Elasticities are *unitless*, which make them attractive to social scientists: we can compare elasticities across all goods, since the units are the same. We can see this by looking at the definition of the price elasticity of demand:

$$\eta = (\Delta Q^d / \Delta P) * (P / Q^d)$$

Since the price (P) and quantity demanded (Q^d) appear in both the numerator and denominator, the units of each cancel, and there are no units for an elasticity calculation. So, we use elasticities rather than slopes to measure the responsiveness of consumer purchases to changes in prices and other economic variables. By using elasticities, we can compare apples and oranges!

To summarize our discussion so far, elasticities represent how responsive consumers are to changes in price. An elastic demand curve represents consumers who are more responsive to price changes, and an inelastic demand curve represents consumers who are less responsive to price changes. We can compare elasticities across all goods. Remember that the major determinant of the elasticity of demand is the availability of substitutes. If substitutes are available, then when the price of a good increases, consumers buy something else, and the good is relatively elastic.

The price elasticity of demand can be used to explain a great deal of situations, including why gasoline stations in Manhattan charge higher prices for gasoline the day prior to Spring Break: on this day when several thousand students are preparing to leave town to go home (or to Padre Island!), the elasticity of demand for gasoline is relatively inelastic. Station owners know this, and increase the price of fuel to take advantage of the situation.

Veterinarians often change higher prices for rich people with poodles than for poor people with Australian shepherd mixes. Why? Because rich people are more likely to be willing and able to pay higher prices for vet services than poor people. The elasticity of demand for medical services is lower (more inelastic) for rich persons than for poor.

Airplane tickets almost always cost more if they are purchased on the same day as the flight. Why? Because travelers who have not made flight arrangements prior to the day of the flight have an inelastic demand for airline travel: they are flying in the case of an emergency or an urgent situation, and would be willing to pay higher prices for the flight. The elasticity of demand for airlines tickets becomes more inelastic as the day of the flight approaches, and airlines take advantage of this by increasing prices as flight time approaches.

Another example is the prices of tickets for performances at McCain Auditorium. For faculty, season tickets are several hundred dollars per year, whereas for students, the tickets are less than one hundred dollars. Why? Because students have more substitutes than faculty: Aggieville!

For practice using the elasticity concept, let's calculate an arc elasticity of the demand for wheat. The definition of the price elasticity of demand is:

$$\eta = \%\Delta Q^d / \%\Delta P = (\Delta Q^d / \Delta P)*(P/Q^d)$$

In words, this is equivalent to the percentage change in quantity demanded as a result of a percentage change in price. Suppose that the price of wheat increases from $3/bu to $5/bu, resulting in a decrease in the quantity of wheat demanded from $Q_1 = 20$ billion bushels to $Q_2 = 16$ billion bushels.

$P_1 = \$3/bu$ $Q_1 = 20$ billion bushels
$P_2 = \$5/bu$ $Q_2 = 16$ billion bushels

To calculate the elasticity of demand using the formula above, we first need to know the changes in price and quantity.

$$\Delta P = P_2 - P_1 = 5 - 3 = 2$$
$$\Delta Q = Q_2 - Q_1 = 16 - 20 = -4$$

The next step in the elasticity calculation requires us to select a price and a quantity to plug into the elasticity formula. Which P should we use? P_1 or P_2? Since using either of these two prices would result in a different calculation, we use the average price. This can be seen in the arc elasticity formula:

Figure 8.19

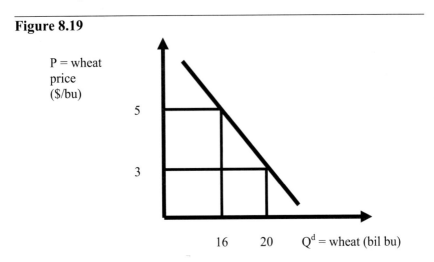

P = wheat
price
($/bu)

5

3

16   20 Q^d = wheat (bil bu)

$$\eta = \%\Delta Q^d / \%\Delta P = [(Q_2 - Q_1)/(P_2 - P_1)]*[(P_1 + P_2)/(Q_1 + Q_2)]$$

Recall that this formula uses the average (or mean) prices and quantities for the price and quantity levels. Since the average price is equal to $[(P_1 + P_2)/2]$, and the average quantity is equal to $[(Q_1 + Q_2)/2]$, the twos cancel each other out, resulting in the equation given above.

The Law of Demand states that if the price increases, consumers will purchase less wheat, resulting in a decrease in the quantity of wheat demanded. Therefore, the sign of the price elasticity of demand will always be negative. The magnitude of the elasticity depends on the availability of substitutes for wheat. Consumer could switch from wheat bread and tortillas, for example, into corn bread and tortillas. Cattle feedlots will minimize costs by substituting out of the relatively expensive wheat and into other grains. Using the formula above, we can now quantify the responsiveness of consumers to a change in the price of wheat:

$$\eta = (Q_2-Q_1)/(P_2-P_1)*(P_1+P_2)/(Q_1+Q_2)$$
$$= (16-20)/(5-3)*(3+5)/(20+16) = -0.44$$

The Law of Demand informs us that the sign of the price elasticity of demand must always be negative. To investigate the magnitude of the price elasticity of demand, we take the absolute value of the elasticity to convert the elasticity into a positive number.

258

$$|\eta| = 0.44$$

This elasticity tells us how much quantity demanded changes given a change in price. The price elasticity relates to the demand curve shown in figure 8.19, since the demand curve is defined as the relationship between quantity demanded and price. The price elasticity of demand (η) is also a relationship between quantity demanded and price. As we will see in the next section, since the magnitude of the price elasticity of wheat is low, wheat is relatively inelastic: there are few good substitutes for wheat.

8.6.2 Responsiveness Classifications.

The price elasticity of demand (η) summarizes consumer behavior. Specifically, it summarizes the responsiveness of the quantity demanded to price changes. We will now explore the relative magnitude of consumer responsiveness to the price of different goods. For example, the quantity demanded of food remains fairly constant, since food is a physiological necessity. If the price of food increased, most consumers would eat the same amount. This is a situation that economists call **Inelastic Demand**. Goods that are characterized by inelastic demands are goods that consumers do not change in response to changes in price. Necessities of all types have relatively inelastic demands: food, housing, tobacco, gasoline, etc.

Inelastic Demand = A change in price brings about a relatively smaller change in quantity demanded.

Recall the definition of elasticity:

$\eta = \%\Delta Q / \%\Delta P$.

In the case of a good with an inelastic demand, we know that the price movement is greater than the change in quantity demanded ($\%\Delta Q < \%\Delta P$). Therefore, when a good is inelastic, $|\eta| < 1$, as shown in figure 8.20. The good depicted in figure 8.20 is inelastic, or relatively unresponsive to price: the magnitude of the elasticity of demand is relatively small. If the price of the good increased by one percent, then the quantity demanded will decrease by less than one percent.

Figure 8.20

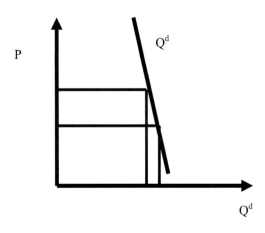

Consider the responsiveness of consumers to changes in the price of another good: ribeye steaks, sold at the Hays House in Council Grove, Kansas. If the restaurant increases the price of one specific cut of meat, customers will substitute out of the relatively expensive steaks and into other menu items (filets, pork chops, or fried chicken). Since substitutes are available, consumers are responsive to changes in price, and ribeye steaks are an example of an **Elastic Demand**.

Elastic Demand = A change in price brings about a relatively larger change in quantity demanded.

A one percent increase in the price of an elastic good results in a greater then one percent decrease in the quantity demanded. In the case of an elastic good, $|\eta| > 1$, since $\%\Delta Q > \%\Delta P$. In a graph of an elastic good such as ribeye steaks, the change in quantity demanded is larger than the change in price.

Substitutes exist for ribeye steaks, so the demand is elastic. Recall that the demand for food as a whole is inelastic, since there are no good substitutes. Examples of goods that are characterized by an elastic demand include: Florida oranges, Idaho potatoes, McDonald's Big Macs, and Budweiser beer.

(Quick Quiz 8.16: explain why each of the goods listed has an elastic demand).

Figure 8.21

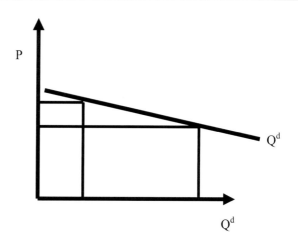

The third and last category of price elasticity of demand is **Unitary Elastic Demand**.

Unitary Elastic Demand = The percentage change in price brings about an equal percentage change in quantity demanded.

Mathematically, this can be represented as:

$$\eta = \Delta Q/\Delta P*(P_1+P_2)/(Q_1+Q_2) = 1.$$

In this case, the quantity demanded of the good falls by the same percentage that the price increases. Table 8.3 summarizes the three categories of the price elasticity of demand.

Table 8.3.Demand Elasticity Classifications.

Unitary	$|\eta| = 1$
Inelastic	$|\eta| < 1$
Elastic	$|\eta| > 1$

The magnitude of the price elasticity depends on the availability of substitutes. Alternative purchases increase over time, resulting in the conclusion that the price elasticity of demand becomes more elastic

261

(consumers become more responsive to changes in prices) as time passes. For example, suppose that the price of electricity increases. Could a consumer change energy sources in the short run? No. Therefore, the demand for electricity in the short run is inelastic: households purchases of kilowatt hours are likely to stay at approximately the same level.

Over time, however, consumers can substitute out of electricity by purchasing natural gas heaters and kitchen appliances. Some households invest in solar power, wind power, and other alternative sources of power. Since consumers have more choices as time passes, the demand for electricity becomes more elastic over time.

8.6.3 The Elasticity of Demand and Total Revenue.

The pricing strategy of a business firm depends crucially on the price elasticity of demand. Consider a firm that is attempting to maximize total revenues (TR = P*Q, where P is the per-unit price and Q is the quantity sold). Figure 8.22 shows the demand curve for an inelastic product and an elastic product. The inelastic demand case suggests that a firm can increase total revenues by decreasing output and increasing price: the price increase will outweigh the decrease in output sold. This can be seen with the help of some simple math:

$$TR = PQ$$

$$\Delta TR = \Delta(PQ) = \Delta P \Delta Q$$

When demand is inelastic, as it is in the upper graph of figure 8.22, the positive price increase (ΔP) is larger than the negative quantity decrease (ΔQ), so the change in total revenue is positive when quantity sold is reduced. Given an inelastic demand, a firm will reduce its output to increase revenues.

Figure 8.22

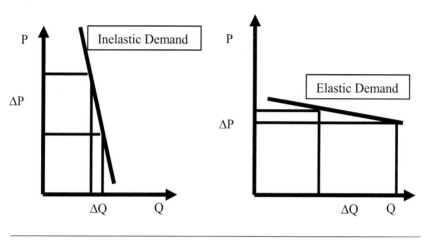

The strategy of reducing output would backfire for a firm facing an elastic demand: the reduction in quantity would be greater than the price increase, resulting in a decrease in total revenues. This is because the decrease in quantity (ΔQ) is larger than the increase in price (ΔP).

(Quick Quiz 8.17: describe the impacts of an agricultural policy that reduces the number of acres of land planted to wheat in the USA.)

The relationship between the price elasticity of demand and total revenues explains why business firms are so interested in the elasticity of demand for the goods that are sold by the firm: pricing strategy requires knowledge of how customers will respond to a change in price.

8.6.4 Own-Price and Cross-Price Demand Elasticities.

We saw in a previous section that elasticities of supply could be calculated for (1) the good's own price, and (2) the price of a related good.

Own-Price Elasticity of Demand = Measures the responsiveness of the quantity demanded of a good to changes in the price of that good.

A related good is one that has an impact on the consumption of a good. The Cross-Price Elasticity of Demand measures how the demand of one good changes when the price of a related good changes:

Cross-Price Elasticity of Demand = Measures the responsiveness of the quantity demanded of a good to changes in the price of a related good.

The cross-price elasticity is written as: $\eta_{XY} = \%\Delta Q^d_Y / \%\Delta P_X$. This formula states that the cross price elasticity of demand is the percentage change in quantity demanded of good Y given a percent change in price of good X. If two goods X and Y are unrelated, then the change in the price of X has no effect on the consumption of good Y, and the cross price elasticity is equal to zero (η_{XY}). There are two types of related goods in consumption: **Substitutes** and **Complements**.

Substitutes in Consumption = Goods that are consumed "either/or." (e.g. wheat bread and white bread).

An example of substitutes in consumption are corn and milo in feeding cattle: a feedlot can purchase either of these two feed grains, since they are nearly nutritionally equivalent. If the price of corn increases, then the quantity demanded of milo increases, as feedlots substitute out of corn and into milo. Thus, the cross price elasticity of demand is positive for substitutes.

$$\eta_{XY} = \%\Delta Q^d_Y / \%\Delta P_X > 0$$

Another example of substitutes is electric appliances (stoves, furnaces, and hot water heaters) and natural gas appliances. Most homes in Kansas have either gas or electric appliances, depending on the relative prices of natural gas and electricity. **Complements** are goods that are consumed together, for example bread and butter; or a tractor and a plow.

Complements in Consumption = Goods that are consumed together (e.g. peanut butter and jelly).

If the price of bread increases, consumers will purchase less bread and less butter. The change in the quantity of butter demanded will decrease when the price of bread increases. Therefore, the cross price elasticity of butter with respect to bread is negative:

$$\eta_{XY} = \%\Delta Q^d_Y / \%\Delta P_X < 0$$

We mentioned above that unrelated goods have no relation to each other. Unrelated good might include ice cream, and houses: the quantity of homes purchased is unlikely to be related to the price of ice cream. Similarly, the price of houses has no impact on the demand for ice cream. In this case, the cross price elasticity of demand is equal to zero.

$$\eta_{XY} = \%\Delta Q^d_Y / \%\Delta P_X = 0$$

8.6.5 The Relationship between Elasticity and Slope.

As with supply curves, the elasticity of demand is related to the slope of a demand curve, but not equal to it. Caution should be exercised when comparing the slopes of two demand curves in different graphs. The slope may reflect different scales on the horizontal and vertical axes, and thus be misleading when comparing elasticities. Only when the actual elasticities are calculated can we compare elasticities across goods.

7. Change in Demand; Change in Quantity Demanded.

In Section One, we derived a demand curve from the consumer equilibrium graph by successively lowering the price of a good: macaroni and cheese. We saw that the demand curve is the relationship between price and quantity demanded, *ceteris paribus* (holding all else constant). The demand curve reflects a consumer's willingness and ability to purchase a good given the price of a good. To demonstrate the difference between a change in demand and a change in quantity demanded, we will investigate the demand curve for beef. If the price of beef changes, this results in a movement along the demand curve, called a **Change In the Quantity Demanded**. For example, if the price of beef decreased, holding everything else constant, then consumers will eat more beef.

(Quick Quiz 8.18: how do we know that the quantity of beef demanded will decrease?)

Change in Quantity Demanded = When a change in the quantity of a good purchased is a result of a change in the price of the good. A movement along the demand curve.

265

The movement along a demand curve is due to a change in the price of the good, or a change in quantity demanded, as depicted in figure 8.23.

Figure 8.23

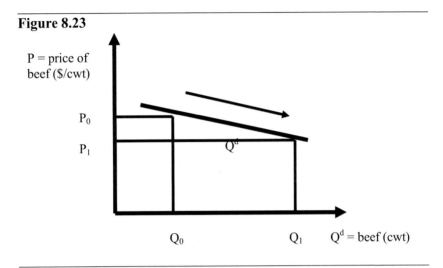

P = price of beef ($/cwt)

P_0

P_1

Q^d

Q_0 Q_1 Q^d = beef (cwt)

If anything other than the good's own price changes, then there is a shift in demand, known as a **Change in Demand**.

Change in Demand = When a change in the quantity of a good purchased is a result of a change in an economic variable other than the price of the good. A shift in the demand curve.

For example, an increase in income causes the entire demand curve to shift out, since an increase in purchasing power will result in consumers buying more beef at every price. This is a change in demand, due to consumers being able to afford to eat more beef, as shown in figure 8.24.

8.7.1 Examples of Demand Changes.

1. The Price of Corn and Soda Demand.

What does the price of corn have to do with the price of soda? Corn is a major input in the production of soda (corn syrup is the sweetener!), so as the price of corn increases, the price of soda increases. Does this cause a shift or a movement in demand? This is a change in the price of soda, so it is a movement along the demand curve for soda, seen in figure 8.25.

Figure 8.24

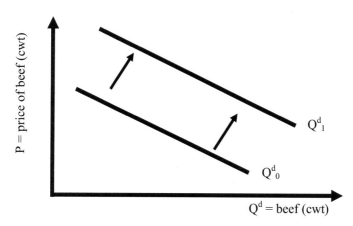

Figure 8.25

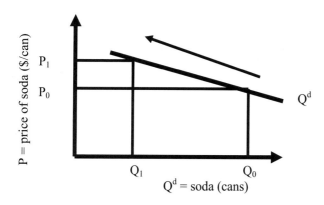

1. The Impact of Cold Weather on Cattle.

Cattle can be killed or made ill when very cold weather hits Kansas. This would result in a reduction of the amount of cattle available, as cattle become more scarce. This, in turn, results in an increase in the price of beef, which causes a movement along the demand curve, as shown in figure 8.26.

3. The Price of Milo's Impact on the Demand for Corn.

Recall that milo and corn are near perfect substitutes: either one can be used by a feedlot to fatten cattle.

Figure 8.26

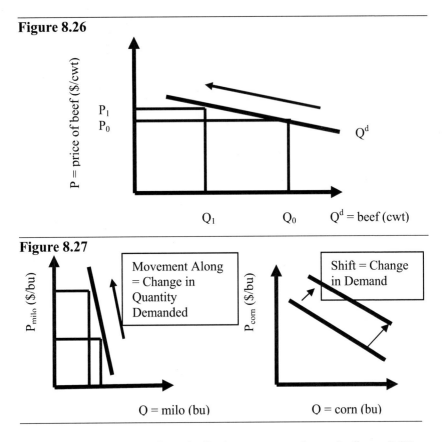

Figure 8.27

If the relative price of milo increases, as shown in figure 8.27, this results in a movement along the demand for milo, and a shift in the demand for corn, or an increase in the demand for corn.

4. College.

Suppose that the price of a college degree increases (tuition hikes). This is a price change, so it is a movement along the demand curve, or a change in quantity demanded, as shown in figure 8.28. Some students will shift out of college and into employment when the price of college is increased.

Figure 8.28

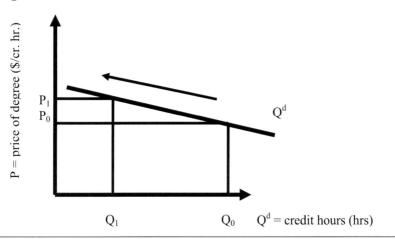

5. **The Effect of a Decrease in Income on the Demand for Veterinary Services.**

If an economic variable other than the price changes, it results in a change in demand, or a shift in the demand curve, as is seen in figure 8.29. If the standard of living in a community declined, for example, then the purchasing power of individuals and households falls, and less is spent on veterinary services. Now that we have had some practice at shifting demand curves around, we will turn to the determinants of demand in the last section of this chapter.

Figure 8.29

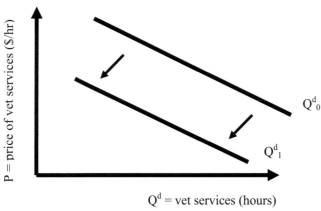

8. Determinants of Demand.

We have seen that the own price of a good (P_{own}) is the most important determinant of demand. Other determinants of demand include the price of related goods ($P_{related\ goods}$), income (M), and tastes and preferences (T), expectations of future prices (E), and population (Pop) as written in this demand function:

$$Q^d = f(P_{own}, P_{related\ goods}, M, T, E, Pop)$$

There are other determinants as well, but we have captured the most important ones here. We will now take a closer look at each of these determinants of demand. The first demand determinant is the good's own price. We have studied the Law of Demand: if the price of a good increases, then the quantity demanded decreases, *ceteris paribus*.

(Quick Quiz 8.19: when the price of a good changes, is it a change in demand or a change in quantity demanded?)

8.8.1 Prices of Related Goods.

The second determinant of demand is one that we have been introduced to when we studied the cross price elasticity of demand: the price of related goods: substitutes and complements. We saw that substitutes are goods that can be purchased either/or: corn and milo are both feed grains, and are substitutes in the production of beef. Depending on the relative price of corn and milo, feedlot managers will purchase either one.

Two quick examples of substitutes: (1) if the price of corn increases, consumers (feedlots) substitute out of corn and into milo. If the price of corn increases, the quantity demanded of corn decreases, and the demand for milo increases; (2) if the price of natural gas increases, the demand for oil will increase.

Complements are goods that are used together, such as bread and butter. If the price of butter increases, the quantity demanded of butter decreases, and the demand for bread will decline as well.

8.8.2 Income.

Changes in income have a significant impact on the demand for goods and services. Think of the vast differences between the types of goods that a homeless person consumes and a very rich person consumes. Increases in the standard of living have a huge impact on the type and magnitude of goods and services that consumers purchase. A good example of the impact of income on consumption is wheat exports from the United States. Over 60% of wheat produced in Kansas is exported to other nations, much of it to low-income nations. In a low-income nation in SubSaharan Africa or Asia, incomes are at subsistence levels. Therefore, any increase in income will be spent primarily on food. When income levels rise in China and Pakistan, the USA exports more wheat to these countries, making wheat producers in Kansas better off.

The relationship between income and consumption is very important to agriculture, because as our standard of living increases, we shift our purchases from goods like Top Ramen and macaroni and cheese to steak and roses. The demand for goods produced in Kansas depends strongly on income.

Over 100 years ago, a German statistician named Ernst Engel studied the relationship between income and what consumers spend their money on. He studied the relationship between income and consumption, holding all else constant, or:

$$Q^d = f(M \mid P_{own}, P_{related\ goods}, T, E, Pop)$$

The **Engel Curve** shows the relationship between income and quantity demanded, ceteris paribus.

Engel Curve = The relationship between consumer income and quantity of a good consumed, *ceteris paribus*.

Engel studied the consumption patterns of individuals, which led him to discover a relationship called Engel's Law that is highly significant to agriculture.

Engel's Law = states that as income increases, the proportion of income spent on food declines, *ceteris paribus*.

Notice that Engel's Law says that the *proportion* of income spent on food, not the *total magnitude* spent on food. This means that as people become wealthier, they spend more dollars on food, but at a declining rate. Engel's Law has major implications for agriculture: it states that production agriculture decreases relative to the rest of the economy. This is exactly what has happened over the course of American history: the percentage of the population engaged in farming is now less than two percent of the total population.

We can get a better idea about Engel's law by looking at the Engel curve for food in figure 8.30.

The Engle Curve shows the relationship between income (M) and the quantity of food purchased (Q^d). Near the origin, where income is equal to zero, we see that an increase in income of one dollar will result in most of that income being spent on food. This is because food is a necessity,

Figure 8.30

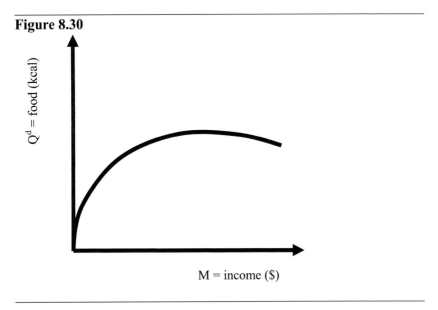

and at low levels of income, most of the budget will be spent on food. As income levels increase, purchases of food continue to increase (the slope of the Engel Curve is positive), but at a decreasing rate (the steepness of the slope falls). This demonstrates the increasing purchase of nonfood items as income increases. At a certain point, food purchases actually achieve a maximum and begin to fall. This shows that wealthy individuals may not spend as much money on food as individuals with lower levels of income. There is much statistical evidence that shows that this is true.

(Quick Quiz 8.20: does the Engel Curve show that middle-income families eat less than low-income families? Explain why or why not.)

Let's take a closer look at Engel's Law by deriving two Engel Curves, using our example of the K-State student who purchases only

272

two goods: macaroni and cheese (Y_1), and pizza (Y_2). We will start at a weekly income of $40, a price of macaroni and cheese of two dollars per box (P_{Y1} = $2/box), and a price of pizza of five dollars per pizza pie (P_{Y2} = $5/pie). To summarize:

M = $40/week

Y_1 = mac-n-cheese P_{Y1} = $2/box

Y_2 = pizza P_{Y2} = $5/pie

Next, we will see how the consumer's equilibrium purchases change with a change in income. We will increase the income available for food expenditures from $40/week to $60/week, and then to $80/week, as in figure 8.31.

Figure 8.31

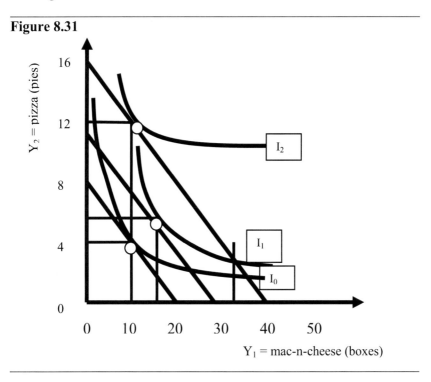

The small circles indicate the consumer equilibrium points at each level of income. The K-State student buys more pizza as income is increased. The graph also shows that the consumption of macaroni and cheese increases as income is increased from $40/week to $60/week.

273

However, when income is increased further to $80/week, the purchases of macaroni and cheese decline.

(Quick Quiz 8.21: show how the budget lines were drawn for each level of income)

(Quick Quiz 8.22: how is the consumer's equilibrium found in the graph? State the equilibrium condition for the consumer.)

The three equilibrium points are listed in table 8.4.

Table 8.4. Consumer Purchases and Income.

M Income ($/week)	Y_1 $Q^d_{\text{mac -n- cheese}}$ (boxes)	Y_2 Q^d_{pizza} (pies)
40	10	4
60	15	6
80	10	12

Recall that the Engel Curve is the relationship between income and quantity demanded. Given the data in table 8.4, we can graph Engel Curves for both macaroni and cheese and pizza, as depicted in figure 8.32.

Figure 8.32

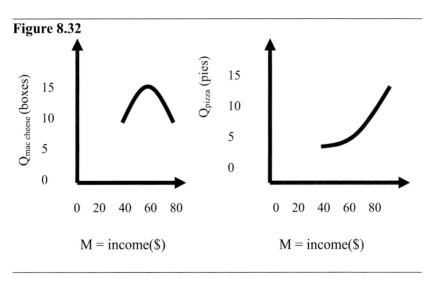

Now, lets look at the relationship between income (M) and quantity demanded, holding all else constant (remember the mathematical expression for this?)

$Q^d = f(M \mid P_{own}, P_{related\ goods}, T, E, Pop)$

The graph on the bottom of figure 8.32 shows how pizza consumption increases as income increases. The relationship between income and pizza purchases is positive, meaning that more pizza is purchased as income increases. Economists call the type of good whose consumption increases as income increases a **Normal Good**.

Normal Good = A good whose consumption increases in response to an increase in income. Also called a superior good.

Normal goods might include such goods as food, clothing, and automobiles. Other goods exhibit decreased consumption levels as income increases: **Inferior Goods**. Inferior goods could include used clothes, or macaroni and cheese: as incomes rise, consumers substitute out of these goods and into other goods.

Inferior Good = A good whose consumption declines in response to an increase in income.

In the left side of figure 8.32, we see that the consumption of macaroni and cheese increases as income increases from \$40/week to \$60/week (macaroni and cheese is a normal good in this range), but declines from as income rises from \$60 to \$80 per week (macaroni and cheese is an inferior good in this range). This makes sense: as people earn more money, they buy more foods that are inexpensive (macaroni and cheese, ramon noodles, spaghetti, etc.). When income reaches a certain level, consumers will begin to shift out of inexpensive foods and into more expensive goods, such as steak and seafood.
A **Luxury Good** is one that increases at an increasing rate when income increases. Pizza consumption in figure 8.32 is an example of this. A luxury good is a specific type of normal good, since the relationship between income and quantity consumed is positive.

Luxury Good = A good whose consumption increases at an increasing rate in response to an increase in income.

A **Necessity Good** is also a normal good, but one where consumption increases at a decreasing rate as income increases:

275

Necessity Good = A good whose consumption increases at an decreasing rate in response to an increase in income.

The relationship between income and consumption is crucial to Kansas farmers, as was highlighted in the introductory chapter. As the standard of living increases in low-income nations such as China and Korea, consumers substitute out of less expensive calorie sources, such as grains, and into more expensive calorie sources, such as beef and chicken. This increase in meat consumption has a large, positive effect on the income of farmers and ranchers in Kansas.

Meat consumed in Asia is imported from the United States. Also, it takes approximately seven pounds of grain to produce one pound of meat. Therefore, increases in the consumption of meat increase the demand for feed grains, which are produced in the Great Plains. Any increase in the development of low-income nations that leads to an increase in income will enhance the demand for meat consumption, which in turn will result in an increase in the well-being of agriculturalists in Kansas.

Economists summarize the relationship between income and consumption with the **Income Elasticity of Demand** (:).

Income Elasticity of Demand = The percentage change in the demand for a good in response to a one percent change in consumer income.

The mathematical formula for the elasticity of demand is:

$$\mu = \%\Delta Q^d / \%\Delta M = (\Delta Q/Q)/(\Delta M/M).$$

The formula above is a "point elasticity;" it can be used to find the income elasticity of demand at a given point on the Engel Curve. Most often, we are interested in calculating the income elasticity of demand over a range, so we use the arc elasticity formula, which incorporates the average values of income and quantity demanded:

$$\mu = \%\Delta Q^d / \%\Delta M = \Delta Q/\Delta M)^*(M_1 + M_2/Q_1 + Q_2).$$

Given our definition of the income elasticity of demand, we can classify goods into three categories, based on the responsiveness of consumers to changes in income (table 8.5).

Table 8.5. Good Responsiveness to Income.

Normal Goods	$\mu > 0$	$\%\Delta Q^d > 0$
Luxury good	$\mu > 1$	$\%\Delta Q^d > \%\Delta M$ (normal good)
Necessity good	$0 < \mu < 1$	$\%\Delta Q^d < \%\Delta M$ (normal good)
Inferior good	$\mu < 0$	$\%\Delta Q^d < 0$

One conclusion that can be drawn from our study of the relationship between income and consumption is that agricultural producers and processors can make themselves better off by following the saying: "Give the consumers what they want!" As the standard of living increases in the United States, consumers will shift out of inferior goods, and into luxury goods. In agriculture, luxury goods include:

-Organic fruits and vegetables
-Free-range chicken
-Hormone-free beef.

To make money in agriculture: don't waste any time or effort opposing this type of good, just "Give the consumers what they want!" and revenues will increase. There is a large and increasing demand for expensive agricultural goods in high-value markets. This is related to the tastes and preferences that consumers have.

8.8.3 Tastes and Preferences.

The tastes and preferences of consumers are a major determinant of the demand for goods in the USA, and these change over time. For example, tobacco use has dropped off dramatically for the entire population in the USA, although smoking among young persons is higher now than it was thirty years ago. Food safety has become a much more important determinant of consumer demand for agricultural products, due do outbreaks of salmonella in poultry and *E. coli* in beef. Organic fruits and vegetables are a small but rapidly growing sector of the food market. Consumer tastes and preferences are always changing, based on trends, relative prices, and other factors.

8.8.4 Expectations of Future Prices.

The expectations of future prices have an impact on the demand for a good. For example, if the price of gold is expected to increase in the future, what would you do: buy or sell gold? If you could buy gold today at $100/ounce, and sell it later for $170/ounce, you could make a lot of money! This is why the expected future prices of agricultural products affect demand today. If the price of a good or commodity is expected to decrease, then the demand for the good will decrease, as individuals attempt to sell the commodity before the price decrease.

Buying and selling goods and commodities is how traders make a living on the Chicago Board of Trade, Chicago Mercantile Exchange, and the New York Stock Exchange (NYSE). This is also one of the major subject areas of the field of agricultural economics.

8.8.5 Population.

Population is the final determinant of demand. Population growth has a direct and important impact on consumption: more people buy more goods, particularly necessities such as food. This is similar to an increase in income in low-income nations. If the population of Ethiopia increases, then the demand for wheat will increase.

This concludes our discussion of the determinants of demand. In Chapter Nine, we will see how markets operate by combining the supply and demand curves into one graph, to study the interaction between producers and consumers.

Chapter Eight Summary

1. Supply is the amount of a good available in a given location at a given price.
2. The Marginal Cost curve above the minimum Average Variable Cost curve is the supply curve of the individual firm.
3. The market supply curve is the horizontal summation of all individual supply curves.
4. A supply schedule shows the relationship between the price of a good and the quantity of a good supplied.
5. The Law of Supply states that the quantity of goods offered to a market varies directly with the price of a good, *ceteris paribus*.
6. An elasticity is the percentage change in one economic variable with respect to a percentage change in another economic variable.
7. The Elasticity of Supply is the percentage change in the quantity supplied with respect to a percentage change in price [$\varepsilon = \%\Delta Q^s/\%\Delta P$]. An inelastic supply curve is relatively unresponsive to changes in price ($\varepsilon < 1$); an elastic supply curve is relatively responsive to changes in price ($\varepsilon > 1$); a unitary elastic supply curve is one where a percentage change in price results in an equal percentage change in quantity supplied ($\varepsilon = 1$);
8. The elasticity of supply becomes more elastic as time passes.
9. Elasticities are unitless. Therefore, we can compare elasticities across different goods.
10. The own-price elasticity of supply measures the responsiveness of quantity supplied of a good to changes in the price of that good.
11. The cross-price elasticity of supply measures the responsiveness of quantity supplied of a good to changes in the price of a related good.
12. The change in quantity supplied occurs when the change in quantity of a good sold is a result of a change in the price of a good. Graphically, this is a movement along a supply curve.
13. A change in supply occurs when the change in quantity of a good sold is a result of a change in an economic variable other than the price of a good. Graphically, a shift in the supply curve.
14. Determinants of supply include: (1) input prices, (2) technology, (3) prices of related goods, and (4) the number of sellers.

15. Complements in production are goods that are produced together. Substitutes in production are goods that compete with the same resources in production.
16. Demand is the consumer willingness and ability to pay for a good.
17. The Demand Curve is a function connecting all combinations of prices and quantities consumed for a good, *ceteris paribus*.
18. The Demand Schedule presents information on price and quantities purchased.
19. The market demand curve is the horizontal summation of all individual demand curves.
20. The Law of Demand states that the quantity of a good demanded varies inversely with the price of a good, *ceteris paribus*.
21. The price elasticity of demand relates how responsive quantity demanded is to changes in price [$\eta = \%\Delta Q^d / \%\Delta P$]. An inelastic demand curve is one where a change in price results in a relatively smaller percentage change in quantity demanded ($|\eta| < 1$). An elastic demand is one where a change in price results in a relatively larger change in quantity demanded ($|\eta| > 1$). A unitary elastic demand curve is one where the percentage change in price results in an equal percentage change in quantity demanded ($|\eta| = 1$).
22. The own-price elasticity of demand measures the responsiveness of the quantity demanded of a good to changes in the price of the good.
23. The cross-price elasticity of demand measures the responsiveness of the quantity demanded of a good to changes in the price of a related good.
24. Substitutes in consumption are goods that are consumed "either/or." Complements in consumption are goods that are consumed together.
25. A change in quantity demanded results from a change in the price of a good. A change in quantity demanded is a movement along a demand curve.
26. A change in demand results from a change in an economic variable other than the price of a good. A change in demand is a shift in the demand curve.
27. Demand is determined by: (1) the price of the good, (2) prices of related goods, (3) income, (4) tastes and preference, (5) expectations of future prices, and (6) population.
28. The Engel curve shows the relationship between consumer income and the quantity of good consumed, *ceteris paribus*.

Engel's Law states that as income increases, the proportion of income spent on food declines.

29. The income elasticity of demand is the percentage change in the demand for a good in response to a percentage change in consumer income [$\mu = \%\Delta Q^d/\%\Delta M$].

30. A normal good is one whose consumption increases in response to an increase in income ($\mu > 0$). An inferior good's consumption declines in response to an increase in income ($\mu < 0$). A luxury good's consumption increases at an increasing rate in response to an increase in income ($\mu > 1$), while a necessity good's consumption increases at a decreasing rate in response to an increase in income ($\mu < 1$).

Chapter Eight Glossary

Arc Elasticity. A formula that measures responsiveness along a specific section (arc) of a supply or demand curve, and measures the "average" price elasticity between two points on the curve.

Change in Demand. When a change in the quantity of a good purchased is a result of a change in an economic variable other than the price of the good. A shift in the demand curve.

Change in Quantity Demanded. When a change in the quantity of a good purchased is a result of a change in the price of the good. A movement along the demand curve.

Change in Quantity Supplied. When a change in the quantity of a good sold is a result of a change in the price of the good. A movement along the supply curve.

Change in Supply. When a change in the quantity of a good sold is a result of a change in an economic variable other than the price of the good. A shift in the supply curve.

Complements in Consumption. Goods that are consumed together (e.g. peanut butter and jelly).

Complements in Production. Goods that are produced together (e.g. beef and leather).

Cross-Price Elasticity of Demand. Measures the responsiveness of the quantity demanded of a good to changes in the price of a related good.

Cross-Price Elasticity of Supply. Measures the responsiveness of the quantity supplied of a good to changes in the price of a related good.

Demand. Consumer willingness and ability to pay for a good.

Demand Curve. A function connecting all combinations of prices and quantities consumed for a good, *ceteris paribus*.

Demand Elasticity. The percentage change in quantity demanded relative to the percentage change in price.

Demand Schedule. Information on prices and quantities purchased.

Elastic. A change in price brings about a relatively larger change in quantity.

Elasticity. The percentage change in one economic variable with respect to a percentage change in another economic variable.

Elasticity of Demand. The percentage change in the quantity demanded with respect to a percentage change in price.

Elasticity of Supply. The percentage change in the quantity supplied with respect to a percentage change in price.

Engel Curve. The relationship between consumer income and quantity of a good consumed, *ceteris paribus*.

Engel's Law. A Law that states that as income increases, the proportion of income spent on food declines, *ceteris paribus*.

Income Elasticity of Demand. The percentage change in the demand of a good in response to a one percent change in consumer income.

Inelastic. A change in price brings about a relatively smaller change in quantity.

Inferior Good. A good whose consumption declines in response to an increase in income.

Law of Demand. The quantity of a good demanded varies inversely with the price of the good, *ceteris paribus*.

Law of Supply. The quantity of goods offered to a market varies directly with the price of the good, *ceteris paribus*.

Luxury Good. A good whose consumption increases at an increasing rate in response to an increase in income.

Market Demand. The horizontal summation of all individual demand curves for all individual consumers in the market.

Market Supply. The horizontal summation of all individual supply curves for all individual producers in the market.

Necessity Good. A good whose consumption increases at a decreasing rate in response to an increase in income.

Normal Good. A good whose consumption increases in response to an increase in income. Also called a superior good.

Own-Price Elasticity of Demand. Measures the responsiveness of the quantity demanded of a good to changes in the price of that good.

Own-Price Elasticity of Supply. Measures the responsiveness of the quantity supplied of a good to changes in the price of that good.

Substitutes in Consumption. Goods that are consumed either/or. (e.g. wheat bread and white bread.

Substitutes in Production. Goods that compete for the same resources in production. (e.g. wheat and barley).

Supply. The amount of a good available in a given location at a given price.

Supply Curve. The marginal cost curve above the minimum average variable cost curve.

Supply Schedule. A schedule showing the relationship between the price of a good and the quantity of a good supplied.

Supply Elasticity. The percentage change in quantity supplied relative to the percentage change in price.

Unitary Elastic. The percentage change in price brings about an equal percentage change in quantity.

Chapter Eight Review Questions

1. The individual firm supply curve is:
   a. the horizontal summation of the market supply curve
   b. the MC curve above the maximum ATC
   c. the MC curve above the minimum ATC
   d. the MC curve above the minimum AVC

2. The market supply curve is:
   a. the MC curve above the minimum ATC
   b. the horizontal summation of all individual firm supply curves
   c. the vertical summation of all individual firm supply curves
   d. not enough information provided to answer

3. The Law of Supply states that:
   a. producers will always maximize profits
   b. the price of a good and quantity supplied have a positive relationship
   c. supply equals demand
   d. the Law of Diminishing Returns affects supply

4. An elasticity measures:
   a. how prices affect inflation
   b. the Law of Supply
   c. how economic influences the stock markets
   d. how responsive one variable is to another variable

5. The elasticity of fruit is _____ relative to the elasticity of apples.
   a. more elastic
   b. less elastic
   c. the same level of elasticity
   d. not enough information provided to answer

6. If the price of a good increases 1%, and quantity supplied increases 2%, then the good is:
   a. elastic
   b. inelastic
   c. unitary elastic
   d. can not tell from the information given

7. If a change in the price of apples results in a change in the quantity supplied of oranges, then the goods are:
   a. own-price elastic b. cross-price elastic c. related d. unrelated

8. If the price of fish increases, then there is a change in:
   a. the supply of fish
   b. the quantity supplied of fish
   c. the amount of fish sold
   d. can not tell from the information given

9. Each of the following is a determinant of supply except:
   a. number of sellers
   b. technology
   c. tastes and preferences
   d. input prices
10. An individual demand curve for pizza can be derived with the following:
    a. prices of pizza, one other good, and income
    b. price of pizza and two other goods
    c. income
    d. price of pizza alone
11. If the price of milo increases:
    a. consumers will buy more milo
    b. consumers will buy less milo
    c. consumers will buy the same amount of milo
    d. can not tell with the information given
12. Which has the least elastic demand curve?
    a. apples
    b. fruit
    c. food
    d. oranges
13. If a firm faces an inelastic demand curve, then it will desire to:
    a. maintain output at the current level
    b. increase output to increase revenues
    c. decrease output to increase revenues
    d. purchase more inputs
14. If the price of pork increases, then the following will result:
    a. a change in pork demand and a shift in pork demand
    b. a change in pork demand and a movement along the pork demand curve
    c. a change in quantity of pork demanded and a shift in pork demand
    d. a change in quantity of pork demanded and a movement along the pork demand curve
15. If the price of gold is expected to increase in the future, then:
    a. the demand for gold will increase today
    b. the demand for gold will decrease today
    c. the quantity demanded of gold will increase today
    d. the quantity demanded of gold will decrease today
16. The income elasticity of demand for food is:
    a. $0 < \mu < 1$ b. $\mu < 0$
    c. $\mu > 1$ d. $\mu = 0$

CHAPTER NINE
MARKETS

The previous chapter discussed supply and demand independently. We have seen that the production and sale of a good (supply) depends crucially on the price of the good, as well as several other determinants. The consumption of a good (demand) also depends on the price of the good, together with other economic factors that influence consumer spending. In this chapter, we tie together supply and demand by discussing *markets*: the interaction of supply and demand.

Prices are determined by the interaction of supply and demand in markets. Markets determine the price of a good, and as a result have a huge influence on society. Recall that in a free market economy, relative prices determine the flow of goods and resources between producers (firms) and consumers (households). We have seen that production decisions of what to produce, how much to produce, and how to produce are all determined by relative prices. Consumer choices also depend on relative prices, as consumers seek to maximize utility by selecting the goods that provide the highest levels of satisfaction at the lowest cost.

Given the supreme importance of prices in a free market economy, producers who have knowledge of how market prices are determined, and how prices are likely to change in the future, will possess the ability to make better economic decisions. Producers who understand how and why the prices of goods and resources change over time will be able to utilize this information to increase the profitability of their firm. Consumers will also make better choices if they understand the market forces that determine price changes. This chapter describes and explains how buyers and sellers interact in markets, which provides useful information to students who learn the concepts of supply and demand well.

1. What is a Market?

A **Market** is simply an institution where buyers and sellers interact. A **Market** is not necessarily a **Marketplace**, which is a physical location where buyers and sellers interact, such as a farmer's market or the commodity trading pits of the Chicago Board of Trade.

Marketplace = A physical location where buyers and sellers meet to trade goods.

A **Market**, on the other hand, can be located in a physical space such as the Manhattan Town Center Mall, but it need not be. Buying and selling goods on the internet (for example, Amazon.com and Ebay.com) is a market, but the buyers and sellers do not actually have to be in the same physical location. Therefore, a **Market** is the interaction between the buyers and sellers of a good:

Market = The interaction between buyers and sellers.

It is this interaction between buyers and sellers that determines the price of a good, and the quantity of the good that is purchased and sold. One key feature of markets is that they are *voluntary*: the exchange of goods and services is left up to the individual buyers and sellers. In the next section, we will see how the voluntary actions of numerous producers and consumers lead to market equilibrium.

2. Market Equilibrium.

Markets work by bringing together producers, who desire to sell their product at the highest possible price, with consumers, who desire to purchase goods at the lowest possible price. Although the goals of buyers and sellers are opposite from one another, voluntary trades allow for the objectives of both groups to be met. This section will describe how the behavior of numerous individual buyers and sellers results in a situation where there is no tendency to change, or **Equilibrium**:

Equilibrium = A point from which there is no tendency to change.

The supply and demand curves that were derived in Chapter 8 are shown together in figure 9.1. Recall that the supply curve represents the horizontal sum of all of the individual firms' marginal cost curves above the average variable cost curve. The supply curve represents the quantity of a good that producers are able and willing to offer for sale at a given price. The graph of the supply curve shows the relationship between the price of a good and the quantity supplied by firms, holding all other determinants of supply constant (input prices, technology, prices of related goods). The *voluntary* nature of the supply curve should be emphasized: firms offer the quantity of a good to the market voluntarily in order to maximize profits.

The demand curve represents the horizontal sum of all individual consumer demand curves. Individual demand curves show the quantity of a good that a consumer is willing and able to pay for a good at a given price. Therefore, the market (aggregate) demand curve represents the relationship between the price and quantity demanded of a good, holding all else constant (*ceteris paribus*). The demand curve is derived from the *voluntary* behavior of consumers seeking to maximize utility, holding all factors that influence demand other than own price constant (income, prices of related goods, population, expectations of future prices, tastes and preferences, etc.).

Figure 9.1

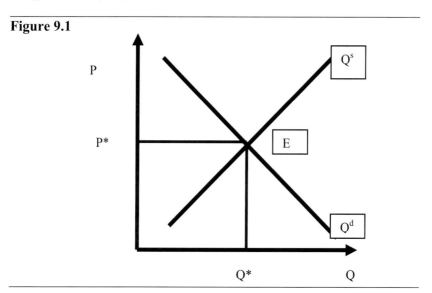

The **Market Equilibrium** is found at the intersection of the supply and demand curves, or point E in figure 9.1. At this point, the quantity supplied by firms at a given price (Q^s) is equal to the quantity demanded by consumers at a given price (Q^d).

Market Equilibrium = The point where the quantity supplied by producers at a given price is equal to the quantity demanded by consumers.

At point E (and only at point E), the following market equilibrium condition holds:

$$Q^* = Q^s = Q^d.$$

There is only one price that equates the quantity of a good supplied to the market by producers with the quantity purchased on the market by consumers. This price is called the **Equilibrium Price**, which is P* in figure 9.1.

Equilibrium Price = The price at which the quantity supplied equals the quantity demanded.

The equilibrium price is also called the **Market Price**, since it is the price that is determined in the market.

Market Price = The price where quantity demanded is equal to quantity supplied.

The **Equilibrium Quantity** is Q*, where the quantity supplied is identically equal to the quantity demanded.

Equilibrium Quantity = The point where quantity supplied is equal to quantity demanded.

We have defined the intersection of supply and demand to be the market equilibrium. Next, we will investigate why every price other than P* is not an equilibrium price, and every quantity other than Q* is not an equilibrium quantity. Any point in figure 9.1 other than point E is a **Disequilibrium** point, because buyers and sellers will not settle at any point other than the equilibrium point.

Disequilibrium = A market situation in which the market price does not result in equality of supply and demand.

The voluntary behavior of buyers and sellers will result in a movement toward equilibrium (point E), where the quantity supplied equals the quantity demanded. The tendency for the market to gravitate towards equilibrium can be best explained with an example: consider the market for wheat in Kansas, depicted in figure 9.2.

The supply curve of the Kansas wheat market (Q^s) is the relationship between the price of wheat and the quantity of wheat offered for sale to the market by Kansas wheat producers, *ceteris paribus*. Intuitively, the supply curve represents the cost of production of wheat in Kansas. Low-cost producers are located to the left, where the supply curve is low, and high-cost producers are located to the right, at higher prices.

Figure 9.2

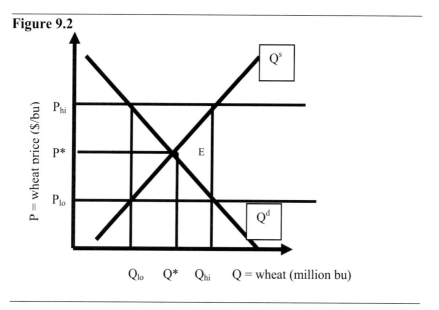

(Quick Quiz 9.1: how is the supply curve for Kansas wheat derived?)

The demand curve for Kansas wheat (Q^d) is the relationship between the price of wheat and the quantity of what consumers are willing and able to purchase, *ceteris paribus*. In the case of the Kansas wheat market, the consumers are millers who purchase Hard Red Winter Wheat (the class of wheat most commonly grown in Kansas) to grind into flour for baking bread. Intuitively, the demand curve represents the consumers' willingness and ability to pay for wheat. Scarcity causes the demand curve to slope downward from left to right: as more wheat becomes available, millers offer lower prices as their wheat needs are met.

(Quick Quiz 9.2: how is the demand curve for Kansas wheat derived?)

(Quick Quiz 9.3: why do we hold everything other than price constant in the graph of supply and demand? Is this a good thing to do?)

We are now in a good position to show why the Kansas wheat market will always gravitate toward the equilibrium point, E. Suppose that the price of wheat in Kansas is P_{hi}. At this relatively high price of wheat, the Law of Demand tells us that consumers (flour millers) will decrease their purchases of wheat. Specifically, at price P_{hi}, wheat consumers will purchase exactly Q_{lo} million bushels of wheat. Wheat

291

producers, however, expand wheat production when the price of wheat is relatively high: Kansas wheat farmers will provide Q_{hi} million bushels to the market at this higher price. At price P_{hi}, the quantity supplied (Q_{hi}) exceeds the quantity demanded (Q_{lo}). This situation is called a **Surplus**:

Surplus = A market situation in which producers are willing to supply more of a good than consumers are willing to purchase at a given price ($Q^s > Q^d$).

A surplus occurs at any price higher than the equilibrium price (P*). In a surplus situation, there is more wheat available for sale than millers are willing to purchase. We often see this situation in the summer, after harvest has been completed: large piles of wheat are found near elevators. Suppose that you are the manager of a grain elevator in Western Kansas, and have a huge pile of wheat on the ground, since the elevator is full. At the current price (P_{hi}), no millers are buying any wheat. You feel pressured to sell the wheat as quickly as possible, since rain or moisture will result in sprouting, which will considerably lower the value of the wheat. What do you do? Lower the price of wheat in order to sell it!

As the price of wheat is lowered from P_{hi}, producers will reduce the quantity of wheat offered to the market along the supply curve, and consumers will increase the quantity demanded of wheat along the demand curve. Producers will lower the price of a good until they are able to sell their product, and eliminate the surplus. The price will continue to be lowered until the quantity of wheat supplied (Q^s) becomes in line with the quantity of wheat demanded (Q^d). This occurs at the equilibrium price (P*) and the equilibrium quantity ($Q^* = Q^s = Q^d$).

This story holds true not only for Kansas wheat, but for any good or service: if the price of a good is greater than the equilibrium price, producers will lower the price until equilibrium is reached. Any price higher than P* is a disequilibrium price, since there is a tendency to move towards the equilibrium point (E). Once equilibrium is reached, there is no tendency to change, since quantity supplied is equal to quantity demanded.

Now suppose that the price of wheat in Kansas falls to P_{lo}. At this relatively low price, wheat producers will cut back production to Q_{lo}, and wheat consumers (millers) will increase quantity demanded to Q_{hi}. This situation is called a **Shortage**, since the quantity demanded (Q_{hi}) is greater than the quantity supplied (Q_{lo}).

292

Shortage = A market situation in which consumers are willing and able to purchase more of a good than producers are willing to supply at a given price ($Q^s < Q^d$).

Shortages occur at all prices below the market equilibrium price (P*). Now suppose that you are a wheat miller who has contracted with several bread bakers for a large quantity of flour, to be delivered as soon as possible. At the price P_{lo}, you are unable to acquire any wheat, due to the shortage. What would you do? Offer a higher price to increase the amount of wheat available! By offering a higher price, the millers cause the quantity supplied to increase along the supply curve, as wheat merchandisers find new supplies of wheat, perhaps from Oklahoma and Colorado. The quantity demanded decreases along the demand curve as the price is raised. The price will continue to be "bid up" by wheat consumers until the equilibrium point E is reached. This occurs not only in the market for wheat, but for any good where a shortage occurs. Thus, any price below P* is a disequilibrium price, since buyers will gravitate toward the equilibrium point.

At any price higher or lower than the equilibrium price, market forces (the behavior of buyers and sellers) will bring the price back into equilibrium at the market equilibrium price and quantity. Market prices are always changing, due to changes in the economic variables that shift the supply and demand curves. We will find out how these changes in supply and demand change equilibrium prices and quantities later in this chapter.

With some practice, you will be able to daze and amaze your friends and family members by predicting price movements in the economy with the use of the simple supply and demand analysis that you have just learned! If you get really good at it, you could even make a lot of money as a grain merchandiser, commodity trader, or stock broker! These individuals often use very simple supply and demand analysis to "buy low and sell high!" In any business or job, supply and demand are extraordinarily useful to determine how market forces will affect the price and quantity of inputs and outputs. In the next section, we will get more practice at supply and demand with the use of a mathematical model of a market.

3. Mathematical Markets.

One reason that economics is an attractive field of study is that there are three ways to describe market phenomena: (1) graphs, (2) "stories", or verbal explanations, and (3) mathematical models. In the previous section, we described the Kansas wheat market in both graphical and verbal terms. We will now use simple algebra to describe a market. The mathematical model uses the same information that the other two approaches use to describe supply and demand.

Suppose that the supply of wheat can be represented by the equation:

$$P = 1 + 0.1Q^s,$$

where P is the price of wheat in dollars per bushel, and Q^s is the quantity supplied of wheat in million bushels. This equation is called an **Inverse Supply Function**, since price (the independent variable) is a function of quantity supplied (the dependent variable). Mathematically, we could describe a supply function as: $Q^s = f(P)$, since price is given and producers determine how much to produce given the independent variable, price. Recall that graphs of supply and demand are "backwards," since price is located on the vertical axis and quantity supplied is located on the horizontal axis. Thus, to make a function easier to graph, we use the **Inverse Supply Function**, where $P = f(Q^s)$.

Inverse Supply Function = A supply function that is represented with price (the independent variable) as a function of quantity supplied (the dependent variable): $P = f(Q^s)$.

Similarly, we define an Inverse Demand Function to be a demand function with the dependent variable (Q^d) and the independent variable (P) reversed:

Inverse Demand Function = A demand function that is represented with price (the independent variable) as a function of quantity demanded (the dependent variable): $P = f(Q^d)$.

Suppose that the inverse demand function for wheat is given by the algebraic equation:

$$P = 5 - 0.1Q^d$$

To find equilibrium, we can set the two equations equal to each other, since P = P:

$$1 + 0.1Q^s = 5 - 0.1Q^d$$

Next, recall that in equilibrium, $Q^* = Q^s = Q^d$, so we can replace the quantities supplied and demanded with the equilibrium quantity:

$$1 + 0.1Q^* = 5 - 0.1Q^*$$

We can now subtract one from each side of the equation, and add $0.1Q^*$ to each side of the equation to get:

$0.2Q^* = 4$, or

$Q^* = 20$ million bushels of wheat.

The equilibrium price can be found by substituting this equilibrium quantity (Q^*) into the inverse supply function:

$P = 1 + 0.1Q^s = 1 + 0.1(20) = 1 + 2 = \$3/bu.$

We can check this result by plugging the equilibrium quantity into the inverse demand equation:

$P = 5 - 0.1Q^d = 5 - 0.1(20) = 5 - 2 = \$3/bu.$

The equilibrium in the wheat market is: ($P^* = \$3/bu$, $Q^* = 20$ million bushels). This same result could be found graphically, by graphing the supply and demand functions, and locating the equilibrium at the intersection of supply and demand, as in figure 9.3.

Figure 9.3

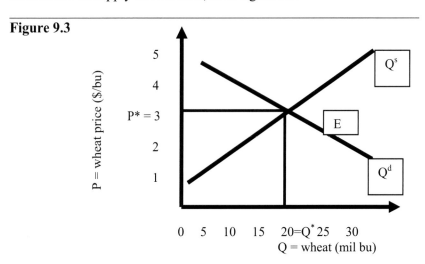

This is the type of mathematical model that economists build to study agricultural markets. Price and quantity data are gathered from markets such as the Kansas City Board of Trade or the Chicago Mercantile Exchange, and an economist can study how changes in policies, weather, or any other economic variable will influence the prices and quantities of agricultural goods.

Using a model such as this, an economist can find out the implications of how a change in the price of wheat will affect the wheat market. For example, suppose that the price of wheat increases above the equilibrium level to \$4/bu. Before we look at the graph in figure 9.3 or use the mathematical model, we know that a price above the equilibrium level will increase production, decrease consumption, and a surplus will occur. To calculate the levels of quantity supplied and demanded, we simply plug in the price of \$4/bu into the inverse supply and inverse demand equations:

$$4 = 1 + 0.1Q^s$$
$$3 = 0.1\,Q^s$$
$$Q^s = 30 \text{ million bushels,}$$

$$4 = 5 - 0.1Q^d$$
$$1 = 0.1\,Q^d$$
$$Q^d = 10 \text{ million bushels.}$$

The surplus quantity $(Q^s - Q^d)$ can also be calculated:

Surplus $= (Q^s - Q^d) = 30 - 10 = 20$ million bushels of wheat.

This procedure can also be used to calculate a below-equilibrium price that leads to a shortage. Suppose that the price of wheat in Kansas drops to \$2/bu. Quantities are found with the use of the inverse supply and inverse demand equations:

$$2 = 1 + 0.1Q^s$$
$$1 = 0.1\,Q^s$$
$$Q^s = 10 \text{ million bushels,}$$

$$2 = 5 - 0.1Q^d$$
$$3 = 0.1\,Q^d$$
$$Q^d = 30 \text{ million bushels.}$$

The shortage quantity $(Q^d - Q^s)$ can also be calculated:

Shortage = $(Q^d - Q^s)$ = 30 – 10 = 20 million bushels of wheat.

This procedure can be repeated for changes in supply or demand brought about by economic variables, as we shall see in the next section.

4. Comparative Statics.

The study of markets provides the managers of business firms with a powerful method of understanding and analyzing how prices for the firm's inputs and outputs change over time. This knowledge can lead to better decision making, and higher levels of profitability for the firm. We have seen how the interaction of supply and demand result in an equilibrium market price and quantity. Now we will see how a change in supply and/or demand will impact the market equilibrium.

Economists call this type of study **Comparative Statics**: we will compare one equilibrium point with another. Since an equilibrium is a point from which there is no tendency to change, equilibrium is a static, or constant, point. Comparative statics compares one equilibrium point before an economic change to another equilibrium point after the economic change has taken place.

Comparative Statics = A comparison of market equilibrium points both before and after a change in an economic variable.

We will study the impacts of changes in demand, changes in supply, and then changes in both supply and demand simultaneously. After careful consideration of these comparative statics, you will be able to analyze any economic policy, change, or situation in a powerful and meaningful way!

9.4.1 Demand Changes.

Suppose that the per-capita income of China increases, as this huge Asian economy moves away from its Communist past towards a free market economy. As we have discussed previously, this is likely to have a positive impact on the demand for beef produced in Kansas: consumers with increasing income levels tend to substitute out of inexpensive calorie sources such as grains and into more expensive goods such as beef and seafood. This increase in demand is shown in figure 9.4.

Figure 9.4

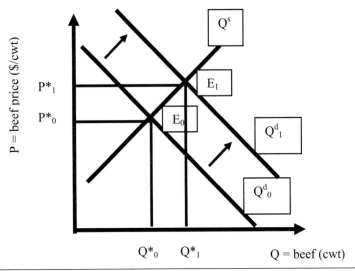

This outward shift in the demand curve is a change in demand (not a change in quantity demanded) since the source of the change was a nonprice variable (an increase in income in China). The equilibrium changes from E_0 to E_1 as a result of the demand change. Notice that as the demand curve shifts upward and to the right, it sweeps across the supply curve from one equilibrium point to another. This increases the price of beef from P^*_0 to P^*_1, and as a result causes a change in quantity supplied, or a movement along the supply curve, as seen in figure 9.4.

A SHIFT IN DEMAND RESULTS IN:
(1) A CHANGE IN DEMAND, and
(2) A CHANGE IN QUANTITY SUPPLIED.

An increase in demand, as shown above, results in an increase in the equilibrium price and quantity of beef. Any economic variable that increases demand for a good will result in a higher price and higher quantity of the good bought and sold. This could be due to an increase in income or population, an expectation that the good's price will increase in the future, or a change in consumer tastes and preferences.

A decrease in demand will have the opposite results: the demand will shift to the left, causing a decrease in both the equilibrium price and quantity of the good. Suppose that the relative price of chicken decreases, causing a substitution out of beef and into chicken. This would result in a decrease in the demand for beef, as shown in figure 9.5.

298

Figure 9.5

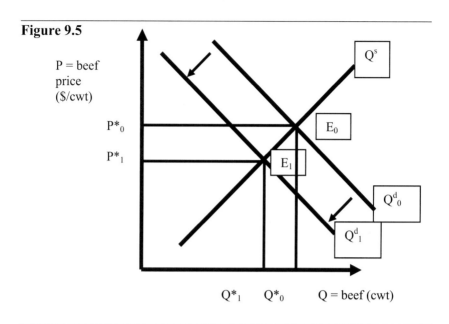

P = beef
price
($/cwt)

P^*_0

P^*_1

E_0

E_1

Q^s

Q^d_0

Q^d_1

Q^*_1 Q^*_0 Q = beef (cwt)

Again, the shift in the demand curve represents a change in demand (shift in the demand curve) and a change in quantity supplied (movement along the supply curve). The equilibrium price and quantity of beef decrease in this situation. We have shown how changes in consumer purchases affect the market price and quantity of a good. Let's turn now to how changes in production will affect the market equilibrium.

9.4.2   Supply Changes.

Suppose that the price of oil increases due to a war in the Persian Gulf with Iraq. As we have discussed previously, petroleum products are a major input into the production of agricultural products such as corn. Corn producers will face a higher cost of production due to this price hike. The marginal cost curve of all corn producers will shift upward due to this increase in the price of an input. Since the market supply curve is the horizontal sum of all individual firm's marginal cost curves, this shift in supply is shown in figure 9.6.

This upward shift in the supply curve is a change in supply (not a change in quantity supplied), since the source of the change was a nonprice variable (an increase in the price of an input, oil, rather than a change in the price of corn). The equilibrium changes from E_0 to E_1 as a result of the supply change. Notice that as the supply curve shifts upward and to the left, it moves across the demand curve from one equilibrium point to another. This increases the price of corn from $P*_0$ to $P*_1$, and as a result causes a change in quantity demanded, or a movement along the demand curve, as seen in figure 9.6.

Figure 9.6

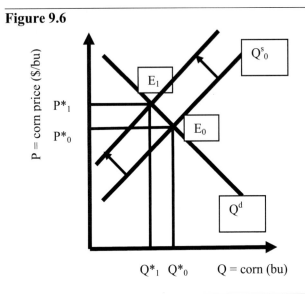

A SHIFT IN SUPPLY RESULTS IN:
(1) A CHANGE IN SUPPLY, and
(2) A CHANGE IN QUANTITY DEMANDED.

The shift in supply in figure 9.6 is a ***decrease*** in supply, since at every price the quantity of corn supplied has decreased. This can be confusing, since an upward shift in the supply curve represents a decrease in supply. The "increase" or "decrease" is measured along the quantity, or horizontal, axis: the corn supply curve shifted to the left, so it is a decrease in supply.

A decrease in supply, as shown above, results in an increase in the equilibrium price and a decrease in the equilibrium quantity of corn. Any economic variable that decreases the supply of a good will result in a higher price and lower quantity of the good bought and sold. This type of shift could be due to a number of things, including an increase in the cost of any input, a tax placed on corn production by the government, or bad weather that has a negative impact on the growing conditions.

An increase in supply will have the opposite results: the supply curve will shift to the right, causing a decrease in the equilibrium price and an increase in the equilibrium quantity of the good. Suppose that a new corn hybrid is developed in the Kansas State University Agronomy Department that yields more bushels per acre than previous corn varieties. This technological change results in an increase in supply, or a rightward shift in the supply curve shown in figure 9.7.

Figure 9.7

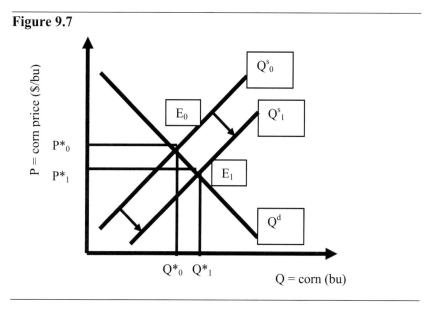

Again, the shift in the supply curve represents a change in supply (shift in the supply curve) and a change in quantity demanded (movement along the demand curve). The equilibrium price decreases and the equilibrium quantity of corn increases in this situation. We have shown how changes in the production of a good affect the market price and quantity of a good. Let's turn now to how changes in production will affect the market equilibrium.

9.4.3 Simultaneous Supply and Demand Changes.

Our examples of comparative statics in the previous two sections have shown one change at a time. In the real world, supply and demand curves are constantly changing, being pushed and pulled by a large number of economic changes. In agricultural markets, supply and demand shift due to weather, input and output prices, exports, imports, and numerous other market determinants. In this section, we will look at supply and demand changing simultaneously.

The production of agricultural products has grown over time, due to technological change. Consumption of food and fiber has also grown,

301

due to increases in population and income. We can show both of these changes in the same graph, as in figure 9.8.

Figure 9.8

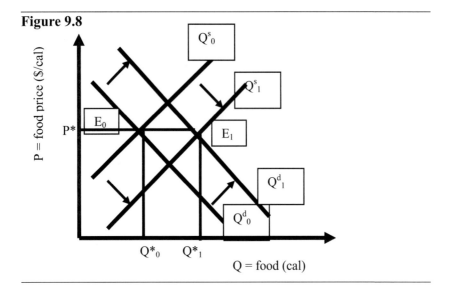

If the supply and demand curves shift by equal quantities over time, the equilibrium changes from E_0 to E_1, as shown in figure 9.8. In this situation, the equilibrium price remains constant at P^*, and the equilibrium quantity increases from Q^*_0 to Q^*_1.

In most agricultural markets in the United States, increases in production have outpaced increases in consumption, as shown in figure 9.9. When supply growth outpaces demand growth, the equilibrium price of food decreases, and the equilibrium quantity of food increases. In US agriculture, since World War II, the relative price of agricultural products has decreased and the output has increased tremendously due to the huge productivity gains made from mechanization, chemical and fertilizer use, and plant and animal breeding. As depicted in figure 9.9, consumers are made better off in this situation, since more food is available at a lower price.

If demand increases at a faster rate than supply, then the equilibrium price will increase, reflecting the increase in scarcity of the good.

(Quick Quiz 9.4: graph the situation where the supply of a good increases faster than the demand for the good. What happens to the equilibrium price and quantity of the good?)

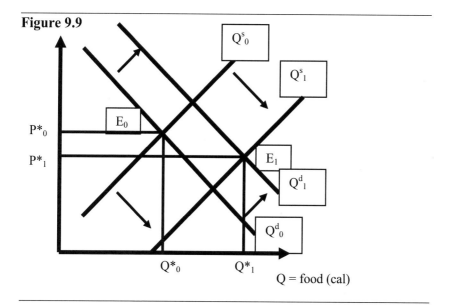

Figure 9.9

Q^s_0

Q^s_1

E_0

P^*_0

P^*_1

E_1

Q^d_1

Q^d_0

Q^*_0 Q^*_1

Q = food (cal)

5. Price Policies.

In many nations, the government will intervene in agricultural markets due to political pressure from either agricultural producers or the consumers of food. The government has the authority to legislate the prices at which goods can be bought and sold. If the government believes that the price of an agricultural product is too low, it can pass a law that mandates a **Price Support** for the good. On the other hand, if the government believes that the price of a good is too high, it can legislate a **Price Ceiling**. This form of government intervention has been common in agricultural markets.

9.5.1 Price Supports.

When the prices of agricultural goods are low, producers often place pressure on politicians to do something about low farm prices. A common reaction of governments is to pass a law that legislates a **Price Support**, or a minimum price below which the market price can not go.

Price Support = A minimum price set by the government for a specified good or service.

The government must enforce this market price intervention, otherwise the surplus would quickly set in motion market forces that would take the market back to the equilibrium point, where the quantity supplied is equal to the quantity demanded. Figure 9.10 shows a price support for wheat, which is higher than the equilibrium market price ($P^s > P*$).

Figure 9.10

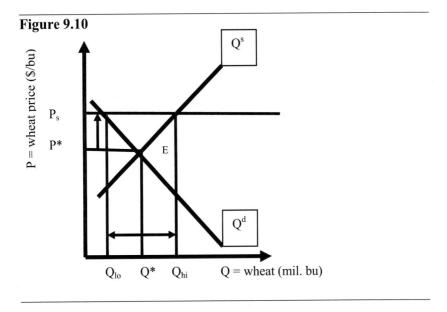

If the government passed a law that said that all wheat must be sold at a price at or above the price support level, this would cause an increase in the price of wheat as shown in figure 9.10. This increase in price results in an increase in quantity supplied, as producers will produce more wheat, and move upward along the supply curve. This is a change in quantity supplied, rather than a change is supply, since the price is the cause of the change, resulting in a movement along the supply curve. Similarly, the price rise causes a decrease in quantity demanded, due to the movement along the demand curve resulting from the increase in price from the equilibrium level to the price support level.

If free markets were allowed to operate, the surplus ($Q^s > Q^d$) would result in downward pressure on the price of wheat until the original equilibrium was reached. The government must enforce this price support by removing the surplus to maintain the price at P^s. The government must stand ready to purchase any quantity of wheat at the price support level, to keep producers from lowering the price. The government will purchase the full quantity of the surplus ($Q_{hi} - Q_{lo}$), and

304

remove this wheat from the market. There are several things that the government could do with the surplus wheat, including:

1. Give it away to US consumers through domestic food programs
2. Give it away to foreign consumers through food aid programs
3. Export the wheat to other nations
4. Destroy the wheat (dump it in the ocean).

At various times, the US government has practices all four strategies. Note that if the price support (P^s) were lower than the equilibrium market price (P^*), nothing would happen. This is because the law states that wheat must be purchased at or above the price support level, and since the market price is above the price support level, the law is not binding.

The price support is good for wheat producers, since they receive a higher price for a larger number of bushels produced. Consumers are made worse off by the price support, since they must now pay a price that is higher than equilibrium. Taxpayers are also made worse off, since they must purchase the surplus and give it away. The United States had a complicated system of price supports, which began with the passage of the Agricultural Adjustment Act of 1933, and ended recently with the Freedom to Farm Bill of 1996.

Price supports had become obsolete in the US agricultural economy, because they raised the price of agricultural goods above the free-market, world price level. Since over half of wheat and feed grains that are produced in the United States is exported, the price supports were making our food products expensive relative to exports from other nations. The USA was losing some export deals with other nations due to the artificially high prices for food and feed grains. Since 1996, price supports were removed and the agricultural sector has come much closer to a free market. Price supports are minimum prices put in place to protect producers. When the government desires to protect consumers, maximum prices, or price ceilings, are often used, as will be explained in the next section.

9.5.2 Price Ceilings.

Price ceilings are simply a government mandated maximum price:

Price Ceiling = A maximum price set by the government for a specified good or service.

When prices rise rapidly, consumers often place pressure on their legislators to do something about the high prices. For example, in the 1970s, the prices of food rose rapidly, creating much pressure for the government to help the common consumer through market price interventions. President Richard Nixon placed price ceilings on beef and other food products. We will use the graphical analysis presented in figure 9.11 to determine the impacts of a price ceiling on producers and consumers.

With the imposition of the price ceiling on beef, producers and consumers cannot buy or sell meat at any price above the maximum price (P_{max}). Note that if the price ceiling were set at a price greater than the equilibrium price, nothing would happen. When the price ceiling (P_{max}) is set below the market price (P^*), however, it has consequences. The price decrease causes movements along both the supply and demand curves.

Figure 9.11

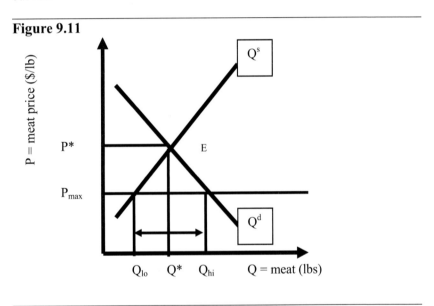

At a lower price, consumers purchase more wheat due to the Law of Demand, resulting in an increase in quantity demanded from Q^* to Q_{hi}. Producers will reduce the quantity of meat supplied at the lower price, and a change in the quantity supplied results in a reduction in meat supplied from Q^* to Q_{lo}. This creates a shortage ($Q^s < Q^d$).

What is interesting about this form of government intervention is that the policy may or may not make consumers better off than they were prior to the legislated price ceiling. The reason is that there is less meat available to consumers at the low price of P_{max}. Profit-maximizing producers will decrease the supply of meat at the lower price, creating the shortage. If the law does not allow price increases, then the shortage will not self-correct, as it would in a free market situation, through a process of consumers bidding up the price back to the equilibrium level, where the quantity supplied equals the quantity demanded.

When the price ceiling is in place, the consumers who are able to purchase meat are made better off, because they pay a lower price for meat. However, there is a group of consumers who are unable to locate and purchase meat due to the shortfall in production. This group of consumers is made worse off by the policy, since they are unable to eat meat!

Markets are enormously useful and adaptable institutions. Government intervention into markets typically has unanticipated consequences which distort the market mechanism. In the case of the price support, put in place to assist producers, the taxpayers and consumers must pay a large sum of money to the recipients of the price support. A price ceiling results in a shortage of the good, and some unsatisfied consumers. Government intervention takes away the "self-correcting" nature of markets, which will always result in the attainment of equilibrium, or a situation where the quantity supplied is equal to the quantity demanded.

Now that we have some practice at shifting supply and demand curves around, we will turn our attention to the structure of agricultural industries, or the number of firms in an industry, in the next chapter.

Chapter Nine Summary

1. Prices are determined by the interaction of supply and demand in markets. A market is simply an institution where buyers and sellers interact. A marketplace is a physical location where buyers and sellers meet to exchange goods. The interaction between buyers and sellers determines the price of a good and the quantity of the good purchased and sold.

2. Market equilibrium is the point where the quantity supplied at a given price is equal to the quantity demanded. The equilibrium price is the price at which quantity supplied equals quantity demanded. The equilibrium quantity is the point where quantity supplied equals quantity demanded. Disequilibrium is a market situation in which the market price does not equate supply and demand.

3. Economic forces will result in the price always gravitating toward the equilibrium price.

4. A surplus is a market situation where quantity supplied is greater than quantity demanded.

5. A shortage is a market situation where quantity demanded is greater than quantity supplied.

6. The inverse supply function is represented by a price as a function of quantity supplied. The inverse demand function is represented by a price as a function of quantity demanded.

7. Comparative statics is a comparison of market equilibrium points before and after a change in an economic variable.

8. A price support is a minimum price set by the government for a specified good or service.

9. A price ceiling is a maximum price set by the government for a specified good or service.

Chapter Nine Glossary

Comparative Statics. A comparison of market equilibrium points both before and after a change in an economic variable.

Disequilibrium. A market situation in which the market price does not result in equality of supply and demand.

Equilibrium. A point from which there is no tendency to change.

Equilibrium Price. The price at which the quantity supplied equals the quantity demanded.

Equilibrium Quantity. The point where quantity supplied is equal to quantity demanded.

Inverse Demand Function. A demand function that is represented with price (the independent variable) as a function of quantity demanded (the dependent variable): $P = f(Q^d)$.

Inverse Supply Function. A supply function that is represented with price (the independent variable) as a function of quantity supplied (the dependent variable): $P = f(Q^s)$.

Market. The interaction between buyers and sellers.

Marketplace. A physical location where buyers and sellers meet to trade goods.

Market Equilibrium. The point where the quantity supplied by producers at a given price is equal to the quantity demanded by consumers.

Market Price. The price where quantity demanded is equal to quantity supplied.

Price Ceiling. A maximum price set by the government for a specified good or service.

Price Support. A minimum price set by the government for a specified good or service.

Shortage. A market situation in which consumers are willing and able to purchase more of a good than producers are willing to supply at a given price ($Q^s < Q^d$).

Surplus. A market situation in which producers are willing to supply more of a good than consumers are willing to purchase at a given price ($Q^s > Q^d$).

Chapter Nine Review Questions

1. If the quantity supplied is greater than quantity demanded, there is a:
   a. trade deficit
   b. equilibrium
   c. shortage
   d. surplus
2. If the price is higher than the equilibrium price, then:
   a. quantity demanded is greater than quantity supplied
   b. quantity supplied is greater than quantity demanded
   c. the price will increase over time
   d. can not answer with information given
3. An inverse demand function:
   a. is incorrect
   b. has price as a function of quantity demanded
   c. has quantity demanded as a function of price
   d. must be inverted to graph the function
4. An increase in income results in:
   a. no change in demand
   b. a change in quantity demanded
   c. a shift in demand
   d. a movement along the demand curve
5. An increase in the price of fertilizer will alter the market for wheat by:
   a. a leftward shift in demand
   b. a rightward shift in demand
   c. a leftward shift in supply
   d. a rightward shift in supply
6. A price support results in:
   a. off-farm migration
   b. shortages
   c. surpluses
   d. lower prices
7. A price ceiling will result in:
   a. higher returns to producers
   b. higher prices
   c. surpluses
   d. shortages

CHAPTER TEN
THE COMPETITIVE FIRM

In the previous chapter, we investigated how the interaction of buyers and sellers determines the market price and quantity of a good or service in a free market economy. In this chapter, we will study **Market Structure**, or how an industry is organized. The number of sellers in the industry determines the structure of a market. The structure has a large influence on the prices and quantities of goods and services that are sold in a market. If there are only a few firms in an industry, their behavior and business strategies will be quite different than firms in an industry with numerous competitors, as we will find out in what follows.

1. Market Structure.

The structure of a market refers to how many firms there are in a given industry. This is quite variable across industries in a free market economy: we purchase electricity from a single firm with no choice. Computer software is provided primarily by Microsoft, with a few other options such as Linux. When we buy fast food, there are several different choices (Big Macs; Whoppers; KFC; Taco Bell, etc.). And, when we purchase clothing, there are numerous choices in stores, catalogs, or on the internet.

The automobile industry is dominated by three large firms (General Motors, Ford, and Daimler-Chrysler), who compete with numerous foreign manufacturers (Jaguar!). When Archer Daniels Midland (ADM, "supermarket to the world") buys soybeans to crush into oil, it can purchase beans from thousands of independent soybean farmers throughout the Midwest and Great Plains. However, when grocery stores and restaurants seek to purchase steaks for their customers, there are only three major packers who are in the beef business: IBP, ConAgra, and Excell. Recently, the hog industry has been consolidated into one very large firm when Murphy Family Farms merged with Smithfield.

Given the diversity of market structures, economists are interested in the causes and consequences of the number of firms that comprise an industry. Economists have organized the type of market structure, or industrial organization, into several categories, listed in table 10.1.

Table 10.1. Market Structures.

Structure	Number of Firms	Examples
Monopoly	Single Seller	Westar for gas and electricity; City of Manhattan for water.
Oligopoly Industry.	Few Sellers	Car industry; Beef Packing
Monopolistic Competition	Numerous Sellers of Branded Goods	Gasoline Stations; Grocery Stores.
Perfect Competition	Numerous Sellers	Agricultural Goods: wheat, corn, cattle.

Monopoly is the extreme case of a single firm in an industry. Westar Energy (formerly KPL) is the sole source of natural gas and electricity in Manhattan, Kansas: consumers can not purchase these energy sources from any other firm. At the other end of the industrial organization spectrum is **Perfect Competition**. In a competitive market structure, numerous firms produce an identical product.

Between these two extremes are **Oligopoly**, which is an industry composed of "few" firms, such as the automobile industry. **Monopolistic Competition** reflects a market structure that combines some features of monopoly with some characteristics of competition. An industry that has numerous firms that produce similar, but not identical products is categorized by monopolistic competition. Beer, toothpaste, soap, and clothes are examples of this type of industry.

In the next two chapters, we will see that the behavior and performance of an industry depend crucially on market structure. Competitive firms strive to maximize profits taking prices as fixed and given. Monopolists, on the other hand, maximize profits by selecting the profit-maximizing price. Firms located between the two extremes of monopoly and competition have some ability to influence price, but not complete authority. The ability to set the price of output is called **Market Power**. Monopolists have complete market power; competitive firms have no market power. As we will see, a firm that enjoys market power is able to increase profits above the competitive firm.

Business firms in agriculture and agribusiness are often in competitive industries. Given the importance of competition to

312

agriculture, this chapter is devoted to a discussion and analysis of firms in Perfect Competition. Chapter Eleven discusses the cases of imperfect competition: monopoly, oligopoly, and monopolistic competition.

2. Characteristics of Perfect Competition.

The first market structure that we will study is that of **Perfect Competition**:

Perfect Competition = A market or industry that has four characteristics: (1) numerous buyers and sellers, (2) homogeneous product, (3) freedom of entry and exit, and (4) perfect information.

The behavior and outcomes of competitive firms depend crucially on these four characteristics. Real-world firms do not meet all four of these characteristics perfectly; the concept of a perfectly competitive firm is an idealized, extreme case. The study of competition allows economists to better understand firm behavior and make useful predictions about how prices change and how firms will respond to those price changes. We will now take a close look at the implications of each of the four characteristics of a competitive firm.

10.2.1 Homogeneous Product.

Firms in a perfectly competitive industry all produce an identical product, or a **Homogeneous Product**, which simply means that the consumer cannot determine which firm produced the good by looking at it:

Homogeneous Product = A product that is the same no matter which producer produces it. The producer of a good cannot be identified by the consumer.

Agricultural commodities are good examples of homogeneous products: wheat, corn, and soybeans are identical across all producers. It would be difficult to ascertain which beef packer produced the meat in the grocery store. However, cattle are distinguished by a brand, which gives livestock buyers the ability to tell the producer of the cattle, making livestock a nonhomogeneous product.

Homogeneous products allow customers to be indifferent between producers: since the products are identical, customers will purchase from the seller with the lowest price. Competitive industries, therefore, do not have firms in steep competition with each other to win over customers, since customers only care about the price of the good.

10.2.2 Numerous Firms.

A perfectly competitive industry has "numerous" firms. The question is, "how many is numerous?" The term, "numerous firms" has a special meaning in economics. Numerous firms means that each individual firm in an industry is so small relative to the entire industry that the firm cannot influence the price of inputs and outputs.

Consider a soybean grower in Southeast Kansas: this individual farmer's soybean output is so tiny relative to the soybean market that the price of soybeans would not be affected, regardless of how many bushels of soybeans were produced, whether it was zero or a bumper crop. This is true of each and every soybean producer, no matter how large or small. So, the soybean industry can be considered to have numerous firms.

This feature of perfectly competitive markets results in a competitive firm being a **Price Taker**, or a firm that has no influence over the price of inputs or outputs.

Price Taker = A situation where the firm is so small relative to the industry that the price of an input or output is fixed and given, no matter how large the quantity of input purchased or output sold is.

Being a price taker means that the firm has no market power: the firm must take input and output prices as given and fixed. This provides freedom to the firm to not have to worry about prices: price levels are outside of the scope of things that the firm can influence.

Conversely, firms that do have market power are called **Price Makers**. These firms have at least some ability to influence the price of inputs and output, due to the large size of the firm relative to the market.

Price Maker = A firm characterized by market power, or the ability to influence the price of an input or output. Restated, a firm facing a downward-sloping demand curve.

Price makers, or firms who have market power, are the subject of Chapter Eleven.

10.2.3 Perfect Information.

In a perfectly competitive industry, all firms have open access to complete information about prices, quantities, and technology. There are no secrets in a competitive industry!

314

Perfect Information = A situation where all buyers and sellers in a market have complete access to technological information and market information (all input and output prices, and all quantities bought and sold).

This characteristic provides a "level playing field" for firms in a competitive industry. All firms share market information. This is true for most agricultural commodities. Farmers have access to market information provided by the United States Department of Agriculture, and the Land Grant University Complex. Technology is also shared by all producers, and production techniques are public information.

In some noncompetitive industries, information is private, not available to all firms in the marketplace. Patents protect innovative firms that develop new production techniques. Privately held market information can be used to earn profits. These sources of privately held information are ruled out in a competitive industry.

10.2.4   Freedom of Entry and Exit.

Firms in a perfectly competitive industry have the ability to enter and exit the industry at any time. Potential entrants can enter an industry without legal or economic **Barriers to Entry and Exit**.

Barriers to Entry and Exit = A legal or economic barrier to the entrance of a new firm into an industry, or to the exit of a firm from an industry.

If an industry is earning profits, this will attract potential entrants to enter and share in the high earnings of the profitable industry. If a profitable industry is subject to a barrier to entry, then other firms will not be able to enter.

For example, Westar has a legal right to produce and sell electricity in Kansas. No other firm can legally sell electricity. Recently, Wal-Mart attempted to locate a "superstore" in Manhattan, Kansas, but the local government would not allow them the legal right to build. These are examples of barriers to entry into an industry. Competitive firms can enter and exit at will: think of the restaurant business in Manhattan, or of wheat producers in Kansas.

The four characteristics of a perfectly competitive industry are used by economists to build a model of a competitive firm that reflects the market conditions facing a firm that meets the four conditions. This model is useful in understanding how firms behave, and enables managers of firms in competitive industries to increase profitability.

3. The Perfectly Competitive Firm.

10.3.1 The Demand Curve Facing a Competitive Firm.

We will now develop a graphical model of a perfectly competitive firm. A competitive firm is small relative to the market; it can not influence the price of the good that it produces and sells. Let's consider an individual wheat producer in Newton, Kansas. Figure 10.1 shows the relationship between the wheat market (on the left) and the individual wheat producer from Newton (on the right).

The interaction of all wheat producers and consumers appears in the supply and demand curves on the left. Market forces will establish an equilibrium point at the intersection of supply (Q^s) and demand (Q^d). In equilibrium, a quantity of Q* billion bushels are produced and sold at a price of P* dollars per bushel. Recall that the demand curve slopes down due to the Law of Demand, and the supply curve slopes up due to the Law of Supply.

Figure 10.1

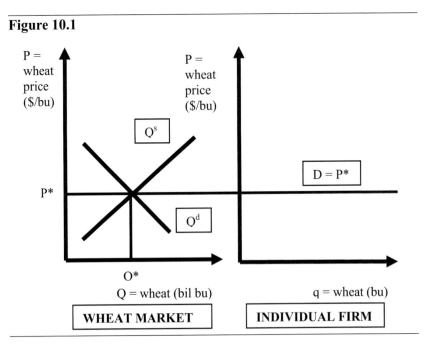

(Quick Quiz 10.1: how is the market demand for wheat derived?)

(Quick Quiz 10.2: how is the market supply of wheat derived?)

316

The units of the graph are crucial: notice that the units for quantity of wheat in the wheat market graph are in billion bushels (Q). This is a large market! The wheat market is truly global in scope, as farmers all over the world produce wheat. Since wheat is traded globally, the supply and demand curves for wheat represent the global market for wheat. The quantity units of the individual producer are in bushels (q).

The graph on the right side of figure 10.1 represents the individual firm. The demand facing the individual firm is perfectly elastic, or flat. This means that the price elasticity of demand is infinite!

$$|\eta| = \infty.$$

To see why this is true, first consider the set of demand curves in figure 10.2.

Figure 10.2

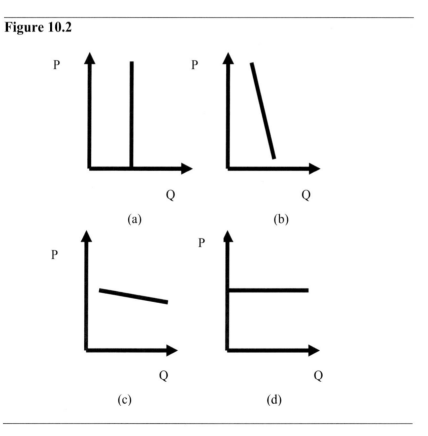

(a)

(b)

(c)

(d)

The demand curve in graph (a) is perfectly inelastic: the consumer purchases the same quantity, regardless of price. No substitutes exist for this good. This demand is perfectly inelastic, or $\eta =$ 0. In graph (b), the demand curve is inelastic ($|\eta| < 1$), since consumers do not change the quantity demanded much in response to price changes. Graph (c) shows an elastic demand ($|\eta| > 1$), where consumers are very responsive to price: if the price increases a small amount, the quantity demanded decreases significantly. Finally, graph (d) depicts a perfectly elastic demand curve ($|\eta| = \infty$).

When demand is perfectly elastic, the price is fixed. This is due to the characteristics of the perfectly competitive industry. The good is homogeneous, so consumers do not care which firm they purchase the good from. Consider what would happen if the individual wheat farmer in figure 10.1 tried to raise the price of wheat one cent above the market price, P*. No elevator or grain buyer would purchase the farmer's wheat at a higher price, even if the price were only slightly larger, since there is a large quantity of wheat available at the market price, P*. At any price higher than P*, the demand facing this firm would fall to zero.

If the individual firm were to charge a price lower than the equilibrium price by one cent, all of the consumers in the market would flock to the producer with the lower price. The demand facing a competitive firm is perfectly elastic, since consumers are extraordinarily responsive to price. Any rational producer would not charge less money than the market price, since the firm can always receive P* dollars per bushel of wheat. The elastic, or flat, demand curve facing the individual wheat producer reflects the ability to sell as much or as little wheat as desired at the prevailing market price. The firm is so small relative to the market that the quantity supplied by the individual firm does not affect the market price.

To see this, consider how large the quantity of wheat is for the individual farmer relative to the world wheat market. The quantity of wheat in the right hand side of figure 10.1 is trivial compared to the billions of bushels of wheat in the world wheat market equilibrium on the left side of figure 10.1.

The demand curve facing the competitive wheat farmer (D) is identical to the price line (P*), since the firm can sell as much or as little wheat as it desires at the market price. The revenues of a competitive firm are quite easy to calculate, since the output price is fixed and given. Recall that total revenues (TR) are defined as the market price (P) multiplied by the quantity produced and sold by the firm (q).

TR = P*q

Total revenues for the wheat producer in Newton are the shaded rectangle defined by the price line and the quantity sold, as shown in figure 10.3.

Average Revenues (AR) are the per-unit level of revenues earned by the firm:

$$AR = TR/q = P*q/q = P$$

Figure 10.3

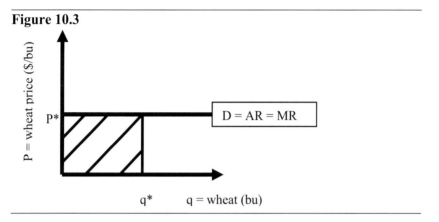

The Average Revenues for the Newton wheat producer are equal to the price (P=AR). Lastly, the Marginal Revenues (MR) for the competitive firm are the change in TR brought about by a small change in output (Δq). Since price is fixed, it does not change, and $\Delta TR = \Delta(Pq) = P\Delta q$, since the only source of change must come from the quantity of output sold (q) since price (P) is fixed.

$$MR = \Delta TR/\Delta q = \Delta(Pq)/\Delta q = P\Delta q/\Delta q = P$$

Marginal Revenues are also equal to price for the competitive firm. This makes good intuitive sense, because the additional (marginal) revenue that the firm receives from the sale of one unit of output is always equal to the constant price (P*). The demand curve for the firm is the same as average revenues, marginal revenues, and the equilibrium market price: $D = AR = MR = P*$.

10.3.2 *Profit-Maximization for a Competitive Firm.*

We have shown in previous chapters that a firm will set marginal revenue equal to marginal cost (MR = MC) to maximize profits. The profit-maximizing condition holds true for the competitive firm, as shown in figure 10.4.

Figure 10.4

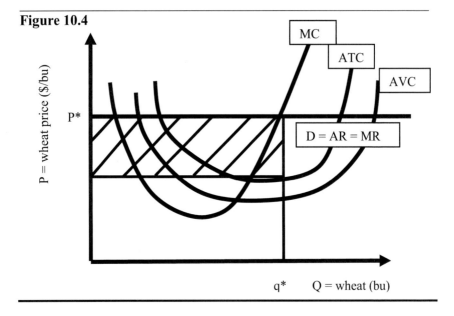

In figure 10.4, the standard "U-shaped" cost curves are shown, together with the market price derived from the intersection of market supply and market demand. The wheat producer maximizes profits by meeting the two conditions of profit-maximization:

(1) MR = MC, and
(2) MC must cut MR from below.

The profit-maximizing level of output is q*, where the two conditions are met. Total revenues for the wheat producer are the large rectangle found by multiplying the equilibrium price by the equilibrium quantity (TR = P*q*).

Profits are found by subtracting all costs of production from the total revenues (π = TR – TC). Total costs are found by substituting the output level (q*) into the ATC curve. This is because ATC = TC/q, so TC = ATC*q. The level of profits for the wheat producer is the shaded area in figure 10.4. In the case shown in the diagram, the firm is making positive economic profits.

(Quick Quiz 10.3: what is the difference between accounting profits and economic profits?

4. The Efficiency of Competitive Industries.

Perfectly competitive industries have many desirable features. Competition results in **Efficiency** of resource use in the economy.

Efficiency = A characteristic of competitive markets, indicating that goods and services are produced at the lowest cost and consumers pay the lowest possible prices.

Efficiency is a desirable result of competition: scarce resources will be used to produce the goods and services that consumers desire at the lowest possible cost. A perfectly competitive industry achieves efficiency in two ways. First, prices charged by competitive firms will be no higher than the cost of production (MC). Numerous firms that produce homogeneous products guarantee this.

If a firm were to try to charge a price higher than the competitive market price, customers would quickly shift to other producers charging the lower market price. Consumers will never by "gouged" by producers trying to raise the price above the competitive level.

The second characteristic of perfectly competitive industries that leads to efficient market outcomes is the freedom of entry and exit. When an industry is earning high levels of profits, potential entrants will begin to produce the good or service that is profitable. This eliminates the possibility of market power, or monopoly prices, from a competitive industry. When a business is unprofitable, it will exit the industry to find a more profitable enterprise.

The agricultural sector of the United States has been subject to decreases in the number of farms since the turn of the century. Why? Because the opportunities to earn a living outside of agriculture have been greater than the opportunities inside of agriculture for many individuals and families over the past 100 years.

This free movement of resources into and out of industries is a unique feature of a free market economy. When an economy is organized with markets, resources flow to the highest return use. Efficiency is attained, meaning that goods are produced at the lowest cost and consumers pay only the cost of production to acquire a good.

To see how this flow of resources takes place, we can take a look at the market for flowers in Johnson County, Kansas. The cities of Overland Park and Olathe are located in Johnson County, which is located just west of Kansas City, Missouri, and happens to be a county with one of the highest per capita incomes in the nation. We will investigate the market for flowers in Johnson County by using graphical analysis in figure 10.5 for both the entire market and an individual florist, "Frank's Flowers."

Figure 10.5

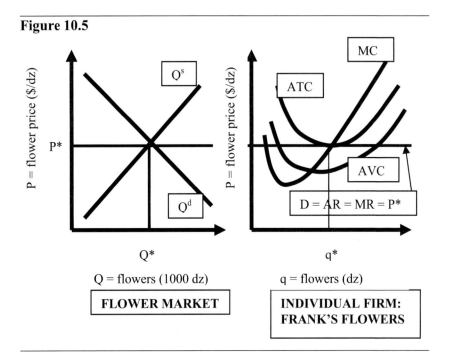

Q = flowers (1000 dz)   q = flowers (dz)

FLOWER MARKET   **INDIVIDUAL FIRM: FRANK'S FLOWERS**

In figure 10.5, we can see the market for flowers in Johnson County: the supply reflects all of the florists in the market, and the demand represents all of the consumers. The market price for flowers is determined by the intersection of supply and demand at P*. All of the florists in the area must charge the same price of P* per dozen flowers, or customers will shift their business to the firms that charge P*. This results in the perfectly elastic demand curve facing Frank.

Frank sells flowers (in dozens) by setting marginal revenue (D = MR = P*) equal to marginal cost (MC) at a quantity of q* dozen flowers. Economic profits are equal to zero, indicating that the resources employed by Frank (K, L, A, and M) are all earning exactly their opportunity cost.

(Quick Quiz 10.4: list and describe the four factors of production for Frank: K, L, A, and M).

(Quick Quiz 10.5: What are opportunity costs? Why are economic profits equal to zero a good outcome?)

The situation depicted in figure 10.5 is a market equilibrium, and a firm equilibrium: the quantity supplied equals the quantity demanded in the market, and the firm is earning zero profits, and price equals marginal cost. The efficiency that results from this outcome is considered to be highly desirable by economists: the resources employed by Frank's firm are earning the highest rate of return possible, since they are earning at least as much as their next best alternative use, or their opportunity cost. Consumers are paying the exact cost of production for a dozen flowers. Suppose that there is an increase in population in Johnson County, and examine what happened to this equilibrium situation in figure 10.6.

Figure 10.6

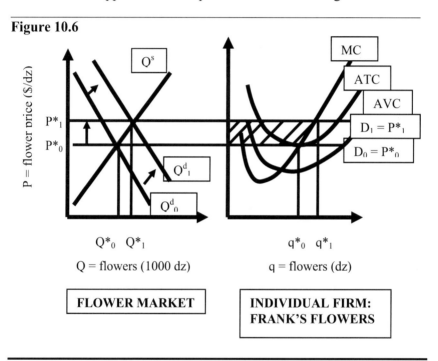

Q^s

P^*_1

P^*_0

Q^d_1

Q^d_0

$Q^*_0 \quad Q^*_1$

Q = flowers (1000 dz)

MC

ATC

AVC

$D_1 = P^*_1$

$D_0 = P^*_0$

$q^*_0 \quad q^*_1$

q = flowers (dz)

P = flower price ($/dz)

| FLOWER MARKET | INDIVIDUAL FIRM: FRANK'S FLOWERS |

With an increase in population in Johnson County, the demand for flowers will increase. The larger demand is shown in the market graph (on the left of figure 10.6) as a shift in demand upward and to the right. This is an increase in demand, rather than an increase in quantity demanded, since the cause of the change was population, a variable other than the price of flowers. The shift in demand results in a movement along the supply curve to the new equilibrium point, or an increase in quantity supplied. The new equilibrium price is P^*_1 and quantity is Q^*_1: the increase in population resulted in an increase in the price of flowers in the county, and an increase in the quantity of flowers sold.

323

The increase in price translates into an increase in economic profits for Frank: in the right panel of figure 10.6, we can see the positive economic profits in the shaded rectangle (B = TR – TC). The market price increased from $P*_0$ to $P*_1$, while the costs of production remained the same as they were prior to the population increase.

Positive economic profits will be earned not only by Frank, but also by every florist in Johnson County. These positive profits explain a lot of economic behavior in Kansas. To take a local example, this analysis shows why businesses in Manhattan favor (1) increased enrollment at K-State, (2) a good football team (think of the Aggieville merchants on game day!), (3) more troops stationed at Fort Riley, (4) an active industrial park in Manhattan that recruits new firms to locate their businesses in Manhattan, and (5) new golf courses and housing developments that will attract new individuals and families to Manhattan. To businesses, population growth is a good thing!

Our story, however, is not over. The high level of earnings by Frank and the other florists will result in entry of other firms into the floral industry: in a free market economy, resources flow to the highest return. This means that K-State graduates with a degree in Horticulture will locate in Johnson County and open up floral businesses to take advantage of the profitable conditions there. This entry of new firms will shift the supply curve of flowers to the right (an increase in supply) as long as positive economic profits exist. The supply of flowers will continue to shift to the right until the original price ($P*_0$) is reached, as in figure 10.7.

Figure 10.7

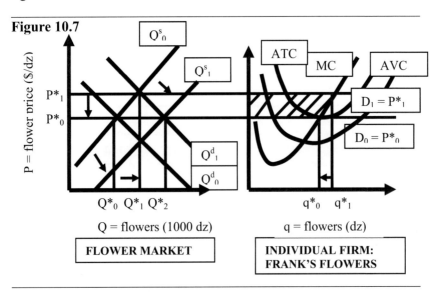

FLOWER MARKET

INDIVIDUAL FIRM: FRANK'S FLOWERS

324

The increase in supply results in an increase in the equilibrium level of output from Q^*_1 to Q^*_2, and a decrease in the equilibrium price back to the original level, P^*_0. This lowers the price line facing Frank, since there are new florists in Johnson County who receive some of Frank's original business. Frank maximizes profits by setting marginal revenue equal to marginal cost at the lower price, P^*_0, and produced the original level of output, q^*_0. Frank is now back at his original equilibrium point! Frank's positive economic profits attracted new firms, which attracted some of Frank's customers and reduced profits back to the equilibrium level of zero profits.

In a competitive industry, the competitive equilibrium will always result in firms earning zero profits, due to the entry and exit of firms into and out of the industry. Aggieville provides a good example of this: think of all of the small businesses that enter and exit the Aggieville area in the course of a single year!

The above analysis can also show how a decrease in demand results in the exit of firms from an industry. In Frank's case, if the demand for flowers fell, this would result in a lower market price for flowers, which would lower the perfectly elastic demand curve facing Frank. If the price drop were small, and price remained above the shut down point (P > min AVC), then Frank would stay in business to minimize costs in the short run. However, if price were to fall below the shut down point, Frank would have to shut down, or exit the industry, and the resources originally employed by Frank would move to other enterprises.

The exit of scarce resources from unprofitable industries is efficient from a societal point of view, although it can be devastating to the persons involved. In a free market economy, the consumers determine what is to be produced and not produced: if the demand for a good is not sufficient for the number of firms producing the good, then some resources will flow out of the unprofitable industry and into enterprises with higher earning opportunities.

(Quick Quiz 10.5: use the two-panel graph of a market and a firm to show the impact of an increase in the price of chicken on the beef market.)

We have explored the behavior of a competitive firm, and shown that competition brings about desirable results for society. In the next section, we will investigate the strategies that competitive firms undertake to maximize profits in the long run.

5. Strategies for Perfectly Competitive Firms.

Competitive firms are price takers, so pricing strategies would not be a good use of resources for the firm's manager. Since the market price is determined by the supply and demand in the entire market, the price is outside of the individual competitive firm's control. Similarly, the goods produced by competitive firms are homogeneous, so quality competition does not matter to the competitive firm. This means that advertising and other marketing activities are not profitable activities for competitive firms.

These outcomes are desirable for producers and consumers: no resources are "wasted" on advertising and marketing, so consumers pay only the production costs of the good. But, if price and product quality are outside of the firm's control, what can a competitive firm do to maximize its earnings in the long run? *MINIMIZE COSTS!*

A competitive firm's best strategy is to lower the costs of production at every opportunity. This could involve adopting new technologies and/or purchasing inputs at the lowest possible price. In a competitive industry, firms must continue to keep up with the other firms in the industry in order to stay in business. If other firms reduce costs, the firm will have to match these cost reductions, or face lower profits in the future. This explains why agricultural producers are often developers of new technology in the form of new equipment, farm management practices, and farming methods.

Technological change allows for higher levels of output to be produced with the same level of inputs, which results in lower per-unit costs of production. The impact of a firm adopting a new technology in the flower business can be seen in figure 10.8.

The technological change lowers the costs of production from MC_0 to MC_1. This allows the florist to go from a position of zero economic profits at the original equilibrium (q^*_0) to positive economic profits at the new equilibrium (q^*_1). If Frank's Flowers adopts this technology before the other florists in Johnson County, he will earn positive profits. These high earnings will draw new entrants into the industry, which will increase the supply of flowers in the market until the market price drops to a new equilibrium price at the minimum ATC curve. So, profits are temporary in a competitive industry: positive profits induce entry, and entry causes supply to increase until the profits are dissipated.

Figure 10.8

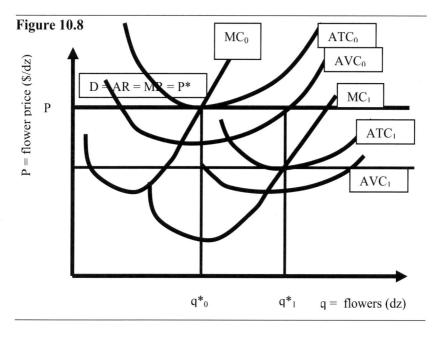

The conclusion of this analysis is that the ***early adopters*** of technological change capture the benefits of technological advance. Firms who do not adopt the technology will be forced out of business, as their costs remain high and the market price drops. This is the best strategy recommendation for a firm in a competitive industry, such as an agricultural firm: develop and adopt technology as rapidly as possible. The saying, "If you snooze, you lose" is particularly pertinent to agricultural firms: these businesses must continuously adopt more efficient production methods in order to remain profitable in the long run.

Much of the research in agriculture is conducted at Land Grant Universities such as Kansas State University. This if often funded by producer groups such as the Kansas Livestock Association and the Kansas Wheat Growers for exactly this reason: the best strategy for firms in competitive industries is to remain on the "cutting edge" of production technology. This is what the large agricultural research complex at K-State provides to Kansas producers.

Not only do producers who adopt technology benefit, but the consumers of agricultural products (everyone who eats!) benefit from research and development of food and fiber, since technological change continuously lowers the price of these goods.

Isn't competition cool? Economists have a great deal of confidence in the ability of markets to allocate scarce resources efficiently: resources are drawn into industries where profits are high, and resources exit industries where profits are negative. Society is made better off through this continuous process of adjustment to new market conditions. Producers earn the maximum profits possible by investing factors of production in the most profitable areas, and consumers pay the lowest possible prices for goods and services.

Alas, the real world is more complicated than the competitive models that we have studied in this chapter. Not every industry meets the four characteristics of perfect competition. Many real-world industries have fewer firms than the competitive ideal. In the next chapter, we will investigate the performance of markets that are imperfect, such as monopolies.

Chapter Ten Summary

1. The market structure of an industry refers to the number of sellers in the industry.
2. A monopoly has only a single firm in an industry.
3. A perfectly competitive industry has numerous firms which produce an identical product.
4. An oligopoly in composed of a "few" firms.
5. Monopolistic competition combines some factors of monopoly with some characteristics of competition. Monopolistic competitors produce similar, but not identical products.
6. Market power is the ability of a firm to set price. Monopolists have complete market power; competitive firms have no market power.
7. A perfectly competitive firm has four characteristics: (1) numerous buyers and sellers, (2) homogeneous product, (3) freedom of entry and exit, and (4) perfect information.
8. A homogeneous product is identical to the output of all firms in the industry, regardless of the firm that produces it.
9. A price taker is a firm so small relative to the industry that it has no influence over price. A price maker has the ability to influence price.
10. Perfect information is a situation where all buyers and sellers in a market have complete access to all technological and market information.
11. Barriers to entry and exit of a firm into an industry are legal or economic barriers to the entrance of a firm into an industry or to the exit of a firm into an industry.
12. The demand curve facing an individual competitive firm is perfectly elastic.
13. Profit maximization conditions for a competitive firm are to set MR=MC, and MC must cut MR from below.
14. Efficiency is a condition indicating that goods and services are produced at lowest cost and consumers pay lowest possible prices.
15. A competitive firm's best strategy for maximizing profits is to minimize costs.

Chapter Ten Glossary

Barriers to Entry and Exit. A legal or economic barrier to the entrance of a new firm into an industry, or to the exit of a firm from an industry.

Efficiency. A characteristic of competitive markets, indicating that goods and services are produced at the lowest cost and consumers pay the lowest possible prices.

Homogeneous Product. A product that is the same no matter which producer produces it. The producer of a good cannot be identified by the consumer.

Market Power. The ability to affect the price of output. A firm with market power faces a downward-sloping demand curve.

Market Structure. The organization of an industry, typically summarized by the number of firms in an industry.

Monopolistic Competition. A market structure defined by: (1) numerous sellers, (2) a product of close, but differentiated, substitutes, (3) some freedom of entry and exit, and (4) some availability of knowledge and information.

Monopoly. A market structure characterized by a single seller.

Oligopoly. A market structure characterized by a few large firms.

Perfect Competition. A market or industry that has four characteristics: (1) numerous buyers and sellers, (2) homogeneous product, (3) freedom of entry and exit, and (4) perfect information.

Perfect Information. A situation where all buyers and sellers in a market have complete access to technological information and market information (all input and output prices, and all quantities bought and sold).

Price Maker. A firm characterized by market power, or the ability to influence the price of an input or output. Restated, a firm facing a downward-sloping demand curve.

Price Taker. A situation where the firm is so small relative to the industry that the price of an input or output is fixed and given, no matter how large the quantity of input purchased or output sold is.

Chapter Ten Review Questions

1. Which type of firm has complete market power?
   a. monopolist
   b. competitive firm
   c. oligopolist
   d. monopolistic competitor
2. Which good is a homogeneous product?
   a. furniture
   b. automobile
   c. wheat
   d. toothpaste
3. A competitive firm is a:
   a. oligopolist
   b. price maker
   c. price taker
   d. monopolist
4. The demand curve facing an individual competitive firm is:
   a. perfectly elastic
   b. perfectly inelastic
   c. the aggregate demand curve
   d. equal to the supply curve
5. Competition results in:
   a. monopoly prices
   b. prices higher than the cost of production
   c. cut-throat price wars that leave consumers worse off
   d. efficient prices
6. A competitive firm's best strategy for maximizing profits is to:
   a. set a monopoly price for the product
   b. differentiate the product
   c. reduce output to increase price
   d. minimize costs

CHAPTER ELEVEN
MARKET POWER: MONOPOLY AND OLIGOPOLY

We have seen how competitive markets and free, voluntary trade between buyers and sellers results in efficiency in resource use. In this chapter, we will discuss noncompetitive markets, within which firms have the ability to influence the price of output. This occurs when a competitive industry does not exist, because there are not "numerous" firms in the industry. When there are only a few firms in an industry, competition between firms does not always result in a competitive situation. Since competition is efficient, our discussion now turns to situations where free markets may not be efficient: consumers may pay prices higher than the cost of production, and potential producers may be unable to enter an industry due to barriers to entry. We begin our discussion with an explanation of **Market Power**.

1. Market Power.

Market Power is simply the ability of a firm to charge a price greater than the cost of production, or the competitive market price.

Market Power = The ability to affect the price of output. A firm with market power faces a downward-sloping demand curve.

Recall from the previous chapter that if a competitive firm were to raise the price of the good that it produces and sells, it would sell nothing: all of the customers would immediately shift to other firms who sell the product at the competitive price. When there are numerous firms in an industry, this price competition will always force each firm to charge the competitive market price, or cost of production (P=MC).
When there are only a few firms in an industry, however, price competition is not necessarily the outcome. When the number of firms is small, firms may be able to increase the price higher than the competitive level, making consumers pay more than the cost of production. Since this outcome is inefficient, the government has legislated laws against the use of market power: the Sherman Antitrust Act. This legislation is intended to protect consumers from a firm exercising its market power. As we shall see, market power is not always a bad thing: in some situations, market power is the natural outcome of free market forces.

But, we are getting ahead of ourselves. Let's first investigate a Monopoly, or an industry comprised of a single firm.

2. Monopoly.

A **Monopoly** is easy to define and understand: a single firm is the entire industry. No other firms produce the same good.

Monopoly = A market structure characterized by a single seller.

(Quick Quiz 11.1: is McDonalds a monopoly, since it is the only firm that produces and sells a Big Mac?)

While it is true that McDonalds is the only firm that sells the Big Mac, economists do not consider McDonalds a monopolist, since there are many firms that produce hamburgers. A monopoly is the only producer of a good that has *NO CLOSE SUBSTITUTES*. McDonalds has many close substitutes: Burger King, Wendys, etc. In a monopoly, the firm is identical to the industry: no other firm produces a good that is similar to the monopolist's product. Since the monopolist is not subject to competition, the monopolist is considered to be a **Price Maker**, instead of a **Price Taker**:

Price Maker = A firm characterized by market power, or the ability to influence the price of an input or output. Restated, a firm facing a downward-sloping demand curve.

A monopoly has characteristics that are quite different than the competitive firm, since these two types of market structure are on opposite ends of the spectrum (see table 10.1). We summarize a monopolist's characteristics in table 11.1.

As seen in table 11.1, the monopoly situation is opposite in every way from the competitive industry. The single firm of the monopoly produces a good for which there are no close substitutes, whereas a competitive firm produced a good that is identical in every way to the product of the numerous other firms in the same industry. Competitive firms are characterized by freedom to enter and exit the industry, whereas potential entrants into the monopoly industry face a legal or financial barrier to entry that does not allow a firm to produce and sell the same product as the monopolist. Lastly, the monopoly can withhold market information from others, the opposite the perfect information situation of the competitive firms.

Table 11.1 Monopoly and Competition.

Monopoly	Competitive Firm
One seller	Numerous sellers
No close substitutes	Homogeneous product
Barriers to entry and exit	Freedom of entry and exit
Unavailability of information	Perfect information

Next, we will investigate the profit-maximizing behavior of a monopolist to determine monopoly prices and quantities, and compare them to the competitive equilibrium prices and quantities. Let's begin with the demand curve facing Westar Energy (formerly KPL). Businesses and Firms in Manhattan must purchase electricity from Westar, since the firm has a legal monopoly on the production and sale of electricity in this region. The firm is the industry, so the market demand curve is the same as the demand curve facing the firm, as can be seen in figure 11.1. The demand curve shown there is the market demand curve. Electricity is sold in units of kilowatt hours (kwh).

Figure 11.1

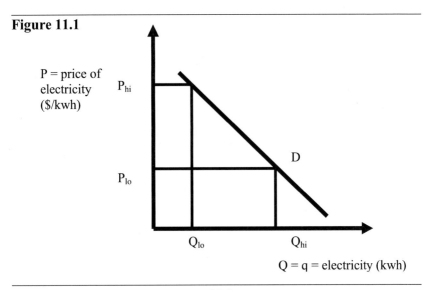

P = price of electricity ($/kwh)

P_{hi}

P_{lo}

D

Q_{lo} Q_{hi}

Q = q = electricity (kwh)

(Quick Quiz 11.2: how is the market demand curve for electricity derived?)

(Quick Quiz 11.3: what does the demand curve facing a competitive firm look like?)

Notice that the notation for the monopolist's demand curve is unique: we have labeled the quantity of electricity demanded both Q (used to indicate a market quantity) and q (used to indicate a firm's quantity). This is the key feature of a monopoly, as has been emphasized: the firm is the industry.

Several features of a monopoly can now be made clear. The monopolist's goal is to maximize profits. This is the identical goal of all firms, regardless of market structure: a competitive firm tries to maximize profits, as does a monopolist. So, a monopolist may be perceived by society as a firm that behaves differently than other firms, but the underlying objective is the same!

The monopolist is called a Price Maker, but in fact, the monopolist does not have complete control to set price. The monopoly is subject to the willingness and ability of consumers to purchase the product, or the demand curve. If the price of electricity were set higher than a price that consumers are willing to pay for it, then the monopolist would not sell any electricity.

The demand curve facing a monopolist is given, so the monopolist can either: (1) set a price, and let consumers determine how much to purchase at that price, or (2) set a quantity, and let consumers determine the price. The monopolist has no control over the demand curve, since it is determined by consumer behavior. Therefore, the monopolist can set either price or quantity, but not both.

For example, in figure 11.1, if Westar sets a high price (P_{hi}), then it will sell only a small quantity of electricity (Q_{lo}). If the monopolist sets a low price (P_{lo}), then it will sell a large quantity of electricity (Q_{hi}). Contrast this with the competitive case, where any firm can sell as much or as little as it desires at a constant price. To sum up our discussion so far, the monopolist desires to produce and sell a product (such as electricity) to maximize profits. The monopolist is not a price-taker, so must determine a price at which to sell the product. The monopolist cannot set any price, but is constrained by the demand curve (the consumers' willingness to pay for the good).

The cost structure of a monopolist is the same as for any firm: the cost curves are the familiar "U-shaped" curves that we have worked with in this course. The revenues for a monopolist, however, differ greatly from the revenues of a competitive firm. To show this, let's first

335

take a look at the revenues of a competitive firm, to contrast with the monopoly case. Recall that the demand curve facing a competitive firm such as a wheat producer is perfectly elastic, or horizontal, as in figure 11.2.

Figure 11.2

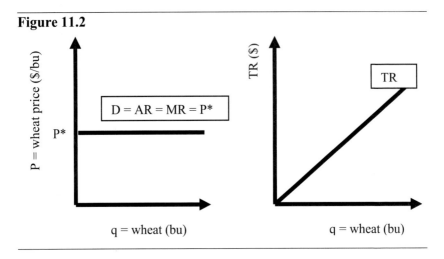

Since the total revenues are the quantity sold multiplied by the price of the product (TR = P*Q), the total revenue line is upward sloping, and of constant slope. This reflects the fact that the competitive wheat firm can sell any quantity of wheat at the given market price, P*. This is due to the assumption that a competitive firm is so small relative to the market that any action that a single firm takes is so small that price is unaffected.

Contrast the demand curve of a competitive firm with those of a monopolist shown in figure 11.3. Suppose that the inverse demand function for electricity is given by:

$$P = 10 - q$$

where P is the price of electricity and q is the quantity of electricity sold, in kilowatt hours (kwh).

By graphing this demand curve, we can easily see why the monopolist is unable to set the price of electricity at any level it wants to, without regard to consumer willingness to pay. The monopolist is constrained by the demand curve. If Westar charged $10/kwh, it would not sell any electricity! By lowering the price of electricity to $8/kwh, the firm will sell 2 kilowatt hours of electricity, for a total revenue of $16.

Figure 11.3

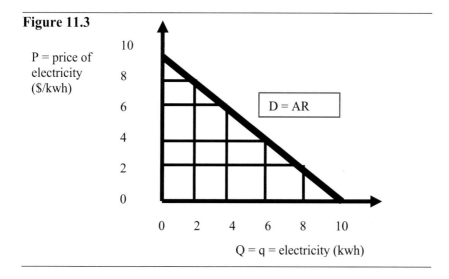

As the price of electricity is lowered, consumers will purchase more, due to the Law of Demand. At a price of $0/kwh (electricity is given away free), Westar sells 10 kilowatt hours of electricity: the total revenues are zero, since no price was charged. A table of possible prices, quantities, and total revenues is shown in table 11.2.

Table 11.2. Revenues for Westar Energy.

Price ($/kwh)	Quantity (kwh)	Total Revenues ($)	Average Revenues ($/kwh)	Marginal Revenues ($/kwh)
10	0	0	--	--
9	1	9	9	9
8	2	16	8	7
7	3	21	7	5
6	4	24	6	3
5	5	25	5	1
4	6	24	4	-1
3	7	21	3	-3
2	8	16	2	-5
1	9	9	1	-7
0	10	0	0	-9

These revenue curves for Westar are drawn in figure 11.4. For the monopolist Westar, average revenues are equal to the demand curve (D = AR), as depicted in the left side of figure 11.4. This result comes from the definition of total revenues (TR = Pq). Average revenues are the revenues per unit of output, or total revenues divided by the quantity produced and sold:

$$AR = TR/q = Pq/q = P.$$

Since average revenues are equal to the price of the good, the demand curve is identical to the average revenue curve. Remember the relationship between average and marginal? The average always "chases" the marginal. Putting this idea to use, if the average revenue curve is decreasing, then the marginal revenue curve is located below the average revenue curve, as shown in figure 11.4.

The marginal revenue curve represents the rate of change, or slope, of the total revenue curve (MR = ΔTR/ΔQ). Since marginal revenues are declining, then the slope of the total revenue curve declines throughout. The marginal revenue curve crosses the x-axis at a quantity of q_0 units of output. This is the same quantity of output where the slope of the total revenue curve becomes negative. To maximize revenues, the monopolist would sell 5 units of output, since that is the highest level of revenues (TR = 25) that could be earned by the firm.

Figure 11.4

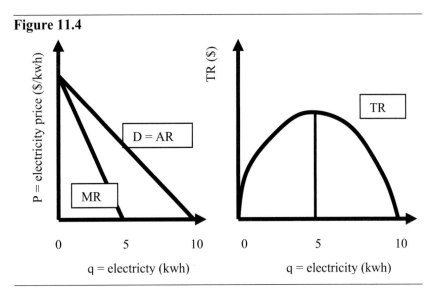

q = electricty (kwh)   q = electricity (kwh)

Recall, however, that to maximize profits, the firm must also include the costs of production in the decision of how much output to produce. Depending on the cost structure, it may cost the firm too much to profitably produce 5 units of output. We need to add costs to the revenues to determine the profit-maximizing level of output for the monopolist. The "standard" cost curves are shown in figure 11.5, together with the average revenue and marginal revenue curves. The profit-maximizing condition for the monopolist is to set MR = MC.

The profit-maximizing solution for the monopolist is an example of incremental decision-making: the firm sets MR = MC at q* kilowatt hours of electricity. The profit-maximizing price of electricity can be found by taking the quantity where MR = MC (q*), and plugging it into the demand curve to find P*. At this quantity, the firm earns positive economic profits by selling q* kilowatt hours of electricity at P* dollars per kilowatt hour. Profits are found by the rectangle below P* and above ATC*, to the left of q*.

Figure 11.5

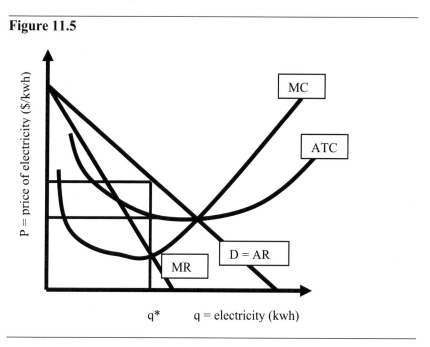

(Quick Quiz 11.4: what would happen if Westar charged a price higher than P*? Lower?)

It can be seen that profits are maximized at q* kilowatt hours. If one additional unit of electricity were produced and sold, the size of the profit rectangle would decrease, since the MC curve is higher than the MR curve at all quantities greater than q*. If one fewer units of electricity were sold, profits would be lower, since MR > MC at all

339

quantities to the left of q*. Monopolists search for the maximum revenue by offering different price levels, and finding out what the demand and total revenues are at each price level.

The economic intuition behind the monopolist's solution is to restrict output in order to receive a price above the competitive level. By restricting output, the monopolist is making its good scarcer, and thus, more valuable. Notice in figure 11.5 that the price that the monopolist charges is significantly higher than the cost of production (MC) at quantity q*. This is why economists and society favor competitive markets over monopoly: the monopoly solution is inefficient, since price is greater than the cost of production. The legal system has laws in place to try to "break up" or regulate monopolies, due to their adverse effect on consumers.

Monopolies exist for several reasons, including: (1) large fixed costs, (2) locational monopolies, and (3) patents. If a firm must incur large fixed costs prior to the sale of a good, it is called a **Natural Monopoly**.

Natural Monopoly = A situation where a single firm has large fixed costs.

Think of Westar, the electricity provider for Manhattan. Prior to the sale of electricity, Westar must build and operate a power generator, together with a distribution network, which are both extremely large and costly. The marginal cost of producing one additional kilowatt hour is quite small, relative to these large fixed costs. If Westar charged only the marginal cost of production, it would not cover its total costs. Therefore, firms that have huge fixed costs are in a situation where only one firm can exist in an industry. Price competition between two or more firms would drive price down to the competitive level, and run both firms out of business.

This is why many public utilities such as electricity, natural gas, local telephone service, mail, and water are either regulated monopolies, or goods provided by governments. In these cases, huge fixed costs require firms to charge prices greater than marginal costs to recover their production costs.

Locational monopolies are firms that own a unique location and can charge a high price for the uniqueness of the good, such as the golf course at Pebble Beach, California, which has fairways on the Pacific Ocean. Prime real estate locations can also charge high prices to willing customers who desire to locate homes and businesses in the best areas.

Patents are government licenses issued to the developers of new products and/or techniques. Any inventor can apply for a patent which grants exclusive use of a product or technique to the inventor for a period of 17 years. This is a legal barrier to entry which gives the firm a monopoly for 17 years, if no close substitutes for the product exist. An agricultural example of a monopoly of this type is Monsanto, the developer of RoundUp herbicide. This chemical is extraordinarily good at killing plants. The patent on RoundUp gave Monsanto the exclusive right to produce and sell the product in the United States.

The reason that patents are given to firms is to allow them to recoup their high research and development (R&D) costs. Patents do make goods more expensive to consumers, but many argue that research and development would not occur in a world with no patents, which give firms the exclusive right to produce and sell a good.

In the real world, there are few industries that fit the strict requirements of monopoly and competition. Real-world industries are typically somewhere in between these two opposite forms of market structure. In the next section, we will explore a market structure that combines aspects of both monopoly and competition.

3. Monopolistic Competition.

Many industries in the real world have many firms that produce similar, but not identical goods. These industries are called Monopolistic Competitors by economists.

Monopolistic Competition = A market structure defined by: (1) numerous sellers, (2) a product of close, but differentiated, substitutes, (3) some freedom of entry and exit, and (4) some availability of knowledge and information.

The key ingredient of monopolistic competition is *product differentiation*, or competition to attract customers by making a good different from the other goods in the industry. The firms in this type of industry compete with numerous other firms, so their behavior is unnoticed by other firms. Almost all consumer products fall into this form of market structure: gasoline stations, cake mixes, grocery stores, toothpaste, soap, beer, toilet paper, etc. Advertising and marketing are the key outcomes of monopolistic competition, in which firms attempt to show consumers how their product differs from the competition.

Since the products in a monopolistic competition industry are not homogeneous, the firm faces a downward-sloping demand curve. The slope, or elasticity, of demand depends upon the degree of uniqueness of the good, and the consumers' loyalty to the product. For example, if consumers of Coke would rather pay more for Coke than switch to Pepsi, then the elasticity of demand for Coke is relatively inelastic. On the other hand, if consumers perceive Pepsi to be a good substitute for Coke, then the demand curve for Coke would be relatively elastic.

While the characteristics of goods across firms differs in monopolistic competition, the prices do not vary much: if price differences get to be large, consumers will switch to the close substitutes offered by competing firms. In other words, firms do not have much control over price in monopolistic competition. Figure 11.6 shows the graphical analysis of such a firm: the demand curve is downward sloping, showing the market power of the monopolistic competitor. The cost structure of the firm is the standard "U-shaped" curves that we have become familiar with.

Figure 11.6

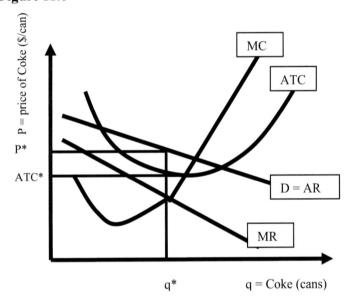

It can be seen in figure 11.6 that the monopolistic competitor is similar to a monopolist: it sets MR = MC, produces q* units of output, and sells them at a price P*. Profits are positive: the rectangle between the price (P*) and average total cost (ATC*) lines, and to the left of q*. The difference between a monopolist and a monopolistic competitor is that the monopolistic competitor has less influence over price, and must use other strategies to compete with firms that produce similar products.

The monopolistic competitor has two major strategies to increase profits. First, reduce costs. This is the same as the competitive firm: do

342

anything possible to lower production costs, including adoption of new technology or purchasing inputs at lower prices. Second, the monopolistic competitor will attempt to influence demand through advertising and marketing efforts. If consumers believe that a certain brand of toothpaste will make their teeth whiter and control cavities, then the demand for that brand of toothpaste will shift to the right (increase). This type of strategy is called, "Nonprice Competition."

Nonprice Competition = Where firms compete over good characteristics other than price, such as quality, quantity, services, etc.

Competition to win customers over to a certain brand is often intense. Interestingly, there is no "fierce competition" between firms in a competitive industry. Since price is fixed and given to a competitive firm, there is no need to compete with rival firms. In fact, competitive firms often help each other out, or form alliances, or industry groups.

Think of wheat harvest when a wheat farmer is ill, and cannot operate a combine. Neighbors typically pitch in to help out their friend (and competitor!). On the other hand, the rivalry between monopolistic competitors is intense: the automobile manufacturers in Detroit, Michigan often hold much information privately, for fear that the other car companies will steal their new products and ideas. Coke and Pepsi do battle on prime time television, and on college campuses to convince consumers that their product is better than the rival's cola.

Monopolistic competition has been used as a criticism of free market capitalism. The reason is that under this type of market structure, many resources are "wasted" on advertising and marketing. Millions of dollars are paid to Michael Jordan and other superstars to endorse a product (Just Do It!). Command economies, such as China, often produce just one type of clothing, and save the resources in advertising, marketing, etc. Many individuals believe that the variety of goods offered in a free market economy is not wasteful, but rather, is giving consumers what they want. If consumers were not willing to pay for and pay attention to advertising, we know that the advertising industry would not survive in a market system. Is advertising wasteful? It just depends on your viewpoint: since economists try to purge value judgments from their analysis, we will remain neutral on this issue.

Monopolistic competition is a form of market structure that lies between the two extremes of monopoly and competition. It lies closer to competition, since there are numerous firms. In the next section, we will investigate a form of market structure that is closer to monopoly, since there are only a few firms in the industry.

343

4. Oligopoly.

An **Oligopoly** is a market structure where production activities are conducted by a few large firms:

Oligopoly = A market structure characterized by a few large firms.

The key characteristics of firms in an oligopoly is that firms are *rivalrous* and *interdependent*: the behavior of one firm has an impact on the other firms in the industry. Contrast this with a competitive industry, where firms are completely independent as price takers: a competitive firm can sell as much or as little output as it would like at a fixed price. No real rivalry takes place in competitive industries, since every individual firm can sell at a given price. Monopolists are also independent, since they are the only firm in the industry. Oligopolists must take into consideration the actions of other firms. Firms in an oligopoly are considered to have market power, and their ability to set price is determined by their own actions and the actions of the other firms in the industry.

For example, agricultural implement manufacturers form an oligopoly. There is much interdependence between these implement producers: both price and nonprice competition are prevalent. John Deere must pay close attention to Case-IH in order to maximize profits. If one firm decreases the price to try to get customers to shift over to their product, the other firm will most likely match the price cut to retain its customers. If the price is lowered by both firms, then both firms earn lower levels of profits! Both firms would be better off maintaining a higher price. Similarly, if one firm raises its price, it will lose some customers to the other firm unless the price hike is matched. Profit levels and market shares are determined by all firms in an oligopoly, rather than just the one firm acting alone.

The central strategy of an oligopolist is to form an alliance with the other firms in the industry in order to maintain prices at a level higher than the competitive market price. Firms are said to **Collude** when they agree to keep prices high.

Collusion = When the firms in an industry jointly determine the price of the good.

Collusion is a form of monopoly: if all of the firms in an oligopoly were able to agree to act as a single firm, then the monopoly solution would result. In this sense, the collusive solution is the monopoly solution. This form of business strategy is illegal in the United States: the Sherman Antitrust Act outlaws price cartels and trusts.

11.4.1 Cartels.

Next, we will study the behavior and implications of a **Cartel**.

Cartel = A group of independent firms that join together to regulate price and production decisions.

Our study of cartels provides an excellent review of competition and monopoly. Cartels arise from the attempt of several firms in an industry to band together and approximate a monopoly. While this form of market structure is illegal within the United States, it is legal in other nations. The Organization of Petroleum Exporting Countries (OPEC) is a famous international cartel that limits oil production in its member nations to drive up the world price of oil.

Implicit cartels can form when several firms in an industry set the same price for their output. This has been claimed the case with gasoline stations in Manhattan, Kansas. The price of gasoline in Manhattan is typically five cents higher than neighboring stations in Junction City and Topeka. Why does this occur? If the gasoline stations in Manhattan all charge the same price, then they can each earn profits greater than the competitive level! If one of the gasoline stations were to cut the price of gasoline, then a "price war" could occur, where the price of gasoline was bid down to the competitive market price. Thus, the oligopoly of gas stations in Manhattan is characterized by interdependence: what one firm does affects all of the other firms in the industry.

Let's investigate a potential cartel of beef packers. As we have seen in earlier chapters, there are only three large beef packers in the United States: IBP, ConAgra, and Excell. Much attention is paid to the market structure of the packing industry by cattle producers and the government, since there is such a large concentration of market power in only three firms. Figure 11.7 shows the supply and demand for meat for the industry on the left, and for an individual packing plant on the right. For our example, we will take a look at the IBP packing plant in Holcomb, Kansas (near Garden City in Southwestern Kansas).

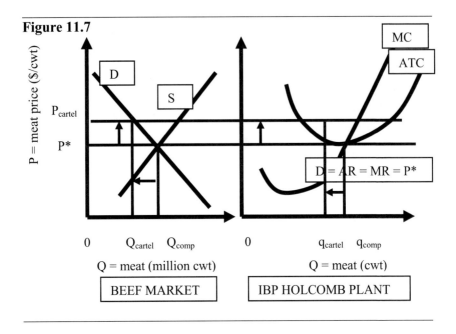

Figure 11.7

P = meat price ($/cwt)

D

S

P_{cartel}

P^*

MC

ATC

$D = AR = MR = P^*$

0   Q_{cartel} Q_{comp}

Q = meat (million cwt)

BEEF MARKET

0   q_{cartel} q_{comp}

Q = meat (cwt)

IBP HOLCOMB PLANT

The competitive solution is shown in figure 11.7 at the intersection of meat supply and meat demand in the market graph on the left (P^*, Q_{comp}). A cartel, if successful, comes up with an agreement to restrict the output of meat from Q_{comp} to Q_{cartel}. Since meat is scarce, this action drives the price up to P_{cartel}. This restricted level of output might be 80 percent of the total market, for example. If the three packers can collude perfectly, they can charge the monopoly price, and act as if they were a single firm. If the real-world firms of IBP, ConAgra, and Excell were to actually collude and form a cartel, it would be illegal.

If these three firms were able to agree to cut back on meat production by 20 percent each, they would earn positive economic profits, as shown in the right side of figure 11.7. The problem with the collusive agreement is that there is a strong incentive to cheat once the agreement has been made. At the collusive price, if the single meat packing plant in Holcomb could slightly increase its production of meat, then it could take advantage of the cartel price and sell more output than the agreed to level. If the single firm could do this at the cartel price, it would set MR = MC at the intersection of those two curves in the right graph.

Remember that in an oligopoly, there are only a few firms (in the case of meat packers, only three!). Therefore, IBP's cheating behavior of increasing production above the 80 percent level (q_{cartel}) puts downward pressure on the price of meat, which erodes the cartel agreement, and leads to a break up of the agreement, and the price falling back down to the competitive level. This aspect of a group of firms that collude to form a cartel limits its effectiveness. The issue is that the cheating firm assumes that all of the other firms stick to the agreement, an assumption that is inconsistent with the firm's own behavior. If all of the firms cheat on the agreement, then the competitive output and price would result. Thus, any cartel must spend money on monitoring other firms to make sure that they don't cheat.

Cartels are unlikely to be effective due to the likelihood that at least one firm will produce more output than the agreed level of output. Once this occurs, other firms will quickly increase production levels to compete with the cheating firm. Strategic behavior among oligopolists can be complicated. The rivalry between firms can lead to aggressive price competition, or effective collusion, or anything in between these two extremes. Economists typically predict that volatility is a major feature of oligopoly. Rivalrous firms may maintain a price agreement for a short period, followed by a price war that keeps the price at a competitive level. We anticipate the price of output in oligopoly to be uncertain as a result. In the next section, we will discuss the benefits and costs of highly concentrated market structures.

5. Is Big Necessarily Bad?

There have been a large number of mergers and acquisitions in the agribusiness industry in the past several years. Many firms have combined to form larger firms, which are often thought of in a bad light by farmers and other market participants. While it is true that if the large firms in concentrated industries have the ability to use market power to charge higher than competitive prices to consumers, then the consolidation of firms into larger entities would be an inefficient outcome for society, and result in a transfer of resources from consumers to the large firms.

There are major economics advantages to the production of goods and services by very large firms, however. The primary benefit to growth in firm size is **Economies to Scale**, which refers to lower production costs at larger levels of output:

Economies to Scale = When the per-unit costs of production decrease as output increases.

There is a tradeoff between large-scale firms in agricultural production and agribusiness. On the one hand, if these large firms exploit their market power by charging prices above the competitive level, then consolidation could be considered a negative aspect of the agricultural economy. On the other hand, to the extent that large firms capture economies to scale, they are contributing to the efficiency of the economy by producing goods in the most inexpensive manner possible.

Mergers and large firms are therefore controversial, as some people are likely to emphasize market power abuses of a large firm, and others are likely to emphasize efficiency gains. Each individual case of consolidation should be considered in isolation, and it is likely to be very difficult to determine the exact impact of consolidation of small farms and firms into larger entities on prices and output levels. Most of the evidence suggests that large firms do not have a great influence on price, due to the potential competition from other firms. Also, there are huge cost savings associated with large production facilities that allow the product to be provided at a low cost. Thus, in most cases, it is likely that the benefits of bigness outweigh the costs.

Just as there are gains to be made from large firms, there are also gains to be made from trading with other nations. The next chapter explores the gains from international trade.

Chapter Eleven Summary

1. Market power is the ability to affect the price of output. A firm with market power faces a downward-sloping demand curve.
2. Monopoly is a market structure characterized by a single seller.
3. The profit-maximizing condition for a monopolist is the set MR=MC.
4. A natural monopoly is a situation where a single firm has large fixed costs.
5. Monopolistic competition is a market structure defined by: (1) numerous firms, (2) a product of close, but differentiated, substitutes, (3) some freedom of entry and exit, and (4) some availability of knowledge and information.
6. Nonprice competition is when firms compete over good characteristics other than price, such as quality, quantity of services, etc.
7. An oligopoly is a market structure characterized by a few large firms.
8. Collusion occurs when the firms in an industry jointly determine the price of a good.
9. A cartel is a group of independent firms that join together to regulate price and production decisions.
10. Economies to scale exist when per-unit costs of production decrease as output increases.

Chapter Eleven Glossary

Barriers to Entry and Exit. A legal or economic barrier to the entrance of a new firm into an industry, or to the exit of a firm from an industry.

Cartel. A group of independent firms that join together to regulate price and production decisions.

Collusion. When the firms in an industry jointly determine the price of the good.

Economies to Scale. When the per-unit costs of production decrease as output increases.

Market Power. The ability to affect the price of output. A firm with market power faces a downward-sloping demand curve.

Market Structure. The organization of an industry, typically summarized by the number of firms in an industry.

Monopolistic Competition. A market structure defined by: (1) numerous sellers, (2) a product of close, but differentiated, substitutes, (3) some freedom of entry and exit, and (4) some availability of knowledge and information.

Monopoly. A market structure characterized by a single seller.

Natural Monopoly. A situation where a single firm has large fixed costs.

Nonprice Competition. Where firms compete over good characteristics other than price, such as quality, quantity, services, etc.

Oligopoly. A market structure characterized by a few large firms.

Price Maker. A firm characterized by market power, or the ability to influence the price of an input or output. Restated, a firm facing a downward-sloping demand curve.

Price Taker. A situation where the firm is so small relative to the industry that the price of an input or output is fixed and given, no matter how large the quantity of input purchased or output sold is.

Chapter Eleven Review Questions

1. Profit-maximization is the goal of which type of firm:
    a. competitive firm
    b. monopolist
    c. oligopolist
    d. all of the other three answers
2. A monopolist produces a good that:
    a. Is a public utility, such as electricity
    b. Has no close substitutes
    c. Has numerous substitutes
    d. Is inferior
3. A natural monopoly has:
    a. Numerous competitors
    b. Large fixed costs
    c. Large variable costs
    d. Zero fixed costs
4. The key characteristics of a monopolistic competitor is:
    a. Freedom of entry and exit
    b. Homogeneous product
    c. Product differentiation
    d. Monopolistic prices
5. A group of firms that join together to regulate price and production decisions is:
    a. The teamsters
    b. An oligopoly
    c. Collusion
    d. A cartel
6. Large firms can take advantage of:
    a. Natural monopoly
    b. Monopoly pricing strategies
    c. Economies to scale
    d. Collusion

CHAPTER TWELVE
THE GLOBAL ECONOMY AND KANSAS AGRICULTURE

1. Globalization and Agriculture.

Anyone who watches the news on television, listens to the radio, or reads a newspaper has been repeatedly bombarded with the terms, "internationalization," "globalization," and "The Global Economy." This focus on international issues has resulted from the rapid and drastic reduction in economic, political, and cultural barriers between nations in the post-Cold War era. A concrete example is the physical tearing down of the Berlin Wall, which separated the Communist Bloc nations from Western Europe. Economic examples of globalization include free trade agreements such as the North American Free Trade Agreement (NAFTA) and the General Agreement on Tariffs and Trade (GATT), and the recent adoption of the Euro as the official currency of most European nations.

While most of us are familiar with current events that have international implications, the underlying causes and consequences of the globalization of our lives is often less clearly understood. Most politicians favor free trade between nations, with a few notable exceptions such as Patrick Buchanon and Ross Perot. While elected officials of all parties and persuasions are supportive of free trade, economists are adamant proponents, obsessed with the idea of goods flowing freely between nations. Indeed, free markets and free trade are the cornerstone and lifeblood of economists, who typically oppose any form of government intervention into the voluntary exchange of goods and services in domestic and international markets.

The objective of this chapter is to explain why international trade occurs, and to share the economists' enthusiasm for free international trade. Put simply, international trade can make everyone better off. Implications of the increasing globalization of the economies of the world on Kansas agriculture will be explored.

2. Interdependence and Gains from Trade.

It doesn't take long to discover the advantages of buying and selling goods from around the world. Consider your breakfast this morning: it most likely included coffee produced from beans grown in

Brazil, and orange juice squeezed from oranges grown in Florida. Our clothes are made from cotton grown in Arizona or Mississippi, and sewn together in Thailand or China. Our Ford pickup trucks were produced from component parts that were manufactured in several different nations around the globe. The paper that these words are printed on was produced from trees grown in Oregon. We rely on goods produced all over the world, which is a good thing, because it allows us to expand the number and variety of goods that we are able to purchase and enjoy. As producers, interdependence allows us to be more productive and efficient, since we can specialize in the production of marketable commodities that we have an advantage in producing.

As Adam Smith explained in his famous 1776 book, *An Inquiry into the Nature and Causes of the Wealth of Nations*, the key idea behind economic interdependence is "advantage:"

> *It is a maxim for every prudent master of a family, never to attempt to make at home what it will cost him more to make than to buy. The tailor does not attempt to make his own shoes, but buys them of the shoemaker. The shoemaker does not attempt to make his own clothes but employs a tailor. The farmer attempts to make neither the one nor the other, but employs those different artificers. All of them find it for their interest to employ their whole industry in a way in which they have some advantage over their neighbors, and to purchase with a part of its produce, or what is the same thing, with the price of part of it, whatever else they have occasion for.*

Smith's simple insight that an individual should "do what he or she has an advantage at" forms the foundation for most economics and international trade. A modern example (Mankiw) of this idea is the question, "should Tiger Woods mow his own lawn?" Tiger Woods is an exceptional athlete, who has earned millions of dollars as a professional golfer. Given Tiger's youth and athleticism, it is very likely that he would quite good at mowing lawns. He may be faster and more efficient at mowing than anyone else. In fact, he may even enjoy mowing grass as a way of unwinding from the stress of fame and fortune earned at a relatively young age.

Given Tiger's ability as a professional golfer, he is most likely be better off spending his time practicing his driving or putting, and allowing someone else to mow the lawn. Tiger's time is extraordinarily valuable, and is better spent investing in what provides his lucrative salary: golf. Tiger can make himself better off by "trading" a portion of his salary for lawn care services, and the individual who cuts Tiger's lawn is better off by accepting payments for mowing the grass (think of the marketing possibilities for this mower!).

Other examples of this principle are common: suppose that Coach Ron Prince is an excellent typist, and can type more words per minute than his secretary. Should Coach Prince type his own letters, since he is so adept with the word processor? No. Economics suggests that Prince should be focused on how to win football games, rather than typing letters. I tell my wife that I am absolutely terrible at cleaning the bathroom, and that she is quite good at it: therefore, we are both made better off if she... (I don't recommend you try this!)

Although this concept appears straightforward, it can be a difficult concept to put in place for many of us. Should farm managers cut their own wheat or hire custom cutters? Should ranchers hire workers to work cattle, or do the work themselves? Should farm managers do their own record keeping or hire it done by an accountant? These questions will be explored further in this presentation.

3. Gains from Trade Example: Kansas Beef and Wheat.

The best way to understand the source of gains from trade and where the benefits of trade come from is to work through a numerical example. Suppose that the year is 1871, and two rugged individuals have made the decision to homestead in Phillips County, Kansas. To make things simple, assume that (1) there are only two persons who live in the county, a farmer and a rancher, (2) there are only two goods available: beef and wheat, and (3) that both individuals like to eat both meat and bread. If the farmer was self-sufficient, he would only be able to eat bread; if the rancher were self-reliant, she could eat all of the beef that she desired, but would be unable to enjoy bread of any type.

If each person were very good at producing one of the two goods, then it would be easy to show that they could both make themselves better off by *specializing* in the production of what they do best, and *trading* with the other person. This is simply Smith's idea of doing what you have an advantage at, or are good at. The concept is intuitively appealing, since humans are born with different abilities and interests, and specialization allows for efficient production, trade allows for a more diverse and interesting consumption package. Both individuals can be made better off by producing what they are good at and trading with the other person.

This simple notion becomes more interesting when one of the individuals is better at producing both goods. Suppose that the rancher has acquired a homestead of very productive river-bottom ground. This allows her to be more productive at producing both beef and wheat, compared to the farmer, whose homestead is located on poor-quality land. The following example will demonstrate that specialization and trade can still benefit both parties, even when the rancher can out-produce the farmer in both beef and wheat! Table 12.1 shows the productivity levels of both the farmer and the rancher, assuming that each can work 40 hours a week, and can raise beef, wheat, or a combination of both.

Table 12.1. Production Possibilities of the Farmer and the Rancher.

	Hours Needed to Make 1 pound of:		Amount Produced in 40 hours (in pounds):	
	Beef	Wheat	Beef	Wheat
Farmer	20	10	2	4
Rancher	1	8	40	5

Figure 12.1. Farmer's Production Possibilities.

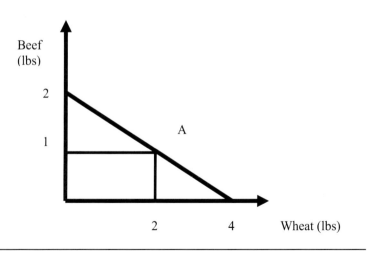

Figure 12.1 shows all of the possible combinations of beef and wheat that the farmer can produce, given the production possibilities

given in table 1. If the farmer produced only beef, he would end up with 2 pounds of beef, and no wheat.

Figure 12.2. Rancher's Production Possibilities.

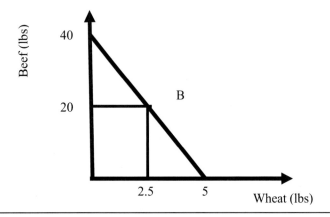

If all of the farmer's hours were spent on wheat production, the farmer would produce 4 pounds of wheat, but no beef. Suppose that the farmer allocates half of his time to the production of each product, so that 20 hours are spent producing beef and 20 hours are devoted to the production of wheat. Point A in figure 1 shows that in this case, the output of beef equals 1 pound and the output of wheat equals 2 pounds.

Similarly, the production possibilities of the rancher are shown in figure 12.2. The rancher can produce more of each product, since she has more productive resources. If the rancher divided her time evenly between the two products, she could produce at point B: 20 pounds of meat and 2.5 pounds of wheat. Next, we will demonstrate how both the farmer and the rancher could be made better off through specialization and trade.

Suppose that the rancher figures out a way of improving the level of consumption of both individuals through trade, without working any more hours. Her suggestion is the following: the farmer could spend 40 hours each week growing wheat. After all, this is the area of production that the farmer is best at. If the farmer were to specialize in the production of wheat, he would produce 4 pounds of wheat in a week. The farmer could trade 1 pound of wheat to the rancher for 3 pounds of beef in return. This would result in a higher level of consumption for both the farmer and the rancher (seems like magic, doesn't it?).

Figure 12.3. Farmer's Consumption with Trade.

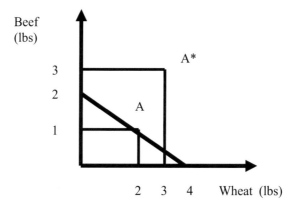

Figure 12.4. Rancher's Consumption with Trade.

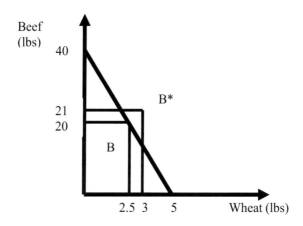

Figure 12.3 shows that with no trade, the farmer was at point A, consuming one pound of beef and 2 pounds of wheat. If the farmer follows the advice of the rancher, then the farmer would produce 4 pounds of wheat, trade one pound of the wheat for three pounds of the meat, and end up at point A*, consuming 3 pounds of both beef and wheat. The farmer is now in a position to consume more of both goods through specialization and trade.

The rancher is made better off through trade, also. This is a good outcome, since the trade was her idea! The rancher started out with no trade at point B in figure 12.4, consuming 20 pounds of beef and 2.5 pounds of wheat. She now switches her production toward her specialty, beef, by allocating 24 hours a week on cattle and 16 hours per week on

357

wheat. This results in the production of 24 pounds of beef and 2 pounds of wheat. The rancher then trades 3 pounds of beef for 1 pound of wheat (remember the proposal from above?). The result is consumption at point B*: 21 pounds of beef and 3 pounds of wheat. The rancher is able to consume more of both products also.

How does this work? Simple: by specializing in what each individual is good at, the total production of goods available to the entire economy is increased. Although both the farmer and the rancher ended up better off with trade than without it, it seems odd that this could be the case when the rancher was actually more productive in the production of both goods. This outcome, that all individuals can be made better off through specialization and trade, holds true in a wide variety of situations and examples, as can be shown by introducing the notion of comparative advantage.

4. The Principle of Comparative Advantage.

The key to understanding how interdependence between individuals in an economy, and international trade between nations, can make everyone better off is to distinguish between the ideas of absolute advantage and comparative advantage. These ideas can be explained by asking the question from out example, "who is better at producing wheat, the farmer or the rancher?" One possible answer is that the rancher is more efficient at producing wheat, since it takes her only 8 hours to produce one pound of wheat, whereas it takes the farmer 10 hours to produce the same amount. Economists use the term **Absolute Advantage** to compare the productivity of two persons, firms, or nations. Whoever is the most productive, or has the lowest cost of production, is said to have an absolute advantage in the production of a good.

Absolute Advantage = Lower costs of production for a specific good or service.

In our simple example, the rancher has an absolute advantage in the production of both beef and wheat.

The second way to answer the question about who is better at producing wheat is to look at what must be given up to produce one pound of wheat. What must be given up to perform an activity is called the opportunity cost of that activity. In our example, each person has 40 hours per week to allocate to the production of beef and wheat. There is a tradeoff between producing these two goods, since an hour spent in the production of beef takes an hour away from the production of what, and vice versa. The opportunity cost of the rancher producing wheat is how many pounds of beef must be given up to produce a pound of wheat. Since it takes the rancher 1 hour to produce 1 pound of wheat, and 1 hour to produce 8 pounds of beef, every hour that the rancher spends producing wheat takes away the possibility of using that hour to produce 8 pounds of beef. Therefore, the "cost" of the rancher producing 1 pound of wheat is the opportunity cost of giving up 8 pounds of beef. This can be seen in figure 4: the slope of the production possibilities line (rise over run) is equal to 8.

For the farmer, the opportunity cost of producing 1 pound of wheat is equal to how much beef must be given up to produce the pound of wheat. The farmer requires 10 hours to produce 1 pound of wheat. If those 10 hours were spent producing beef instead, he could produce 0.5 pounds of beef, since it requires the farmer 20 hours of time to produce 1 pound of beef (table 1). The slope of the farmer's production possibilities line in figure 3 shows the farmer can "trade" one pound of wheat for one-half pund of beef, since the slope is equal to 0.5.

Economists use the term, "**Comparative Advantage**" to describe the opportunity costs of two individuals, firms, or nations.

Comparative Advantage = The superior productive capacity of one nation or region or industry relative to all others, based on opportunity cost.

The producer who has the smallest opportunity cost of producing a good has a comparative advantage in the production of a good. In our example, even though the rancher has an absolute advantage in the production of wheat, the farmer has the comparative advantage! It is not possible for a single person to have a comparative advantage in both goods. Since the farmer has a comparative advantage in producing wheat, the rancher has the comparative advantage in producing beef.

5. Comparative Advantage and Trade.

Differences in comparative advantage, or differences in the opportunity costs between individuals, firms, and nations allow for specialization and gains from trade. Any time that one person has opportunity costs that are different from another person, the total production of the two persons can be increased if they specialize in the production of their comparative advantage. Benefits arise due to each person doing what they are good at, or have an advantage in. As a result, the total production of both products increases, making everyone better off with specialization and trade.

The benefits of increasing production for two individuals also hold for groups of individuals, and populations. This is why nations trade: to buy goods and services from a cheaper source! A nation will produce and export the goods and services that it has a comparative advantage in: for the United States, one of our largest exports is agricultural produce. A majority of wheat and feed grains produced in Kansas are sold overseas. An increasing amount of our beef products is sold to foreign buyers.

Chapter Twelve Summary

1. Absolute Advantage is a situation where one nation has lower costs of production for a specific good or service.
2. Comparative Advantage is a situation where the superior productive capacity of one nation or region or industry relative to all others, based on opportunity cost.
3. Differences in comparative advantage, or differences in the opportunity costs between individuals, firms, and nations allow for specialization and gains from trade.

Chapter Twelve Glossary

Absolute Advantage. Lower costs of production for a specific good or service.

Comparative Advantage. The superior productive capacity of one nation or region or industry compared to all others.

Opportunity Costs. The value of a resource in its next-best alternative use. What an individual or firm must give up to do something (the next best alternative).

Chapter Twelve Questions

1. The nation with the lowest cost of production has a:
    a. Comparative advantage
    b. Absolute advantage
    c. Unfair advantage
    d. Competitive advantage
2. The nation with the lowest opportunity costs of producing a good has a:
    a. Comparative advantage
    b. Absolute advantage
    c. Unfair advantage
    d. Competitive advantage
3. Trade will most likely take place between two nations that are:
    a. Very different
    b. Much the same
    c. Close in proximity to each other
    d. Have similar resources

REFERENCES

Barkema, Alan, and Mark Drabenstott. "Consolidation and Change in Heartland Agriculture." In: *Economic Forces Shaping the Rural Heartland*, Kansas City: Federal Reserve Bank of Kansas City, 1996, pp. 61-76.

Burtless, Gary, Robert L. Lawrence, Robert E. Litan, and Robert J. Shapiro. *Globaphobia: Confronting Fears about Open Trade.* Washington, D.C.: The Brookings Institution, 1998.

Casavant, Kenneth L., Craig L. Infanger, and Deborah E. Bridges. *Agricultural Economics and Management.* New Jersey: Prentice Hall, 1999.

Greider, William. *One World, Ready or Not: The Manic Logic of Global Capitalism.* New York: Simon and Schuster, 1997.

Kuttner, Robert. *Everything for Sale: The Virtues and Limits of Markets.* New York: Alfred A. Knopf, 1997.

Mankiw, Gregory N. *Principles of Economics.* Forth Worth, Texas: The Dryden Press, Harcourt Brace, 1998.

Mason, Paul M. and Michael M. Fabritius. "Using Student Data to Teach Utility Maximizing Behavior." *Classroom Expernomics* Volume 9(Fall 2000).

Penson, John B. Jr., Oral Capps, Jr., and C. Parr Rosson III. *Introduction to Agricultural Economics*, Second Edition. New Jersey: Prentice Hall, 1999.

Robinson, John P. and Geoffrey Godbey. *Time for Life: The Surprising Ways Americans Use Their Time.* State College, PA: Pennsylvania State University Press, 1997.

Thurow, Lester C. *Head to Head: The Coming Economic Battle among Japan, Europe, and America.* New York: Murrow, 1992.

Thurow, Lester C. *The Future of Capitalism: How Today's Economic Forces Shape Tomorrow's World.* New York: Penguin Books USA, 1996.

GLOSSARY

Absolute Advantage. Lower costs of production for a specific good or service.

Absolute Price. An absolute price refers to a price in isolation, without reference to other prices. (Also see **Relative Price**).

Accounting Costs. Explicit costs of production; costs for which payments are required.

Accounting Profits (π_A). Total revenues of a firm minus explicit costs. $\pi_A = TR - TC_A$. (Also see **Economics Profits**).

Agricultural Economics. Economics applied to agriculture and rural areas.

Agriculture. The science, art, and business of cultivating the soil, producing crops, and raising livestock useful to humans; farming.

Arc Elasticity. A formula that measures responsiveness along a specific section (arc) of a supply or demand curve, and measures the "average" price elasticity between two points on the curve.

Average Costs (AC). Total costs per unit of output. $AC = TC/Y$.

Average Fixed Costs (AFC). The average cost of the fixed costs per unit of output. $AFC = TFC/Y$.

Average Physical Product [APP]. The average productivity of each unit of variable input used [$=Y/X$].

Average Revenues (AR). The average dollar amount received per unit of output sold. $AR = TR/Y$.

Average Revenue Product (ARP). The average value of output per unit of input at each input use level. $ARP = APP*P_Y$.

Average Total Costs (ATC). The average total cost per unit of output. $ATC = TC/Y$.

Average Variable Costs (AVC). The average cost of the variable costs per unit of output. $AVC = TVC/Y$.

Barriers to Entry and Exit. A legal or economic barrier to the entrance of a new firm into an industry, or to the exit of a firm from an industry.

Break-Even Point. The point on a graph that shows the condition that Total Revenue (TR) is equal to Total Cost (TC).

Budget Constraint. A limit on consumption caused by the prices of goods and the size of the budget.

Budget Line. A line indicating all the combinations of two goods that can be purchased using the consumer's entire budget.

Capital. Physical capital is defined as machinery, buildings, tools, and equipment.

Cardinal Utility. Assigns specific values, or numbers, to the level of satisfaction gained from the consumption of a specific good. The unit of measurement is the util. (See also **Ordinal Utility**).

Cartel. A group of independent firms that join together to regulate price and production decisions.

Ceteris Paribus. Latin for "holding all else constant." We use this assumption to simplify the real world in order to understand it.

Change in Demand. When a change in the quantity of a good purchased is a result of a change in an economic variable other than the price of the good. A shift in the demand curve.

Change in Quantity Demanded. When a change in the quantity of a good purchased is a result of a change in the price of the good. A movement along the demand curve.

Change in Quantity Supplied. When a change in the quantity of a good sold is a result of a change in the price of the good. A movement along the supply curve.

Change in Supply. When a change in the quantity of a good sold is a result of a change in an economic variable other than the price of the good. A shift in the supply curve.

Collusion. When the firms in an industry jointly determine the price of the good.

Command Economy. A form of economic organization where resources are allocated by whoever is in charge, such as a dictator or an elected group of officials. (Also see **Market Economy** and **Mixed Economy**).

Comparative Advantage. The superior productive capacity of one nation or region or industry compared to all others.

Comparative Statics. A comparison of market equilibrium points both before and after a change in an economic variable.

Complements in Consumption. Goods that are consumed together (e.g. peanut butter and jelly). (Also see **Substitutes in Consumption**).

Complements in Production. Goods that are produced together (e.g. beef and leather). (Also see **Substitutes in Production**).

Constant Returns. For each additional unit of input used, output increases at a constant rate (the rate of change in output remains constant).

Consumer. An individual or household that purchases a product.

Costs of Production. The payments that a firm must make to purchase inputs (resources, factors).

Cross-Price Elasticity of Demand. Measures the responsiveness of the quantity demanded of a good to changes in the price of a related good.

Cross-Price Elasticity of Supply. Measures the responsiveness of the quantity supplied of a good to changes in the price of a related good.

Decreasing Returns. Each additional unit increases the production level, but with a smaller change than the previous unit.

Demand. Consumer's ability and willingness to pay for a good.

Demand Curve. A function connecting all combinations of prices and quantities consumed for a good, *ceteris paribus*.

Demand Elasticity. The percentage change in quantity demanded relative to the percentage change in price.

Demand Schedule. Information on prices and quantities purchased.

Disequilibrium. A market situation in which the market price does not result in equality of supply and demand.

Economic Good. A good that is **Scarce**. (Also see **Noneconomic Good**).

Economic Profits (π_E). Total revenues of a firm minus both explicit and implicit costs. $\pi_E = TR - TC_A$ - implicit costs. (Also see **Accounting Profits**).

Economics. The study of the allocation of scarce resources between competing ends.

Economies to Scale. When the per-unit costs of production decrease as output increases.

Efficiency. A characteristic of competitive markets, indicating that goods and services are produced at the lowest cost and consumers pay the lowest possible prices.

Elastic. A change in price brings about a relatively larger change in quantity.

Elasticity. The percentage change in one economic variable with respect to a percentage change in another economic variable.

Elasticity of Demand. The percentage change in the quantity demanded with respect to a percentage change in price.

Elasticity of Supply. The percentage change in the quantity supplied with respect to a percentage change in price.

Engel Curve. The relationship between consumer income and quantity of a good consumed, *ceteris paribus*.

Engel's Law. A Law that states that as income increases, the proportion of income spent on food declines, *ceteris paribus*.

Equilibrium. A point or situation from which there is no tendency to change.

Equilibrium Price. The price at which the quantity supplied equals the quantity demanded.

Equilibrium Quantity. The point where quantity supplied is equal to quantity demanded.

Factor Demand. The firm's demand for the variable input used in production: MRP in Stage II of Production. Also, the relationship between the price and quantity demanded of a variable input.

Fixed Costs. Those costs that do not vary with the level of output; the costs associated with the fixed factors of production.

Fixed Input. An input whose quantity does not vary with the level of output.

Good. An economic good.

Homogeneous Product. A product that is the same no matter which producer produces it. The producer of a good cannot be identified by the consumer.

Imperfect Substitutes. Inputs that substitute for each other incompletely in the production process. (Also see **Complements** and **Substitutes**).

Immediate Run (IR). A period of time in which all inputs are fixed.

Income Elasticity of Demand. The percentage change in the demand of a good in response to a one percent change in consumer income.

Increasing Returns. When each additional unit of input added to the production process yields more additional product than the previous unit of input.

Indifference Curve. A line showing all of the combinations of two goods that provide the same level of utility.

Industry. A group of firms that all produce and sell the same product.

Inelastic. A change in price brings about a relatively smaller change in quantity.

Inferior Good. A good whose consumption declines in response to an increase in income.

Inverse Demand Function. A demand function that is represented with price (the independent variable) as a function of quantity demanded (the dependent variable): $P = f(Q^d)$.

Inverse Supply Function. A supply function that is represented with price (the independent variable) as a function of quantity supplied (the dependent variable): $P = f(Q^s)$.

Isocost Line. A line indicating all combinations of two variable inputs that can be purchased for a given, or same, level of expenditure.

Isoquant. A line indicating all combinations of two variable inputs that will produce a given level of output.

Isorevenue Line. A line depicting all combinations of two outputs that will generate a constant level of total revenue.

Law of Demand. The quantity of a good demanded varies inversely with the price of the good, *ceteris paribus*.

Law of Diminishing Marginal Utility. Marginal utility declines as more of a good or service is consumed during a specified period of time.

Law of Diminishing Marginal Returns. As additional units of one input are combined with a fixed amount of other inputs, a point is always reached at which the additional output produced from the last unit of added input will decline.

Law of Supply. The quantity of goods offered t a market varies directly with the price of the good, *ceteris paribus*.

Long Run [LR]. A time span such that no inputs are fixed; all inputs are variable.

Luxury Good. A good whose consumption increases at an increasing rate in response to an increase in income.

Macroeconomics. The study of economy-wide activities such as economic growth, business cycles, inflation, unemployment, recession, depression, boom, etc. (Also see **Microeconomics**).

Marginal Costs (MC). The increase in total cost due to the production of one more unit of output. $MC = \Delta TC/\Delta Y$.

Marginal Factor Cost (MFC). The cost of an additional (marginal) unit of input; the amount added to total cost of using one more unit of input. $MFC = \Delta TC/\Delta X$.

Marginal Physical Product [MPP]. The amount of additional, or marginal, total physical product obtained from using an additional, or marginal, unit of variable input $[=\Delta Y/\Delta X]$.

Marginal Rate of Product Substitution (MRPS). The rate that one output must be decreased as production of the other output is increased. Also, the slope of the production possibilities frontier (PPF). $MRPS = \Delta Y_2/\Delta Y_1$.

Marginal Rate of Substitution (MRS). The rate of exchange of one good for another that leaves utility unchanged. The slope of an indifference curve. $MRS = \Delta Y_2/\Delta Y_1$.

Marginal Rate of Technical Substitution (MRTS). The rate that one input can be decreased as use of another input increases. The slope of the isoquant. $MRTS = \Delta X_2/\Delta X_1$.

Marginal Revenues (MR). The addition to Total Revenue from selling one more unit of output. $MR = \Delta TR/\Delta Y$.

Marginal Revenue Product (MRP). The additional (marginal) value of output obtained from each additional unit of the variable input. $MRP = MPP* P_Y$.

Marginal Utility. The change in the level of utility as consumption of a good is increased by one unit. MU = $\Delta TU/\Delta Y$.

Market. The interaction between buyers and sellers.

Market Demand. The horizontal summing of all individual demand curves for all individual consumers in the market.

Market Economy. A form of economic organization where resources are allocated by prices. Resources flow to the highest returns in a free market system. (Also see **Command Economy** and **Mixed Economy**).

Market Equilibrium. The point where the quantity supplied by producers at a given price is equal to the quantity demanded by consumers.

Market Power. The ability to affect the price of output. A firm with market power faces a downward-sloping demand curve.

Market Price. The price where quantity demanded is equal to quantity supplied.

Market Structure. The organization of an industry, typically summarized by the number of firms in an industry.

Market Supply. The horizontal summing of all individual supply curves for all individual producers in the market.

Marketplace. A physical location where buyers and sellers meet to trade goods.

Microeconomics. The study of the behavior of individual decision-making units such as individuals, households, and firms. (Also see **Macroeconomics**).

Mixed Economy. A form or economic organization that has elements of both a **Market Economy** and a **Command Economy**.

Monopolistic Competition. A market structure defined by: (1) numerous sellers, (2) a product of close, but differentiated, substitutes, (3) some freedom of entry and exit, and (4) some availability of knowledge and information.

Monopoly. A market structure characterized by a single seller.

Natural Monopoly. A situation where a single firm has large fixed costs.

Necessity Good. A good whose consumption increases at a decreasing rate in response to an increase in income.

Negative Returns. When each additional unit of input added to the production process results in lower total output than the previous unit of input.

Noneconomic Good. A good that is not scarce; there is as much of this good to meet any demand for it; a free good. (Also see **Economic Good**).

Nonprice Competition. Where firms compete over good characteristics other than price, such as quality, quantity, services, etc.

Normal Good. A good whose consumption increases in response to an increase in income. Also called a superior good.

Normative Economics. Statements that contain opinions and/or value judgments. This type of statement contains a judgment about "what ought to be" or "what should be." (Also see **Positive economics**).

Oligopoly. A market structure characterized by a few large firms.

Opportunity Costs. The value of a resource in its next-best alternative use. What an individual or firm must give up to do something.

Opportunity Set. The collection of all combinations of goods that is within the budget constraint of the consumer.

Ordinal Utility. A concept of consumer satisfaction in which goods are ranked in order of preference: first, second, third, etc. (See also **Cardinal Utility**).

Own-Price Elasticity of Demand. Measures the responsiveness of the quantity demanded of a good to changes in the price of that good.

Own-Price Elasticity of Supply. Measures the responsiveness of the quantity supplied of a good to changes in the price of that good.

Perfect Competition. A market or industry that has four characteristics: (1) numerous buyers and sellers, (2) homogeneous product, (3) freedom of entry and exit, and (4) perfect information.

Perfect Complements. Inputs that must be used together in a fixed ratio. The proportion of each input is fixed in the production process. (Also see **Complements**).

Perfect Information. A situation where all buyers and sellers in a market have complete access to technological information and market information (all input and output prices, and all quantities bought and sold).

Perfect Substitutes. Inputs that are completely substitutable in the production process. (Also see **Substitutes**).

Positive Economics. Statements that are factual; these statements contain no value judgements. Positive economic statements describe "what is." (Also see **Normative Economics**).

Price Ceiling. A maximum price set by the government for a specified good or service.

Price Maker. A firm characterized by market power, or the ability to influence the price of an input or output. Restated, a firm facing a downward-sloping demand curve.

Price Taker. A competitive firm that can not influence the price of a good.

Price Support. A minimum price set by the government for a specified good or service.

Price Taker. A situation where the firm is so small relative to the industry that the price of an input or output is fixed and given, no matter how large the quantity of input purchased or output sold is.

Producer. An individual or firm that produces (makes; manufactures) a product.

Production Function. The physical relationship between inputs and outputs.

Production Possibilities Frontier (PPF). A curve depicting all of the combinations of two outputs that can be produced using a constant level of inputs.

Profits [π]. Total revenues minus total costs: $\pi = TR - TC$. The value of production sold less the cost of producing that output. (**Also see** Accounting Profits **and** Economic Profits).

Rational Behavior. Individuals do the best that they can given the constraints that they face. Rational behavior is *purposeful* and *consistent*.

Relative Price. The price of a good relative to prices of other goods. (Also see **Absolute Price**).

Resources. Inputs provided by nature and modified by humans using technology to produce goods and services that satisfy human wants and desires. Also called *inputs, factors of production, or factors*. Resources include capital (K), labor (L), land (A), and management (M).

Scarcity. Because resources are limited, the goods and services produced from those resources are also limited, which means consumers must make choices, or trade-offs between different goods.

Service. A type of economic good that is not physical. For example, a haircut or a phone call is a service, whereas a car or a shirt is a good.

Short Run [SR]. A time span such that some factors are variable and some factors are fixed.

Shortage. A market situation in which consumers are willing and able to purchase more of a good than producers are willing to supply at a given price ($Q^s < Q^d$).

Shut-Down Point. The point on a graph where Marginal Revenue (MR) is equal to Average Variable Costs (AVC).

Social Science. The study of society and of individual relationships in and to society, generally regarded as including sociology, psychology, anthropology, economics, political science, and history.

Substitutes in Consumption. Goods that are consumed either/or. (e.g. wheat bread and white bread.) (Also see **Complements in Consumption**).

Substitutes in Production. Goods that compete for the same resources in production. (e.g. wheat and barley). (Also see **Complements in Production**).

Supply. The amount of a good available in a given location at a given price.

Supply Curve. The marginal cost curve above the minimum average variable cost curve.

Supply Elasticity. The percentage change in quantity supplied relative to the percentage change in price.

Supply Schedule. A schedule showing the relationship between the price of a good and the quantity of a good supplied.

Surplus. A market situation in which producers are willing to supply more of a good than consumers are willing to purchase at a given price ($Q^s > Q^d$).

Technological Change. Allows a greater level of output to be produced with fewer inputs, or the same level of output to be produced with fewer inputs. An upward shift in the production function.

Total Costs (TC). The sum of Fixed Costs and Variable Costs. TC = TFC + TVC.

Total Factor Cost (TFC). The total cost of a factor, or input. TFC = $P_X * X$.

Total Fixed Costs (TFC). The total costs of inputs that are fixed (inputs that do not vary with the level of output).

Total Physical Product [TPP]. The relationship between output and one variable input, holding all other inputs constant. It is measured in physical terms and represents the maximum amount of output brought about by each level of input use.

Total Revenues (TR). The amount of money received when the producer sells the product. Also called gross income or total sales. TR = TPP* P_Y.

Total Revenue Product (TRP). The dollar value of the output produced from alternative levels of variable input. TRP = TPP* P_Y.

Total Utility. The total level of satisfaction derived from consuming a given bundle of goods and services.

Total Variable Costs (TVC). The total costs of inputs that are variable (inputs that vary with the level of output).

Unitary Elastic. The percentage change in price brings about an equal percentage change in quantity.

Utility. The consumer's satisfaction derived from consuming a good.

Utils. Imaginary units of satisfaction derived from consumption of goods or services.

Variable Costs. Those costs that vary with the level of output; the costs associated with the variable factors of production.

Variable Input. An input whose quantity does vary with the level of output.

INDEX

380